Creating Strategic Value through Financial Technology

Founded in 1807, John Wiley & Sons is the oldest independent publishing company in the United States. With offices in North America, Europe, Australia and Asia, Wiley is globally committed to developing and marketing print and electronic products and services for our customers' professional and personal knowledge and understanding.

The Wiley Finance series contains books written specifically for finance and investment professionals as well as sophisticated individual investors and their financial advisors. Book topics range from portfolio management to e-commerce, risk management, financial engineering, valuation and financial instrument analysis, as well as much more.

For a list of available titles, visit our Web site at www.WileyFinance.com.

Creating Strategic Value through Financial Technology

JAY D. WILSON, JR.

Dr. Cyree—
   I hope you • enjoy the book! I think
it will serve as a nice resource for community
bankers looking to survive and thrive in the
digital age!

Jay D. Wilson, Jr.

WILEY

Published by John Wiley & Sons, Inc., Hoboken, New Jersey.
Published simultaneously in Canada.

For general information on our other products and services or for technical support, please
contact our Customer Care Department within the United States at (800) 762–2974, outside
the United States at (317) 572–3993 or fax (317) 572–4002.

Wiley publishes in a variety of print and electronic formats and by print-on-demand. Some
material included with standard print versions of this book may not be included in e-books or
in print-on-demand. If this book refers to media such as a CD or DVD that is not included in
the version you purchased, you may download this material at http://booksupport.wiley.com.
For more information about Wiley products, visit www.wiley.com.

Library of Congress Cataloging-in-Publication Data is Available:

ISBN 9781119243755 (Hardcover)
ISBN 9781119243878 (ePDF)
ISBN 9781119243861 (ePub)

Cover Design: Stephanie Wiggins
Cover Images: smartphone © LOVEgraphic/Shutterstock;
Bank Icon by Freepik/www.flaticon.com

Printed in the United States of America

10 9 8 7 6 5 4 3 2 1

To Becky, *my supportive wife, who inspires me to be better each day.*

To Connor and Sadie, *my two children, who bring so much joy and keep us entertained.*

Contents

Preface

As the financial crisis and Great Recession illustrated, the health and vibrancy of the banking industry is an important ingredient in a healthy economy. In the United States, community banks play a special role in the economy as they constitute the majority of banks, are collectively the largest providers of agricultural and small business lending, and are often key employers and providers of financing in their local communities. While conditions have improved since the depths of the financial crisis, community banks face difficult market conditions with intense and growing competition from both larger banks and non-bank lenders, a relatively difficult interest rate environment that places pressure on margins, and a heightened regulatory and compliance burden.

Community bankers are also increasingly facing an additional challenge with the rise of FinTech and its vast array of emerging companies and technology innovations in different areas of financial services. FinTech is a challenging strategic threat to assess for banks since competition is coming from startups focused on addressing a number of core banking services. While many bankers view FinTech as a potential threat, FinTech offers the potential to improve the health of community banks for those banks that can selectively leverage FinTech to enhance performance and customer satisfaction and improve profitability and returns. FinTech can also help level the playing field for community banks to compete more effectively with larger banks and non-bank lenders.

This book seeks to illustrate the potential benefits of FinTech to banks, both large and small, so that they can gain a better understanding of FinTech and how it can create value for their shareholders and enhance the health and profitability of their institutions. We provide a map of the FinTech industry and present guideposts for navigating the sector so that different parties (investors, entrepreneurs, and traditional financial services companies like community banks) can enhance customer/product offerings, improve efficiency/cost structure, and ultimately profit by creating strategic value as financial services and technology increasingly intersect.

Section One introduces the reader to FinTech and discusses the reasons behind the excitement and interest in the sector globally and, more specifically, for financial services in the United States. Additionally, we examine how FinTech can help community banks close the performance gap with larger banks and enhance customer services offerings, efficiency, profitability, and valuations in a challenging operating environment. Lastly, we delve into the history of FinTech to determine themes and trends from some of the more mature FinTech companies. For those bankers still skeptical of the power of FinTech, consider the time and money saved by both customers and bankers through the use of the ATM, an earlier FinTech innovation that we discuss in Chapter 3. Imagine the lines at banks before a long holiday weekend if that were the only place to go and get cash, as well as the inconvenience of being unable to obtain cash on a Sunday or holiday because all of the bank's branches were closed.

Section Two discusses several FinTech niches that have great potential for banks. Each chapter focuses on a particular niche (Bank Technology, Alternative Lending, Payments, Wealth Management, and Insurance). We provide an overview of emerging trends in each particular FinTech niche and highlight certain FinTech companies that have developed in these areas. Finally, we discuss key insights that can be gleaned from the successes of these emerging FinTech companies. The case studies presented hopefully provide guideposts for bankers as they assess the vast array of companies in the FinTech ecosystem and that particular niche.

Despite the potential benefits of FinTech for community banks and vice versa, significant challenges exist for community banks considering FinTech opportunities. Community banks typically operate with a leaner technology staff and the appeal of FinTech can often be overshadowed by the breadth of the landscape. Lastly, there can be significant cultural, valuation, and risk differences between banks and FinTech companies, which can make partnerships and mergers between the two difficult.

Consequently, **Section Three** attempts to address some of these issues in greater detail and illustrates how both financial institutions and FinTech companies can create strategic value from improving one or some combination of the three primary valuation elements of cash flow, risk, and growth. For those interested in pursuing FinTech opportunities, they present traditional financial institutions with a number of strategic options, including focusing on one or some combination of the following: building your own FinTech solutions, acquiring a FinTech company, or partnering with a FinTech company. While we do not yet know which strategy will be most successful, we do know that discussions of whether to build, partner, or buy will increasingly be on the agenda of boards and executives of both financial institutions and FinTech companies for the next few years. In Section Three, we discuss a range of topics that should assist banks with analyzing these strategic options, including how to value a FinTech company and the pros and cons of partnership and acquisition strategies, and provide an introduction to the frameworks and return analyses banks can use to analyze and structure potential FinTech partnerships and mergers.

FinTech is an increasingly important topic for bankers seeking to navigate complex and difficult market conditions. As FinTech continues to spread across the financial landscape, banks of all sizes are beginning to craft their responses and prepare to either embrace future innovations as an improvement to their business models or attempt to shield their business models from potential disruption. Banks are starting to realize that they must develop a strategy that considers how to evolve, survive, and thrive as technology and financial services increasingly intersect. For these reasons, a number of banks are seeking to engage in discussions with FinTech companies. The right combination of technology and financial services through a partnership has significant potential to create value for both FinTech companies and traditional financial institutions.

FinTech presents the financial services industry with a unique opportunity to both increase revenue, particularly non-interest income, while also lowering costs and improving efficiency. In order to harness the potential of FinTech, bank managers and directors need to understand which FinTech niches best suit their business model and also how to prioritize FinTech initiatives and compare their potential to other strategic initiatives in order to focus on those areas that generate returns and enhance valuation. Similarly, FinTech entrepreneurs need to understand the financial services and banking landscape to be able to discern whether they should approach the industry as a partner, disruptor, or some combination of the two. Therefore, this book should also benefit FinTech companies and entrepreneurs who will gain a greater understanding of the challenging conditions facing banks, how their innovations can create value, key valuation drivers, and how to structure mergers and partnerships with banks.

Globally, banks face many of the same difficult market conditions and challenges currently affecting U.S. banks. However, it is an exciting time to be in financial services. Similar to innovations like the printing press or the steam engine or assembly-line manufacturing that led to significant changes in their respective industries, FinTech offers a unique opportunity to transform the financial services industry while also improving the greater good and providing better and more efficient services for customers, including many un- and under-banked people around the globe. FinTech also offers those countries with a weak financial infrastructure the opportunity for greater financial inclusion by providing financial services like banking, insurance, and wealth management at lower costs through digital channels. This can have a profound impact on people's lives and create profitable business models for banks and innovative FinTech entrepreneurs.

We are still in the early stages of development of a number of FinTech niches and innovations. For example, an innovative development in banking the last few years has been the use of mobile check deposit, which entails writing a physical check and snapping a picture on the phone. As a user of this product, I must admit that it is very convenient and something that I use often as it saves me a trip to my local bank branch. While this is innovative, it is not a fully digital deposit system as it still requires a paper check and doesn't reduce the time spent writing the check or replace the inconvenience when you are out of paper checks.

As the FinTech industry evolves, it will be interesting to see whether idiosyncrasies like depositing a check persist and also whether this dichotomy continues to exist between FinTech, its many niches, and traditional financial services. One can certainly envision a financial services industry in the future where the remaining successful companies combine the best elements of both traditional financial services and FinTech and the two industries converge.

Thanks for taking the time to read this book and please feel free to reach out with comments or questions. In addition to having a keen interest in community banking and FinTech, I am also an avid tennis player. As such, I forewarn the reader to expect a few tennis analogies and stories in different sections of the book.

Jay Wilson
wilsonj@mercercapital.com
901.685.2120

Acknowledgments

Thanks to my family (my wife Becky, son Connor, and daughter Sadie) for putting up with my time away from them and sometimes my sleepiness while working on the book. Other friends and family have also been sources of encouragement and support as the book came into being, and I would like to extend my thanks to them as well.

The idea for this book was first discussed with Barbara Price, Mercer Capital's chief marketing officer, in mid-2015. More likely than not, this book would not have been the end result of those conversations without Barbara's assistance and encouragement. Additionally, I would like to thank the staff at Wiley for providing editorial guidance and also a listening and an encouraging ear to those initial conversations in mid-2015.

A number of colleagues assisted with the development of the book and I am very grateful for their contributions. Specifically, I would like to thank our marketing associates, Stephanie Wiggins, Connor Bran, and Tammy Falkner, for working on edits and making the charts and cover look great. Also, thanks to my summer 2016 associate, Tripp Crews, who assisted with the preparation of the book by researching and drafting certain sections. He contributed greatly to portions of Chapters 1, 3, 6, and 7, as well as portions of Chapters 4 and 5. Additionally, my colleague, Lucas Parris, and another summer associate, Michael Anthony, provided significant assistance for the insurance technology chapter (Chapter 8). They have my thanks. I would also like to extend my appreciation to all my colleagues at Mercer Capital for encouragement, assistance, feedback, and general support for the book.

Also, thanks to the many clients with whom I have worked over the years. The projects I have worked on for these clients and the resulting relationships have exposed me to a number of different segments and sectors within both community banking and FinTech and this has helped to frame my perspective and insights on a number of issues.

Creating Strategic Value through Financial Technology

ection One of this book introduces the reader to FinTech and discusses the reasons behind the excitement and interest in the sector globally and more specifically for financial services in the United States. Additionally, we examine more specifically how FinTech can have a significant impact on community banks through opportunities to enhance customer service offerings, efficiency, and profitability in a challenging operating environment. Lastly, we delve into the history of FinTech to determine themes and trends from some of the more mature FinTech companies.

Chapter 1 is titled **What Is Financial Technology?** We answer that question and present an overview of current trends in the FinTech industry. We also provide perspective on why FinTech is important and receiving significant attention from investors, regulators, entrepreneurs, and management/boards of traditional financial services companies.

Chapter 2, **Community Banks and FinTech,** discusses traditional bank valuation trends and drivers and shows how incorporating FinTech into your bank's existing strategy can help improve the profitability and valuation of your community bank. This chapter is also important for FinTech entrepreneurs as it demonstrates the potential value proposition for FinTech companies in the community banking sector. Successful FinTech companies need to be able to demonstrate their potential to improve the profitability and valuation of banks in order to attract them as customers or partners.

The Historical Context for Fintech is presented in **Chapter 3.** This chapter walks through the history of FinTech, including ATMs, electronic stock exchanges, and core vendors. We also look at the largest IPOs in the industry's history. This history lesson should help the reader understand what might be important in today's FinTech environment.

What Is Financial Technology?

TECHNOLOGY'S IMPACT ON FINANCIAL SERVICES

Tennis was invented a long time ago. How long ago? Well, it depends upon whom you ask. Similar to a number of other sports, the origins of tennis are unknown. The earliest records of the sport include paintings of European commoners and royals batting a ball around. However, the history of modern (lawn) tennis is clearly documented, as it was first publicly announced in March of 1874 by two British papers. The announcement included a patent for "A Portable Court of Playing Tennis," which included a history of the sport, instructions for how to set up the court, and rules of the game.

While basic tenets and elements of the game have remained similar over the years, tennis continues to evolve with changes to scoring, court surfaces, equipment, and playing styles. A key driver of these changes is the influence of technology. The development of stronger and lighter materials for a variety of industrial purposes would not at first glance be noted as a key driver of change in tennis, but these changes had a significant impact on the game. Graphite and other stronger, lighter synthetic frames are commonplace in the game today. The last wooden racket appeared in a major tournament in the 1980s. The confluence of technology and design affects balls, court surfaces, and even the pristine grass of Wimbledon. Many players now regularly use high-tech training tools to improve their fitness and stroke mechanics.

Despite these significant advances in the game over the years, tennis is not a sport that is linked with technology and a spectator at Wimbledon today would still recognize the sport if shown images from the tournament in the early 1900s. For these reasons, tennis is often referred to by pundits as being "steeped in tradition" and viewed by outsiders as a game that is slow to evolve. They can point to certain things like players still hitting the same basic strokes and the biggest tournaments still being held at some of the same venues (Wimbledon has had a tournament since 1877).

While we do not foresee those in financial institutions like banks, wealth managers, or insurance companies picking up tennis rackets anytime soon, there are a number of parallels between the evolution of tennis and the evolution of financial services. Like tennis, certain basic tenets and activities of financial services (such as depositing money, paying for goods/services, and borrowing/lending funds) have existed in some fashion for many centuries and are not expected to change in the future. However, a number of changes have occurred in the past and will continue to occur within financial services as technology increasingly intersects with financial services.

There is much excitement around technology and its potential applications within financial services as a number of pundits and analysts foresee a growing number of applications and improvements for the sector. Consumers are also increasingly asking for and adopting new technology applications. While the term *TenTech* (short for *tennis tech*) has yet to grace magazine covers and TV headlines, *FinTech* (or *financial tech*nology) has become commonplace in major magazines, newspapers, and TV stories within the financial services sector. The excitement around FinTech is difficult to gauge but the expansion in Google searches of the term *FinTech* and the global dispersion of those searches provide some benchmarks and evidence of the growing level of excitement. (See Figure 1.1 and Table 1.1.)

Given the growing interest in FinTech, let's address a few questions about FinTech: "What is financial technology and who are the players?," "Why is there so much excitement about FinTech?," and "Why is FinTech potentially so important for society?" By examining these key questions, we can gain a keen understanding of the topic.

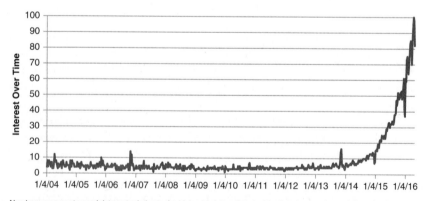

Numbers represent search interest relative to the highest point on the chart for the given region and time. A value of 100 is the peak popularity for the term. A value of 50 means that the term is half as popular. Likewise a score of 0 means the term was less than 1% as popular as the peak.

FIGURE 1.1 Google Search Trends for "FinTech"

TABLE 1.1 Top Search Trends for "FinTech" by Country

1	Singapore	10	Japan
2	Hong Kong	11	Australia
3	South Africa	12	Netherlands
4	South Korea	13	Canada
5	Taiwan	**14**	**United States**
6	Switzerland	15	Argentina
7	India	16	Spain
8	United Kingdom	17	France
9	Germany	18	Italy

Source: Google Trends

WHAT IS FINTECH AND WHO ARE THE PLAYERS?

Historically, FinTech was limited to back-end software of financial institutions (banks, insurance companies, wealth managers, investment banks, etc.). More recently, the term has been expanded to include any technological innovation in finance. We define *FinTech* for purposes of this book as: *companies that primarily use technology to generate revenue through providing financial services to customers either directly or through partnerships with traditional financial institutions.*

With a working definition of FinTech, let's examine the key players and recent trends in the sector. Keep in mind that categorizing a FinTech company can be difficult as it is much like trying to categorize an all-court tennis player as a baseline, serve-and-volley, or counterpunching player. The types of financial services provided by FinTech companies can vary—ranging from technology for traditional financial services such as wealth management, insurance, payments, and banking to newer, innovative areas such as peer-to-peer lending or blockchain technology. There are also a number of technology companies that offer some form of financial services and traditional financial institutions that leverage technology to offer financial services. For example, Apple developed ApplePay, which offers mobile payment services for Apple iPhone users and could on its own be considered a payments or FinTech company. Thus, ApplePay would clearly be classified as a FinTech offering but Apple would likely not be a FinTech company given the expanse of its other non-FinTech products and services with its FinTech offerings comprising only a small proportion of revenues.

Having historically invested heavily in technology, most (if not all) traditional financial institutions offer myriad technology applications. For example, Lloyd Blankfein, the CEO of Goldman Sachs, has referred to

Goldman Sachs as a technology company.[1] Many community banks located in rural markets are often some of the more technologically advanced companies in their community. However, these traditional financial institutions would not be included within our definition of FinTech companies because traditional banking services, rather than technology, serve as the primary revenue driver.

These examples illustrate the difficulty in distinguishing between FinTech and traditional financial services—a trend likely to increase as FinTech companies become more like traditional financial institutions and traditional financial institutions become more like FinTech companies. For example, a few publicly traded banks rely more heavily on technology and less on a traditional physical branch footprint. One such example is Live Oak Bancshares (LOB) or First Internet Bancorp (IBNK). In the online brokerage space, Schwab and E*Trade can be classified as FinTech companies although they have acquired and operate bank subsidiaries offering traditional banking services such as deposit accounts and loans.

While reports vary on exactly how many FinTech companies there are, McKinsey noted that there were approximately 12,000 FinTech companies worldwide.[2] What reports agree on is the number of FinTech companies is growing daily as funding and interest in the sector increases. The universe of publicly traded FinTech companies is a smaller subset, but as seasoned, mature companies, they represent a notable group of FinTech companies. Their public disclosures also provide benchmarking financial information useful in tracking sector trends.

Public FinTech Companies by Niche

On that note, let's take a closer look at the publicly traded FinTech niches. Publicly traded FinTech companies can be broken into three primary niches—Payments, Solutions, and Bank Technology.

- The *Payments* niche includes companies that facilitate and/or support the transfer of money, particularly non-cash transactions. Key sub-niches include *processors* that provide solutions related to the transfer and processing of money and *software/hardware companies* that provide software/hardware that primarily supports the transfer and processing of money. At June 30, 2016, there were 32 publicly traded U.S. FinTech companies in the Payments niche and the total market cap of these companies was $458 billion (with a median market capitalization of $2.8 billion). The top three largest public U.S. FinTech Payments companies include Visa Inc. ($176.9 billion market capitalization at June 30, 2016), MasterCard Inc. ($96.8 billion), and Automatic Data Processing Inc. ($41.9 billion).

■ The *Solutions* niche includes companies that provide technology solutions to assist businesses and financial institutions with financial services. Key sub-niches include *outsourced* companies that are third-party providers of FinTech solutions, *payroll/administrative* companies that improve the human resources function through technology, and *content* companies that provide content/research that supports financial services and decision making. At June 30, 2016, there were 33 publicly traded U.S. FinTech companies within the Solutions niche and the total market cap of these companies was $197.7 billion (with a median market capitalization of $3.4 billion). The top three largest U.S. FinTech Solutions companies included IMS Health Holdings Inc. ($12.5 billion market capitalization at June 30, 2016), MSCI Inc. ($7.4 billion), and Jack Henry & Associates ($6.9 billion).

■ The *Technology* niche includes companies that provide software and services to one of three different financial services subsections, including Banking, Investments, and Healthcare/Insurance. At June 30, 2016, there were 22 publicly traded U.S. FinTech companies within the Technology niche and the total market cap of these companies was $55 billion (with a median market capitalization of $1.6 billion). The top three largest U.S. FinTech Technology companies included Intuit Inc. (market capitalization of $28.6 billion at June 30, 2016), Fiserv Inc. ($24.2 billion), and Fidelity National Information Services Inc. ($24.1 billion).

In addition to the FinTech niches noted above, there are other publicly traded companies in the United States that have significant FinTech offerings and would also meet our definition of FinTech companies such as *online brokers* and *alternative online lenders*. At June 30, 2016, four U.S. FinTech companies within the Online Broker niche were publicly traded (The Charles Schwab Corporation [SCHW], TD Ameritrade [AMTD], E*Trade [ETFC], and Interactive Brokers Group [IBKR]) and the total market cap of these companies was $57.3 billion with a median market capitalization of $10.8 billion. At June 30, 2016, two U.S. FinTech companies (OnDeck Capital [ONDK] and Lending Club Corporation [LC]) within the Alternative Online Lender niche were publicly traded and had market capitalizations of $364 million and $1.6 billion, respectively.

As you can see, the scope of the FinTech industry is vast with a number of publicly traded FinTech companies to analyze in order to track developments and investor sentiment. For bankers, managers, and investors in traditional financial services companies, this rise of FinTech and its vast scope of company type (for both public and private FinTech companies) is a challenging strategic threat to assess. Many FinTech companies are essentially unbundling the bank's core services and leveraging technology to provide a unique solution only to one particular service (such as payments, lending, billing, underwriting, investing, or compliance). While the majority of FinTech companies do not offer all of the services that even a small community bank does, collectively they are a formidable competitor. This presents a difficult problem for banks and other traditional incumbents to combat since competition is coming from a variety of areas and addresses a number of core services.

FinTech and U.S. Financial Institutions

While there are a number of potential applications for technology in other industries, there are a few basic elements of the financial services industry that make it particularly attractive for technology. For example, the business models of traditional financial institutions like banks, insurance companies, and wealth managers are unique from one another but share common characteristics. Because this book is focused on financial institutions specifically, let's explore the common characteristics of financial institutions and the role that FinTech can play.

Profitability   The first common characteristic is profitability. Financial institutions have historically been profitable and collectively are in a highly profitable segment. Savvy technology entrepreneurs and venture capitalists are recognizing that these market conditions in other industries have historically enabled technology companies to develop and prosper.

To gain some perspective on the size and profitability of financial services, consider that the financial services industry adds the largest proportion of value to U.S. GDP (Table 1.2).

With the exception of tobacco, banks were the most profitable (as measured by net income as a percentage of revenue) of any industry. Other related financial services industries, like asset managers and non-bank financial services and insurance companies, were also highly profitable and in the 96th and 93rd percentile respectively (Table 1.3).

Basic Necessity   Another common characteristic of financial institutions is that the financial services they offer are a basic necessity. While one can imagine a world where the delivery vehicle for companies that provide basic financial services is different and largely digital, it is hard to imagine a world without financial services for payments, deposits, lending, borrowing, and investing.

Regulation   Regulation is yet another common characteristic of financial institutions and that regulatory burden has increased over time, particularly

TABLE 1.2 Value Added to U.S. GDP by Industry (billions of dollars)

	2015	% of Total
Gross domestic product	17,947	
Private industries	15,623	
Agriculture, forestry, fishing, and hunting	196	1%
Mining	305	2%
Utilities	288	2%
Construction	717	4%
Manufacturing	2,168	12%
Wholesale trade	1,080	6%
Retail trade	1,050	6%
Transportation and warehousing	528	3%
Information	868	5%
Finance, insurance, real estate, rental, and leasing	**3,636**	**20%**
Professional and business services	2,192	12%
Educational services, health care, and social assistance	1,492	8%
Arts, entertainment, recreation, accommodation, and food services	704	4%
Other services, except government	400	2%
Government	2,324	13%

Source: Bureau of Economic Analysis Release Date: April 21, 2016

TABLE 1.3 Net Income as Percentage of Revenue of Financial Institutions

Industry Name	Net Income–Based Net Margin	Rank (1–95)	Percentile
Bank (Money Center)	24.48%	2	99th
Banks (Regional)	24.33%	3	98th
Financial Svcs. (Non-bank & Insurance)	14.82%	5	96th
Insurance (General)	10.49%	49	49th
Insurance (Life)	7.13%	36	63rd
Insurance (Prop./Cas.)	9.82%	29	71st
Investments & Asset Management	3.69%	8	93rd

Source: Aswath Damodoran, http://pages.stern.nyu.edu/~adamodar/New_Home_Page/datafile/margin.html

since the Great Recession. This offers opportunities for technology solutions that can alleviate regulatory/compliance issues. Heightened regulation also tends to limit a traditional financial institution's ability to innovate, which increases its need and desire for FinTech partners and solutions.

Legacy Systems with Hope of Innovation   Another challenge to innovation is the fact that financial services is such a mature industry and companies rely on a number of legacy technology systems. Legacy technology systems are, in many cases, not enough in today's environment. This has created an opening for new technology companies and applications within the sector to develop. Technology entrepreneurs often look for problems to solve. There are a number of problems related to modernizing the legacy systems of traditional financial institutions and reducing friction for services and applications that customers are increasingly demanding.

Financial institutions are attempting to foster innovation either internally, through partnerships with startups, by sponsoring corporate accelerators/incubators, or by strategic investments/acquisitions. While these traditional financial services companies are increasingly looking to innovate, they are also considering how to innovate responsibly by managing potential risks and selectively determining how to incorporate FinTech into their strategic plan.

Current Environment   For many financial institutions, the prolonged period of lower interest rates is crimping profits and increasing interest in technology that can serve to provide financial services and products more efficiently and at lower costs.

WHY THE HYPE FOR FINTECH?

As technology improves and becomes ubiquitous in our everyday lives, consumers expect better technology offerings of financial services. Regulated and often complex, the nature of financial services presents unique challenges to innovation and society, but particularly the Millennials. Millennials are becoming more comfortable using digital (online and mobile) services in other areas of their lives and are increasingly looking for similar services for their financial lives.

FinTech and financial institutions that effectively utilize FinTech applications will have tailwinds for growth in the coming years, as the trend toward digital continues and Millennials acquire more financial assets. For example, Ernst & Young's "EY FinTech Adoption Index" noted only 15.5 percent of digitally active consumers had used at least two FinTech products in the last six months.[3] This implies a large potential for sector growth for companies that can adapt and adopt technology.

Ease of use ("easy to set up an account") was the top reason cited for the consumer adoption of FinTech per the EY Index. Other reasons for using FinTech were that it offered better user experience and functionality as well as better quality of services. Interestingly, the Index noted that FinTech appealed to wealthier clientele with over 50 percent adoption by those under age 54 and whose earnings were greater than $150,000. The FinTech Adoption Index also noted that the most frequent users tended to be those in urban areas. According to the Index, "Early FinTech adopters tend to be younger, higher-income customers, with adoption concentrated in high-development urban areas such as New York, Hong Kong, and London. These users are some of banking and insurance's most valuable customers and traditional providers must reconsider the way they meet these users' needs if they want to stem the flight to FinTech."

In addition to meeting customer demands, other reasons why FinTech is becoming increasingly important include:

- In order for financial institutions (banks, insurance, asset managers, alternative lenders) to survive and thrive in the future, different parties (investors, traditional incumbents, and entrepreneurs) must work together to modernize the traditional legacy technology infrastructure.
- A significant proportion of the global population is unbanked or underbanked and applying technology to the financial services industry is viewed as one way to both expand and improve services to this significant but underserved proportion of the population. Additionally, financial health and literacy are global issues and a number of FinTech innovations offer opportunities to improve financial health and literacy around the world.
- Millennials are driving change in finance and other industries. Those financial institutions that are well positioned for Millennials will likely outperform those that are not. Millennials tend to be more comfortable using digital channels for financial services. As they acquire more financial assets, financial institutions that can leverage FinTech to meet Millennials' preferences will garner a tailwind for forward growth.
- Recent technology developments have allowed financial technology to rise. For example, the development of the computer chip, personal computer, laptop, and cell phone have all helped lay the foundation for the environment that we see today on which a number of FinTech companies can build. As consumer preferences have shifted toward using technology as a first means of interacting with other vendors, financial services has followed suit.

In summary, the hype surrounding FinTech is largely premised on the financial services industry being both large and profitable and having many potential applications for technology. This combination of large entrenched incumbents with historically profitable business models where customers are increasingly demanding more digital services provides an attractive market for FinTech companies to develop. While it is hard to know what percentage of the global financial services market is available for disruption, the size of the potential market and the possible applications for technology, as well as consumers' desire to use it, are massive.

WHY IS FINTECH POTENTIALLY SO IMPORTANT TO SOCIETY?

As previously noted, FinTech offers the opportunity to expand financial services offerings to un- and underbanked portions of society, and many emerging markets are especially ripe. These ripe conditions include large populations of un- and underbanked people and high concentrations of mobile phone subscribers. FinTech offers those countries the opportunity for greater financial inclusion by providing financial services like banking, insurance, and wealth management at lower costs through mobile channels. This can have a profound impact in people's lives and create profitable business models for innovative entrepreneurs.

One area where FinTech has already started to show its potential to impact society in emerging markets is sub-Saharan Africa. Sub-Saharan Africa itself has a high percentage of mobile bank account users compared to other regions (excluding high-income OECDs) as noted in Figure 1.2. More specifically, mobile bank account users in Kenya and Zimbabwe far outweigh those in comparable countries. In Kenya, 74.7 percent of the adult population has a bank account—a very high number for the region—and the vast majority of those with bank accounts have a mobile bank account (58.4% of the population). In Zimbabwe, 32.4 percent of the adult population has a bank account. The vast majority of those with a bank account have a mobile bank account (21.6% of the adult population).

There are many reasons for this rise in mobile money usage in sub-Saharan Africa, but a desire for financial inclusion, a need to lower transaction costs, and mistrust of financial institutions all serve as key drivers of this rapid growth of mobile money. Africa has a massive unbanked majority, creating a great want of financial inclusion in much of its population. Mobile money makes participation in financial markets accessible to everyone who carries even the most rudimentary type of cell phone with text messaging capabilities.

A need to lower transaction costs also aided the rise of mobile money, as much of the continent still functions as a barter economy. It is also

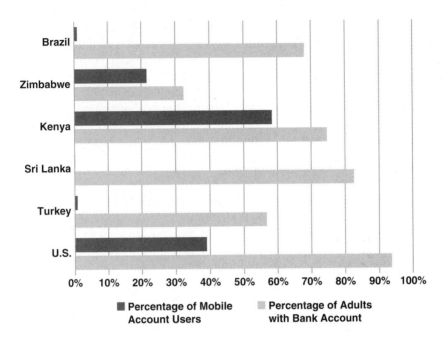

FIGURE 1.2 Disparity in Mobile Banking Account Usage between Sub-Saharan African Countries and Upper-Middle-Income Countries
Source: Global Financial Inclusion Database of the World Bank Group's "The Little Data Book on Financial Inclusion," 2015

impractical for small farmers and merchants to hold their earnings in African banks, as high fees can dissipate their entire income in a year in some cases. Mobile money can significantly reduce these fees for the customer and reduce the servicing expenses of the bank account for the provider. This allows low-income earners the ability to build up larger balances than they would otherwise be able to by holding their money in a traditional bank. The fees charged by African banks, as well as other questionable practices, have created an air of mistrust in many countries, pushing consumer preference toward mobile money.

This rich environment for the growth of mobile money in sub-Saharan Africa has also led to innovations within the continent in efforts to facilitate this growth and create more avenues for the use of mobile money. Perhaps the most useful of these innovations has been the creation of ATMs by mobile service providers that allow customers to withdraw cash by using a onetime PIN sent directly to the customer's phone by text message. Startups that convert bitcoins from foreign currency to Kenyan shillings have also begun to emerge, shielding consumers against exchange rate risk by sending the converted currency straight to the user's mobile wallet. Other FinTech startups are also beginning to create systems that can facilitate and accept small payments to merchants through new business operating systems and software.

The rise of mobile money and e-commerce in sub-Saharan Africa has also been aided by adverse living conditions and disastrous events in the countries that are most receptive to the rise of mobile money. In 2008, post-election violence in Kenya pushed many people toward the use of M-PESA, a FinTech payments company that is the country's largest mobile money system, to transfer money into and out of the violent slums of Nairobi. In Nigeria, fear of the Ebola virus and terrorist groups forced people to stay at home and rely on mobile money systems and the Internet to acquire goods and services. Zimbabwe has also experienced multiple cash shortages in the past several years, encouraging the widespread use of mobile money.

Consistent with the factors driving the successful development of FinTech in sub-Saharan Africa, tremendous opportunities exist for FinTech growth in other emerging and developing regions. Those areas with a high percentage of mobile subscriptions and a low percentage of bank account holders are particularly ripe for FinTech growth. These conditions can be found in Africa and India. In Africa, only 34 percent of the adult population has a traditional bank account while 83 percent has a subscription to a mobile account.[4] Likewise, in India, 53 percent of the adult population has a bank account while 79 percent has a mobile account.[5] The disparity in these two essential tools creates an environment conducive to the future growth of FinTech, as FinTech innovations can be used to close the margin between the two figures. (See Figure 1.3.)

Beyond just emerging and developing markets, though, developed markets like the United States are also ripe for FinTech to help address un- and underbanked populations. The FDIC noted opportunities for FinTech through mobile pay. A survey by the FDIC in 2013 noted that approximately 28 percent of U.S. households were unbanked or underbanked.[6] Despite that, in the United States, the majority of adults have a bank account while a smaller proportion utilize a mobile bank account, which implies the potential exists for mobile account usage to continue to grow among both the banked and underbanked population.

RECENT TRENDS AND MARKET CONDITIONS FOR THE FINTECH INDUSTRY

Realizing the potential for FinTech to grow in both emerging and developed markets, venture capital interest in FinTech has been growing and continues to grow both in North America and globally, as noted in Figure 1.4.

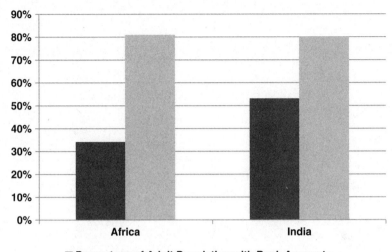

FIGURE 1.3 Percent of Adult Population with Bank Accounts and Mobile
Subscription Comparison between Africa and India
Source: Global Financial Inclusion Database of the World Bank Group's "The Little
Data Book on Financial Inclusion," 2015

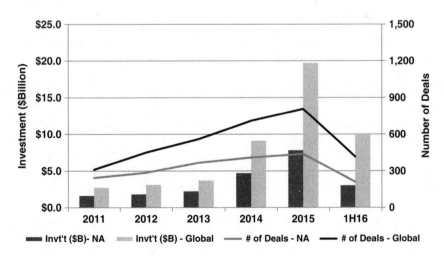

FIGURE 1.4 FinTech Funding Trends (2011– First Half of 2016)
Source: The Pulse of FinTech Report 2Q16, KPMG, and CB Insights, 8/17/2016

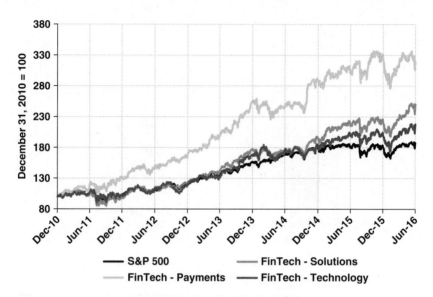

FIGURE 1.5   Public Returns: FinTech Indices vs. S&P 500
Source: S&P Global Market Intelligence and Mercer Capital

FinTech's Rising Valuations and Strong Returns

Additionally, publicly traded FinTech companies have also benefited from the excitement around FinTech, outperforming the broader markets and enjoying rising valuations in recent periods, as shown in Figure 1.5. However, the market has been relatively volatile as investors weigh the prospects for heightened competition from new entrants, ranging from other technology companies to traditional financial institutions, continued evolution of consumer preferences and technology, and emerging risks such as regulatory and business model risks.

Consistent with recent historical growth patterns and near-term outlook and excitement for FinTech, publicly traded FinTech companies remain priced at a premium to the broader markets with the S&P 500 priced at 16.6× estimated forward earnings in mid-2016 (per FactSet). Additionally, valuation multiples have been expanding despite flat-to-declining margins for the FinTech sector (Figures 1.6 and 1.7).

Within the private company realm, FinTech valuations appear to be rising as well with FinTech "unicorns" (i.e., those private companies with an estimated market value of greater than $1 billion) growing and continuing to garner significant investor and media interest.

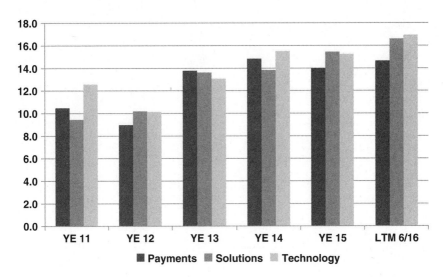

FIGURE 1.6 FinTech Public Company Pricing Multiples: Median Enterprise Value/EBITDA Multiples
Source: Capital IQ, Mercer Capital Research

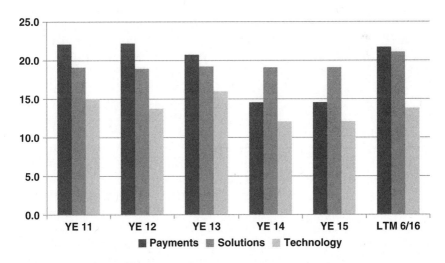

FIGURE 1.7 FinTech Public Multiples: Median EBITDA Margins (%)
Source: Capital IQ, Mercer Capital Research

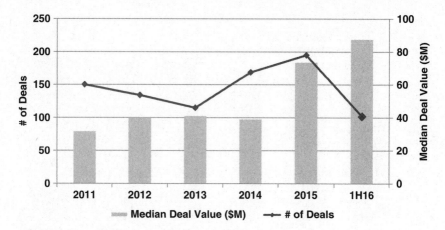

FIGURE 1.8   FinTech M&A Overview (2011– First Half of 2016)
Source: S&P Global Market Intelligence

FinTech's Upward-Trending Exits

The level of interest in FinTech is also paralleling the rising level of exit activity in both mergers and acquisitions as well as IPOs. For perspective, note the number of deals and median deal value increases in recent periods, as shown in Figure 1.8. Pricing details are often not reported for the majority of FinTech transactions, which limits the amount of reliable pricing metrics, but the data indicates a clear, upward pricing trend in recent periods.

IPO activity slowed in late 2015 and 2016. There were eight FinTech IPOs in 2015 and 16 in 2014. Significant FinTech IPOs in 2014 and 2015 included: First Data ($2.3 billion in proceeds); Square ($279 million in gross proceeds); and Lending Club ($1 billion in gross proceeds).

CONCLUSION

Growth and excitement encompasses the FinTech industry with its potential to impact the financial services industry and enhance the lives of people around the world. However, there is evidence that expectations and predictions of FinTech disruption and displacement of traditional incumbents should be tempered by the resiliency of banks. In the mid-1990s, Bill Gates famously called banks "dinosaurs" and noted that banking services were a necessity but banks were not.[7] From that point, Microsoft attempted to access banking but failed to make significant inroads into financial services. These failures by Microsoft and others to attack traditional banks demonstrate the resiliency of traditional banks (at least for the time being).

Many bankers also view the giant technology companies of today such as Amazon, Google, Facebook, and Apple with a wary eye and wonder what their role may ultimately be in the financial services industry. These giants could disrupt not only the traditional banks but many FinTech company business models as well. We have seen recent FinTech-related efforts from these companies such as ApplePay and Google Wallet. However, it will be interesting to watch whether they are content to stay in the background as customers continue to look to traditional financial institutions for financial services or whether will they develop their own unique financial services offerings.

Additionally, FinTech companies and other technology companies face significant regulatory and compliance challenges as they grow their financial services offerings. Regulated industries often create an environment where a few companies with significant scale emerge because those companies can operate profitably, overcoming compliance costs. Consequently, FinTech companies face significant obstacles entering a regulated industry. Regulations can complicate their business plans and stifle innovation. However, regulation can also be a competitive advantage for FinTech companies able to comply because regulations can create significant barriers to entry for those unable or unwilling to comply.

While banks have historically proven to be resistant to the threat from traditional technology companies and FinTech companies thus far, only time will tell whether this resiliency is a temporary blip in the first set of a much longer match with their FinTech competitors or whether the resistance will persist and they will ultimately win the match. As Bill Gates said, "We always overestimate the change that will occur in the next two years and underestimate the change that will occur in the next ten. Don't let yourself be lulled into inaction."[8] Perhaps this statement is more apt for financial services given its complex and regulated nature. It will take longer to evolve, but over time the disruption and full implementation of FinTech will likely impact the industry significantly.

FinTech presents exciting opportunities for traditional banks, particularly community banks, and this book will delve into the details of both the community bank and FinTech sectors seeking to maximize returns to create strategic value for proactive banks and seeking to capitalize on FinTech opportunities.

NOTES

1. "Blankfein: Goldman Sachs Is a Technology Firm," *Bloomberg*, June 3, 2016, http://www.bloomberg.com/news/videos/b/8df546df-20d1-46e5-824b-0702e922 5046.

2. Miklos Dietz, Somesh Khanna, Tunde Olanrewaju, and Kausik Rajgopal, "Cutting Through the Noise Around Financial Technology," *McKinsey & Company*, February 2016, http://www.mckinsey.com/industries/financial-services/our-insights/cutting-through-the-noise-around-financial-technology.

3. "EY FinTech Adoption Index," survey conducted from September 1, 2015, to October 6, 2015, http://www.ey.com/gl/en/industries/financial-services/ey-fintech-adoption-index.

4. "The Future of Financial Services: How Disruptive Innovations Are Reshaping the Way Financial Services Are Structured, Provisioned and Consumed," *World Economic Forum*, June 2015, http://www3.weforum.org/docs/WEF_The_future__of_financial_services.pdf.

5. Ibid.

6. "2013 FDIC National Survey of Unbanked and Underbanked Households," *FDIC*, October 2014, https://www.fdic.gov/householdsurvey/2013report.pdf.

7. Amy Cortese and Kelly Holland, "Bill Gates Is Rattling the Teller's Window," *Bloomberg*, October 30, 1994, http://www.bloomberg.com/news/articles/1994-10-30/bill-gates-is-rattling-the-tellers-window.

8. http://www.brainyquote.com/quotes/quotes/b/billgates404193.html

CHAPTER 2

Community Banks and FinTech

IS FINTECH A THREAT OR AN OPPORTUNITY FOR COMMUNITY BANKS?

In order to understand how FinTech can help community banks create strategic value, let us take a closer look at community banks, the issues facing them, and how FinTech can help improve performance and valuation. As we saw in Chapter 1, when attempting to define a FinTech company, myriad interpretations exist in delineating community banks and it is important to establish a clear representation before analyzing the sector. For purposes of this book, we define a community bank as a bank or thrift with between $100 million and $5 billion in assets.

Community banks are a subset of depository institutions. Depository institutions include banks, bank holding companies, savings banks, mutual savings banks, stock-owned thrift institutions, mutual thrift institutions, and credit unions. While we focus largely on U.S. community banks in this chapter, depository institutions more broadly are facing similar challenges and have several common characteristics: they accept deposits from consumers and/or businesses; their deposits are generally insured by the federal government; they are chartered by the federal government or various states and regulated by agencies of these governments; and they generally deploy the acquired deposits by making loans to customers, either businesses or consumers, or making other investments that provide earnings.

Threats to Community Banks

There are nearly 6,000 community banks with 51,000 locations in the United States (this includes commercial banks, thrifts, and savings institutions). While community banks constitute the vast majority of banks (approximately 90% of U.S. banks have assets below $1 billion),[1] the majority of banking industry assets are controlled by a small number of

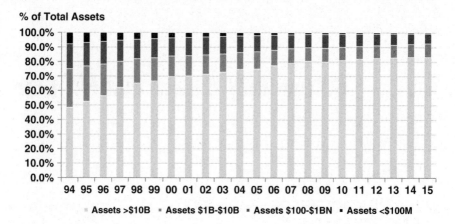

% of Total Assets

Legend: Assets >$10B   Assets $1B-$10B   Assets $100-$1BN   Assets <$100M

FIGURE 2.1   Overview of U.S. Banks
Source: QBPR, www.fdic.gov

extremely large banks. These larger banks have acquired assets quickly and grown at a faster pace in the past few decades than community banks. This has resulted in larger banks taking more market share from community banks. Per Figure 2.1, banks with assets greater than $10 billion controlled approximately 83 percent of total assets in the banking industry compared to 48 percent in 1994.

In addition to competitive pressures related to acquiring assets from larger banks, community banks face headwinds of higher regulatory compliance costs, pressured margins from a historically low interest rate environment, and slower demographic and market trends. These headwinds have contributed to a declining number of community banks and weaker profitability. As noted in Figure 2.2, community bank returns on equity (ROEs) have trended down in recent years due to the significant competitive pressures from larger banks as well as the previously noted industry headwinds.

Along with the difficult market conditions marked by high competition and crimped profitability, many community bankers are also attempting to assess and respond to the potential threat from the vast array of FinTech companies and startups taking aim at the banking sector. For perspective, a group of community bankers meeting with the FDIC in mid-2016 noted that FinTech poses the largest threat to community banks. One executive indicated that the payment systems "are the scariest" as consumers are already starting to use FinTech applications like Venmo and PayPal to send peer-to-peer payments. Another banker went on to note, "What's particularly concerning about [the rise of FinTech] for us is the pace of change and the fact that it's coming so quickly."[2]

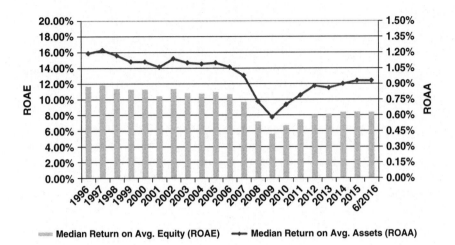

FIGURE 2.2 Community Bank Profitability Trends
Source: S&P Global Market Intelligence

Opportunities for Community Banks

While many bankers view FinTech as a significant threat, FinTech also has the potential to assist the community banking sector. This is significant, particularly in the United States, as community banks compose an important part of the economy, constitute the majority of banks in the United States, and are collectively the largest providers of certain loan types such as agricultural and small business lending. FinTech offers the potential to improve the health of community banks by enhancing performance and improving profitability and ROEs back to historical levels.

Big Banks (defined as those with assets greater than $5 billion and referred to as "Big Banks" hereafter) have outperformed community banks consistently for many years. In the 20-year period from 1996 to 2016, Big Banks reported a higher return on assets (ROA) than community banks in each period except for 2009 (the depths of the financial crisis). In 2015, the median ROA and ROE of the Big Banks was 1.03 and 8.65 percent, respectively, compared to 0.93 and 8.40 percent, respectively, for the community banks.

Interestingly, though, the source of outperformance is not due to net interest margin, perhaps the most common performance metric that bankers often focus on. Community banks had consistently higher net interest margins than Big Banks in each year over that 20-year period (1996–2016). Rather, the outperformance of the Big Banks can be attributed to their generation of greater non-spread revenues (i.e., non-interest income) and lower non-interest expense (i.e., lower efficiency ratios). In each of the last 20 years, the Big Banks have had higher non-interest income as a proportion of assets (Big Banks averaged non-interest income as a proportion of average assets at 1.0% compared to the community bank average of 0.75%) and lower efficiency ratios (Big Banks averaged 59% compared to community banks averaging 67%).

FinTech and Non-Interest Income and Efficiency Ratios While FinTech can benefit community banks in a number of areas, FinTech offers some specific solutions where Big Banks have historically outperformed community banks: non-interest income and efficiency. To enhance non-interest income, community banks may consider a number of FinTech innovations in niches like payments, insurance, and wealth management. Since many community banks have minimal personnel and legacy systems in these areas, they may be more apt to try a new FinTech platform in these niches. For example, a partnership with a robo-advisor might be viewed more favorably by a community bank as it represents a new source of potential revenue, another service to offer their customers, and it will not cannibalize their existing trust or wealth management staff since they have minimal existing wealth management personnel.

FinTech can also enhance efficiency ratios and reduce expenses for community banks. Branch networks are the largest cost of community banks and serving customers through digital banking costs significantly less than traditional in-branch services and interactions with customers. For example, branch networks make up approximately 47 percent of banks' operating costs and 54 percent of that branch expenditure goes to staffing.[3] Conversely, the costs of ATM and online-based transactions are less than 10 percent of the costs of paper-based branch transactions in which tellers are involved.[4]

To illustrate the potential financial impact of transitioning customers to digital transactions for community banks, let's assume that a mobile transaction saves the bank approximately $3.85 per branch transaction.[5] If we assume that FinTech Community Bank has 20,000 deposit accounts and each account shifts two transactions per month to mobile from in-person branch visits, the bank would save approximately $150,000 per month and approximately $1.8 million annually (Table 2.1).

FinTech Community Bank's ability to lower costs due to the transition to mobile transactions helps the bank generate higher earnings, a lower efficiency ratio, and a higher ROA and ROE relative to a "Traditional Community Bank" (Table 2.2).

The Opportunity of Regulatory Technology In addition to the benefits from customers shifting to digital transactions, community banks can utilize

TABLE 2.1 Potential Cost Savings from a Digital-Focused Bank

Costs to Service Deposits	$4.00
Costs to Service Digital Deposits	$0.15
Difference	*$3.85*
# of Deposit Accounts	*20,000*
Transactions Shifted to Mobile/Month	*2*
Pre-Tax Cost Savings per Month	**$154,000**
Pre-Tax Cost Savings to the Bank	**$1,848,000**

TABLE 2.2 Traditional Community Bank and FinTech Community Bank Comparison

	Traditional Community Bank	FinTech Community Bank
Net Interest Income	36,000	36,000
Non-Interest Income	10,000	10,000
Non-Interest Operating Expenses	(31,050)	(28,750)
Pre-Tax, Pre-Provision Income	14,950	17,250
Provision Expenses	(2,160)	(2,160)
Pre-Tax Income	12,790	15,090
Taxes	(4,477)	(5,282)
Net Income	$8,314	$9,809
Return on Average Assets	*0.83%*	*0.98%*
Return on Tangible Equity	*9.24%*	*10.90%*
Average Equity	90,000	90,000
Average Loans	720,000	720,000
Average Earning Assets	900,000	900,000
Average Assets	1,000,000	1,000,000
Net Interest Margin	4.00%	4.00%
Non-Interest Income/Average Assets	1.00%	1.00%
Efficiency Ratio	67.50%	62.50%
Provision Expenses/Average Loans	0.30%	0.30%

FinTech companies focused on "RegTech," or regulatory technology, in leveraging technology to address compliance/regulatory burdens (at lower costs than hiring additional personnel). While shielded from some of the more onerous regulations impacting the Big Banks, community banks have still faced a growing compliance and regulatory burden since the onset of the financial crisis in mid-2008. The majority of bankers cited regulatory compliance (64% of bankers surveyed) as a factor negatively impacting profitability in a recent survey.[6] To better understand the growing regulatory and compliance burden facing community banks, let's consider the following:[7]

- The Call Report, which all banks file quarterly, has lengthened considerably. Up until the mid-1980s, the typical Call Report filing was less than 10 pages. Since that time, it has increased—now totaling over 80 pages.
- Regulations have become more complex with a growing number of new, lengthy pieces of banking legislation. Both the number of new banking acts and the length of those acts has increased in each decade since the 1960s. In the most recently completed decade (2001–2010), there were 10 new banking acts that became law and totaled approximately 2,000 pages of new legislation.

Hiring additional staff to handle this growing regulatory and compliance burden can have a significant impact on bank profitability. For example, Feldman, Schmidt, and Heinecke (2013) at the Federal Reserve Bank of Minneapolis found a reduction in profitability of 45 basis points for increasing staff by two people for the smallest banks (less than $50 million in assets).[8] By leveraging FinTech innovations in the RegTech area, community banks can see reduced compliance costs and enhanced efficiency.

In addition to addressing the key areas where Big Banks have outperformed community banks in recent periods (non-interest income and efficiency ratios), FinTech also offers some other potential benefits for community banks.

Enhanced Scale FinTech can be used to help community banks compete against Big Banks more effectively by minimizing the impact of scale. Scale matters to most financial services companies. The larger they become, the more efficient and profitable they become by enhancing operating leverage and spreading costs over a larger customer base. Smaller banks cannot replicate a large bank's vast branch network or physical footprint. However, by relying on FinTech, smaller banks can more easily replicate a large bank's footprint digitally via the Web or a mobile device. Therefore, FinTech allows a community bank to compete more effectively with a larger bank by attracting, retaining, and providing services to more customers in a more efficient and less costly manner.

Loan Portfolio Diversification FinTech also offers many community banks an opportunity to enhance loan portfolio diversification and regain some market share after years of losing ground in certain segments. Forward-thinking community banks that are able to leverage FinTech may be able to regain market share in areas recently conceded to other players such as consumer, mortgage, auto, and/or student lending. This added market share in non–real estate segments can help address concentration issues and higher credit risks for community banks that already have a high proportion of certain types of loans (i.e., commercial real estate). As shown in Figures 2.3 and 2.4, concentration risk within community banks' loan portfolios has been growing over time as real estate loans (and particularly commercial real estate loans) currently comprise a greater proportion of the loan portfolio than in 1990.

Also, the makeup of a community bank's real estate portfolio today contains a greater proportion of commercial real estate, construction and development, and multifamily lending than historically. By utilizing FinTech offerings, community banks can limit this concentration risk and expand back into other types of lending with digital consumer, mortgage, auto, and/or student-lending offerings.

Customer Retention and Preference Another benefit of FinTech is that it provides an additional touchpoint to improve customer retention and

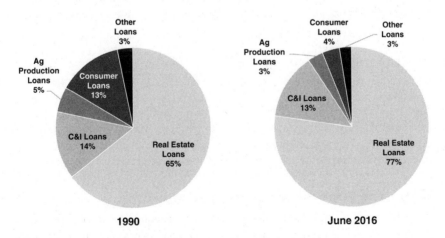

FIGURE 2.3 Community Bank Loan Portfolio Mix (1990 vs. June 2016)
Source: S&P Global Market Intelligence

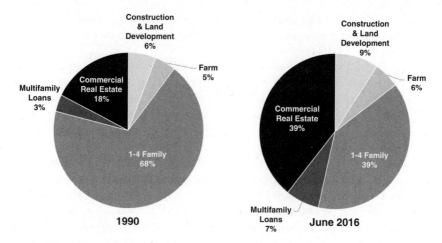

FIGURE 2.4 Community Bank Real Estate Loan Portfolio Mix (1990 vs. June 2016)
Source: S&P Global Market Intelligence

preference. While data is limited, some studies have shown that customer loyalty (i.e., retention) is higher for those customers that use mobile offerings and digital banking (online and mobile) is increasingly preferred by customers.[9] Online banking surpassed branch transactions as the preferred banking method for the first time in 2009 and the gap has only continued to widen.[10] In a 2015 survey, online banking was the most preferred banking method at 32 percent while branch banking had trended down and was only preferred by 17 percent of customers.[11] The number of people preferring mobile was also growing at 12 percent of customers compared to a significantly smaller proportion five years earlier. While digital is clearly growing among customer preference, data has also shown that digital-only customers can be less engaged, loyal, and profitable than those who interact with the bank through a combination of interactions across multiple channels (digital, branches, etc.).[12] So community banks that already rely more heavily on their branch networks should find it beneficial to add digital services to complement their traditional offerings in order to enhance customer retention and preference.[13]

Change Is Inevitable; Growth Is Optional

As technological advances continue to penetrate the banking industry, community banks will need to leverage technology in order to more effectively market to and serve small businesses and consumers in an evolving environment. Community banks will increasingly rely on a model that makes widespread use of ATMs, the Internet, mobile apps, and algorithm-driven decision making, enabling them to deliver their services to customers in a streamlined and efficient manner.

For these reasons, banking and financial services is already the most technologically intense sector today as measured by IT spending relative to revenue and operating expenses. In addition, technology spending is expected to continue to increase going forward. Historically, banks have spent approximately 6–7 percent of revenues on IT. Banks still spend more globally on IT, an average of 5–9 percent of revenues, compared to the 3 percent of revenue IT spend of the insurance and airline industries.[14] Analysts with consulting firm Ovum see no end in this spending pattern, as they predict that IT spending in banks will increase 5 percent annually to $158 billion in 2019 (up from $131 billion in 2015).[15] Top spending initiatives are planned in the areas of security, analytics, and digital banking (an umbrella term for online and mobile), according to industry research.

FINTECH'S POTENTIAL IMPACT ON BANK VALUATION

Having over a decade's worth of experience valuing community banks, I readily acknowledge that each bank's valuation is unique but I attempt to summarize key valuation themes and approaches and demonstrate how FinTech can improve a bank's valuation. Valuing a bank is, by its nature, forward looking with history serving as a guide. Valuation tends to revolve around three primary elements, *earnings/cash flow, risk,* and *growth,* and significant trade-offs can exist among these three elements, particularly when valuing banks.

A bank's earnings, dividend-paying capacity, and growth can be enhanced in the short-to-intermediate term by taking more risk while the impact of that decision (usually credit losses from more aggressive loan underwriting) may not be evident for several years. A well-reasoned bank valuation needs to consider the potential trade-offs and the implications of higher earnings and growth today versus potential risks in the future. Banks considering FinTech niches and partnerships should also weigh the trade-off between growth and risk, as they must strike a balance between attempting to grow revenues and profitability against the potential risk of trying an innovative piece of software or technology.

Two common approaches to valuing a bank are:

■ **Income Approach.** The discounted cash flow (DCF) method is an income approach whereby the bank's value is determined by summing the present value of distributable cash flows generated over the forecast period and the terminal value at end of forecast period. Key elements in a DCF method include distributable cash flow (i.e., existing and internally generated capital that is in excess of a reasonable threshold level), the terminal value that is derived typically from earnings or book value at the end of the forecast period times a multiple of earnings and/or tangible book value and the discount rate.

■ **Market Approach.** Using the market approach, the bank's value is typically determined based upon comparisons to transactions in public banks, whole bank acquisitions, and/or historical transactions in the bank's own stock. The guideline public company or guideline transactions method involves utilizing pricing multiples derived from publicly traded banks or acquired banks bearing similarities to the subject bank, such as business model, asset size, credit quality, geographic region, and profitability. Common bank valuation multiples include price/earnings, price/tangible book value, and core deposit premiums relative to tangible book value (control). Applying the guideline group multiples, inclusive of adjustments for fundamental differences between the subject bank and the guideline groups if necessary, can provide meaningful indications of value. The transactions method may also be helpful as inferences can sometimes be drawn from historical transactions in the bank's stock.

FinTech can be used by community banks to create strategic value and enhance their valuation by improving one or some combination of the three key valuation elements: cash flow, risk, and growth. For example, FinTech can help improve cash flow through either increasing revenues (spread or non-interest income), or reducing expenses, reducing risk through enhanced diversification of product offerings, or increasing potential growth prospects from adding the ability to grow revenues faster through new product offerings or greater customer retention. The trade-off between increased cash flow and potential growth rates versus additional risk will be important to measure and analyze when assessing FinTech niches and their valuation impact.

This enhanced financial performance from leveraging FinTech can significantly impact valuation. Returning to our prior example of the Traditional Community Bank and FinTech Community Bank in Table 2.3, the valuation range for FinTech Community Bank could be 20–25 percent higher at *$125–$150 million* than Traditional Community Bank at *$100–$125 million* (even assuming the same valuation multiple) as shown in the table.

In addition to the valuation benefit from enhanced profitability, FinTech Community Bank's valuation could also benefit from multiple expansion. We previously noted that two key potential benefits from FinTech were to

TABLE 2.3 Price-to-Earnings Multiple Comparison of Traditional Community Bank to FinTech Community Bank

	Implied Financial Performance			Price-to-Earnings Multiple			
	Net Income	ROAA	ROTE	10.0	12.5	15.0	17.5
	7,000	0.70%	7.78%	70,000	87,500	105,000	122,500
Traditional Bank	8,000	0.80%	8.89%	80,000	100,000	120,000	140,000
	9,000	0.90%	10.00%	90,000	112,500	135,000	157,500
FinTech Bank	10,000	1.00%	11.11%	100,000	125,000	150,000	175,000
	11,000	1.10%	12.22%	110,000	137,500	165,000	192,500

improve efficiency by lowering costs and to increase non-interest income. A common approach to valuing a bank is utilizing pricing multiples derived from publicly traded banks bearing similarities to the subject bank such as business model, asset size, credit quality, geographic region, and profitability. Common bank valuation multiples examined among the public banks include price/earnings and price/tangible book value.

To examine the potential impact on the valuation multiple from improving those two performance measures, we examined pricing multiples of publicly traded community banks with assets between $500 million and $1 billion (see Table 2.4) and found that banks that have higher levels of non-interest income and/or lower efficiency ratios tend to achieve higher valuations from a combination of improved profitability and higher multiples. Thus, those banks that are able to effectively leverage FinTech to increase non-interest income and lower efficiency ratios can ultimately enhance shareholder value relative to their counterparts that solely focus on other strategies.

HOW COMMUNITY BANKS CAN HELP FINTECH COMPANIES

In addition to potentially enhancing the profitability and valuation of community banks, a relationship with a community bank can also be beneficial to FinTech companies for a number of reasons. The FinTech company can benefit from being able to test their product or service and improve it before they roll it out to larger banks or more customers, scaling more quickly and at

TABLE 2.4 Summary of Guideline Company Analysis

Public Company Group Description	Price/LTM Core EPS	Price/Tangible Book Value	Core ROATCE
National Banks: Assets $500 Mil–$1 Bil	13.4×	1.02×	8.36%
High Non-Int't Income Banks: Assets $500M–$1BN*	14.2×	1.18×	9.47%
Low Efficiency Ratio Banks: Assets $500M–$1BN**	13.7×	1.19×	9.23%

*Non-Int't Income/Assets >1% in LTM period
**Efficiency Ratio <60% in LTM period
Source: S&P Global Market Intelligence, Market Pricing information as of 6/30/2016

lower acquisition costs from accessing the community bank's customers, and elevating their brand by partnering with a more established brand within the financial services landscape. The knowledge of the bank's management team can also prove invaluable for the FinTech company as it prepares for potential regulatory and compliance scrutiny. Additionally, there are a broader number of smaller community banks located in a diverse range of markets (from urban to rural), which provides a larger and potentially more diverse client pool for FinTech companies.

FinTech entrepreneurs who understand market conditions and the ability of FinTech to enhance performance and valuation of community banks can focus on providing FinTech solutions that meet the needs of community banks and also enhance marketing efforts to potential community bank customers. Historically, the Big Banks have often led the way in rolling out new FinTech innovations. For example, ApplePay was rolled out first to the largest banks and then trickled down to the community banks. However, savvy FinTech entrepreneurs should realize that community banks are a rich market for FinTech as well. Opportunities exist to develop innovations and foster relationships in order to partner with community banks.

CONCLUSION

Despite the potential benefits of FinTech for community banks and vice versa, significant challenges exist for community banks considering FinTech opportunities. Community banks typically operate with leaner in-house management, technology staff, and technology experience to evaluate and pursue FinTech opportunities. Additionally, the appeal of FinTech can often be overshadowed by the breadth of the landscape, which can be overwhelming for a smaller bank and make it difficult for them to pinpoint which niche may be best for them to pursue. Lastly, there can be significant cultural, valuation, and risk differences between banks and FinTech companies, which can make partnerships and mergers between the two difficult.

Consequently, this book will attempt to address some of these issues in greater detail and illustrate how both financial institutions and FinTech companies can create strategic value from improving one or some combination of the three primary valuation elements of cash flow, risk, and growth. To accomplish this, we discuss the FinTech landscape by providing overviews of trends in a number of FinTech niches in order for bankers to consider which areas of FinTech may be the best fit for their institution. For community banks seeking to explore FinTech further, this book discusses specific ways to consider structuring an investment, partnership, or merger and the right metrics to utilize in order to develop a framework for measuring and comparing FinTech opportunities.

NOTES

1. "Community Bank Facts," http://www.icba.org/files/ICBASites/PDFs/cbfacts .pdf.
2. "Fintech Poses No. 1 Threat to Community Banks, Execs Tell FDIC," *Bloomberg BNA*, July 22, 2016, http://www.bna.com/fintech-poses-no-n73014445156/.
3. Jonathan Camhi, "The Next Generation of Bank Branch Employees," *Information Week*, http://www.banktech.com/channels/the-next-generation-of-bank-branch-employees/d/d-id/1298073, accessed April 21, 2015.
4. "Banking's Big Challenge: Breaking Away from the Branch Model," *American Banker*, October 14, 2014.
5. Daniel Huang, "Mobile's Rise Poses a Riddle for Banks," *Wall Street Journal*, December 18, 2014, http://www.wsj.com/articles/mobiles-rise-poses-a-riddle-for-banks-1418945162. While data is limited in regard to the cost comparison of a mobile versus a traditional transaction, this article cites a survey that showed an average cost of $0.17 for digital transactions versus $4.00 for an interaction with a bank teller.
6. Bank Director, 2015 Growth Strategy Survey, http://www.bankdirector .com/issues/growth/2015-growth-strategy-survey-are-banks-missing-out-on-millennials/.
7. Preston Ash, Christoffer Koch, and Thomas F. Slems, "Too Small to Succeed?: Community Banks in a New Regulatory Environment," published by the Dallas Fed in the December 31, 2015, issue of *Financial Insights*.
8. See "Quantifying the Costs of Additional Regulation on Community Banks," by Ron J. Feldman, Jason Schmidt, and Ken Heinecke, *Economic Policy Paper 13-3, Federal Reserve Bank of Minneapolis*, May 30, 2013.

9. Daniel Huang, "Mobile's Rise Poses a Riddle for Banks," *Wall Street Journal*, December 18, 2014, http://www.wsj.com/articles/mobiles-rise-poses-a-riddle-for-banks-1418945162.

10. "ABA Survey: Consumers Prefer Banking Online," September 21, 2009, http://www.mediapost.com/publications/article/113969/survey-consumers-prefer-banking-online.html?edition.

11. "ABA Survey: More Consumers Turning to Mobile Banking," *American Bankers Association*, August 11, 2015, http://www.aba.com/Press/Pages/081115MobileBankingSurvey.aspx.

12. Daniel Huang, "Mobile's Rise Poses a Riddle for Banks," *Wall Street Journal*, December 18, 2014, http://www.wsj.com/articles/mobiles-rise-poses-a-riddle-for-banks-1418945162.

13. Ibid.

14. "Breakthrough IT Banking," *McKinsey on Business Technology*, Spring 2012, www.mckinsey.com/~/media/mckinsey/dotcom/client_service/BTO/PDF/MOBT26_Breakthrough_IT_banking.ashx, accessed June 22, 2016.

15. "Retail Banking Technology," *Ovum.com*, http://www.ovum.com/retail-banking-technology/, accessed June 22, 2016.

CHAPTER 3

The Historical Context for FinTech

INTRODUCTION

The aftermath of the Great Recession left a market environment that was incredibly suitable for FinTech companies to emerge. Key elements of this environment included banks tightening credit standards, a low interest rate environment that effectively offset a significant proportion of the funding advantage that banks have, the proliferation of technology in consumers' everyday lives, rising consumer expectations and trust in digital offerings (e.g., the evolution of digital offerings in retail and entertainment led to higher expectations for digital delivery of financial services), a relatively benign credit environment that has facilitated credit quality for lenders, and a robust funding market for early-stage ventures.

While market conditions are favorable for FinTech presently and a number of pundits are hailing its potential, technology has a long history within financial services and that history is littered with examples of grand successes and failures. By examining the history of technological innovation within financial services before we delve deeper into current trends and outlook for FinTech niches in Section Two of this book, we can determine what has been successful in the past and provide some historical context for what may be successful in the future. Consequently, this chapter provides a historical context for today's FinTech companies, investors, and bankers. It also presents case studies on some selected FinTech companies that have already matured and had success from leveraging technology to provide financial services.

FINTECH HISTORY

Automated Teller Machines[1]

Automated teller machines, commonly known as ATMs, have a ubiquitous, worldwide presence as fast and convenient kiosks where bank customers can withdraw small amounts of cash. ATMs were so revolutionary to the banking industry that former Fed Chairman Paul Volcker stated in a 2009 speech that the ATM has been the "only useful innovation in banking." The roots of the development of the ATM stem from the self-service culture arising in the 1950s and 1960s.

This shift began in Europe in 1967 when some of the earliest ATMs were deployed by British and Swedish banks. In response to unions' calls for more favorable hours for bank tellers, European bankers employed engineers to build automated teller systems that would provide customers with access to cash at all hours of the day. The result of these collaborations was the deployment of the world's first ATMs in 1967, the Bankomat in Sweden and Barclaycash and the Chubb MDR in the U.K. These deployments were made possible by technological innovation that had been advancing through the 1960s—mainly algorithms that allowed these pioneer machines to associate a customer's unique PIN number with his or her bank account and video display units to direct customers through transactions. The biggest issue for these cashpoints (as they were and are commonly referred to in Europe) was creating a computer system that would allow them to connect to the computers in the banks, which is where IBM got involved. IBM began working with Lloyds Bank in 1973 to develop the IBM 2984, the first truly modern ATM.

ATM innovation was not limited to European banks, as an engineer named David Wetzel introduced the first ATM in the United States in 1969. Wetzel's ATM, the Docuteller, was first introduced at Chemical Bank in Rockville Centre, New York, in September 1969. The rudimentary machine would disperse a fixed amount of cash when customers inserted a specially coded card. The introduction of the ATM was so revolutionary to Chemical Bank that it proclaimed, "On September 2, our bank will open at 9 and never close again." In 1971, Docutel, the maker of the Docuteller, and Diebold began manufacturing ATMs in the United States for widespread distribution. U.S. banks began adopting the ATM in efforts to stay ahead of the technology curve. Whereas buzzwords like *blockchain* and *big data* are driving today's FinTech environment, banks saw buzzwords like *self-service* and *automation* as key drivers of ATM adoption. As ATM use and adoption in the United States became more widespread throughout the 1970s, Diebold and NCR became the industry leaders in ATM manufacturing and worked to turn ATMs into the sleek, modernized units they are today. To cap off the first real decade of ATM adoption, in 1979 banks began to utilize computer switching systems that would allow customers of other banks to use their ATMs for a fee. The 1970s laid a solid foundation for ATMs to become a part of everyday American life as innovation continued to improve the machines.

The 1980s saw ATMs mature into sleeker, more modern machines that would become much more reliable and user-friendly than earlier versions. NCR and Diebold continued to dominate the ATM manufacturing industry in the United States and began to add many of the features that we know today. Some of these features included advanced video display units, programmable buttons, cash that was dispensed horizontally, and expanded functionality. Most banks adopted these modernized ATMs by the 1980s, as they were a considerably better use of capital than they had been in their developmental stages. By the 1990s, ATMs became available virtually everywhere in the United States, made possible by the modernization of digital telephoning and use of Windows OS in ATMs. Banks could now run remote diagnostics on their ATMs and virtually manage the internal processes from anywhere. The key implication of this improvement was the creation of *independent ATM deployers* (IADs), which are third-party ATM vendors not associated with any bank. IADs began to place ATMs in high-frequency locations such as malls and convenient stores, further dotting the landscape with the cash machines. Because of these advancements, today there are more than 420,000 ATMs in use in the United States.

One of the more recent innovations includes interactive teller machines. These machines connect customers to live tellers in call centers via video call, allowing customers to receive assistance at ATMs in real time. NCR rolled out 350 of these machines in 2013.

Mobile payments and digital wallets are perhaps today's biggest threat to ATM manufacturers and banks that rely on ATMs for revenue. According to a report from the American Banking Association, only 13 percent of bank customers are using ATMs to manage their accounts, down from 17 percent in 2009.[2,3] Customers also report visiting ATMs less frequently, the most common response being "once every two weeks," down from "once or twice a week" in 2009. This trend is evident in the growth in ATMs as they have been growing at a faster pace globally than in the United States. The United States also appears relatively saturated with a significantly higher number of ATMs per 100,000 people than the rest of the world and also four-to-five times as many ATMs per 100,000 people as there are physical branches per 100,000 people.[4]

Key Takeaway While much of the history and development of ATMs lies in the U.K., Sweden, and the United States, perhaps the future growth of ATMs lies in countries such as Kenya, India, and China. ATM use in countries

TABLE 3.1   Number of ATMs per 100,000 People

				% Annual Change	
	2004	2009	2014	('09/'04)	('14/'09)
U.S.	164.9	173.1	na	1.0%	
World	18.4	28.4	44.0	9.0%	9.1%

Source: World Development Indicators

in the Middle East, Asia, and Africa is skyrocketing as financial inclusion is becoming more widespread in the developing countries of these regions. The data in Table 3.1 shows further evidence of this trend as ATM growth worldwide has outstripped the more mature U.S. market in the last few years.

Electronic Stock Trading

The practice of owning and trading shares of an organization to realize a profit dates back to the era of the Roman Republic, in which the orator Cicero articulated in a speech that a trade group's "shares had a very high price at the time." Many scholars mark the birth of the modern stock market as we know it when the Dutch East India Trading Company began issuing shares of corporate stock to the public in the early 1600s. In the United States, New York brokers formally organized the New York Stock and Exchange board in 1817, which was renamed the New York Stock Exchange in 1863. All that to say the owning and trading of stocks by investors has gone on for a very long time, but technological advances in the last 100 years have led to the widespread proliferation of electronic stock trading. Electronic stock trading has made stock markets more accessible to a wider portion of the population and lowered the cost of trading stocks, leading to the highest levels of trading volume ever seen in markets. However, stocks did not begin trading electronically overnight. Technological advances in the past century, and particularly the past 50 years, have grown electronic trading from its most rudimentary form of the late 19th and early 20th centuries to today's high-speed, automated trading environment.

Before the use of the telegraphic and stock tickertape became widespread, stock prices were communicated through word of mouth and in aggregated summaries that were circulated at the end of a trading day. In 1867, tickertape stock price telegraphs were invented by Edward A. Calahan, an employee of American Telegraph Company. These telegraphs represented the first automation of stock prices and allowed prices to be relayed to investors rapidly and accurately. Brokers and speculators could now gather in centralized locations with tickertapes to buy and sell stocks. By the 1880s, there were around 1,000 of these tickertapes in use around New York City, creating some of the earliest American stock markets. These early markets became known as "bucket shops." A typical bucket shop consisted of one clerk reading the tickertape to another clerk, who wrote the stock prices on a chalkboard while speculators bought and sold shares of the listed stocks. This system led to a great deal of fraud and extortion. In the wake of the Stock Market Crash of 1929, bucket shops disappeared as a result of increased regulation. During this regulation of the markets during the 1930s, modern exchanges such as the New York Stock Exchange and Chicago Board of Trade were created as strictly regulated entities devoid of the chaos that often came in the bucket shops. The creation of these modern exchanges laid the foundation for the widespread proliferation of electronic trading.

Electronic stock trading took another step forward in 1969 when Instinet, the world's first electronic communication network for the buying and selling of securities, went live. Brokers could now post buy and sell offers at any time of the day, even after markets had closed. In 1971, the National Association of Securities Dealers created the NASDAQ, which would automate stock quotes by posting bids and offers on an electronic bulletin board. The NASDAQ vastly lowered the spread on stock prices, initially making it unpopular among brokerages, which made their profits on spreads. The NASDAQ also created the first electronic over-the-counter (OTC) market in which trades did not take place on a physical exchange. Before 1971, OTC trades took place over the phone or the wire, but the proliferation of the NASDAQ allowed quotes to be read and trades to be executed over an electronic network.

The New York Stock Exchange also created its Designated Order Turnaround (DOT) system in 1976, which allowed trades to be sent to specialists on the floor of the exchange. This system was replaced by the SuperDOT in 1984, which had the capability to allow investors or brokers to enter a trade into the system and have it sent to an agent on the NYSE floor upon entrance. The investor or broker would then immediately receive confirmation of the transaction from the system.

Most investors never directly used the SuperDOT, but rather software or online services offered by brokers. After the stock market crashed again in October 1987, the NASDAQ enlarged its small-order execution system (SOES) to give dealers the ability to execute smaller trades electronically rather than over the phone when broker-dealers stopped answering their phones in the aftermath of the crash. This gave rise to individual, electronic "day traders." In the late 1980s, the NASDAQ also launched its first electronic communications network. ECNs, such as Island, began to pop up across the trading landscape, which furthered the rise of day traders, who could set their own prices.

By the mid-1990s, the New York Stock Exchange had begun the process of becoming fully automated with the introduction of wireless handheld computers to receive and execute trades. Today, all stocks on the New York Stock Exchange can be traded electronically, whether for immediate execution or to be sent to the trading floor of the exchange. The SEC also authorized electronic exchanges in 1998, which would allow high-frequency trading to proliferate. High-frequency trading is driven by massive computing power and complex algorithms, allowing trades to be executed in nanoseconds. This provided further liquidity and further narrowed spreads in the market, making trading and investing even cheaper and more accessible. From 2005 to 2009, the proportion of high-frequency trades in total equity trading grew rapidly and peaked in 2009 at approximately 60 percent of total equity trades. Since 2009, high-frequency trading has declined as a proportion of total equity trades to below 50 percent but still well above 2005 levels of 20 percent.[5]

Key Takeaway The automated and electronically driven stock market that we see today did not appear overnight, nor did the stock market as a whole. Through innovation and technological advances, stock trading has evolved to become almost fully automated and exclusively electronic. This has made the stock market more efficient and accessible, giving way to some of the highest trading volumes in history. Given the rapid evolution of the stock market through electronic trading in the past 50 years, there is no way of telling what the future holds, whether it be further innovation and improvement in the market or a holding pattern in which the current technology can further proliferate across the financial landscape.

VISA AND MASTERCARD: THE LARGEST IPOs IN FINTECH HISTORY

Two of the largest IPOs in FinTech history were Visa Inc. and MasterCard Inc. Both Visa and MasterCard operate proprietary payment networks that process payments on debit and credit cards. Both Visa and MasterCard have been extremely successful since their IPOs as well, with market capitalizations of $177 billion and $97 billion at June 30, 2016, respectively, and returns outpacing broader markets and the FinTech industry from IPO through June 30, 2016, as detailed in Figure 3.1.

To gain greater perspective regarding their history and some common themes from their success, let's consider their brief history as well as a few key takeaways from their success.

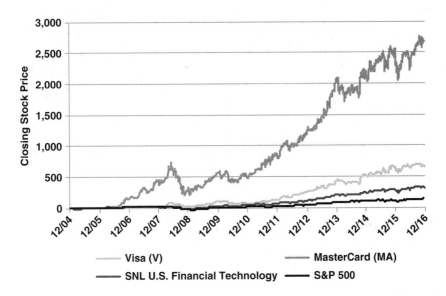

FIGURE 3.1 Total Returns for Visa

Visa

Visa was founded in 1958 after Bank of America launched a consumer credit card program called BankAmericard for middle-class consumers and small to midsize merchants in the United States. It had a rocky start before becoming reasonably profitable but was then challenged by the issuance of a rival card called MasterCharge (a forerunner to MasterCard) by some other California banks. Bank of America's response was to franchise BankAmericards nationwide, which then sparked a trend of other banks responding with their own proprietary cards and franchise systems. Interestingly, the banks were largely focused on issuing the cards to consumers and a number of cards were mailed to various parties.

With so many cards issued, fraud was rampant and a number of the banks were losing money; therefore, in the late 1960s, Bank of America had a meeting among its licensees to find a solution to address the problems of BankAmericard. Coming out of that meeting was the start of the more formal Visa enterprise. It was decided that Dee Hock, who at the time was a VP at a licensee bank but would later become chairman of Visa, was to study the issues. In mid-1970, control of the BankAmericard system passed to a new entity called National BankAmericard Inc., which was later renamed Visa International with Dee Hock as CEO.

Visa was structured as a non-stock, for-profit membership corporation with ownership in the form of nontransferable rights of participation. The organization was intended to operate in a highly decentralized and collaborative manner. It had an interesting paradox in that the financial institutions that were members of the corporation were also fierce competitors as they each issued cards attempting to attract the same pool of customers, but they also had to cooperate such that merchants would be able to take Visa cards issued by any bank at their locations. Thus, Visa had an underlying theme of both intense cooperation and competition among the participating bank partners.[6]

Significant corporate milestones for Visa include expanding internationally in 1974 and introducing the debit card in 1975. In 2007, the regional Visa businesses were merged and the company IPO'd in 2008. It was one of the largest IPOs in history. Presently Visa operates in over 200 countries and its services are available on a multitude of devices (cards, laptops, tablets, mobile devices).[7]

MasterCard

MasterCard was formed as a competitor to BankAmericard by six California banks in 1966. MasterCard's business was primarily conducted through the principal subsidiary, MasterCard International, a Delaware membership corporation that was incorporated in November 1966 until MasterCard Inc., a Delaware stock corporation, was incorporated in May 2001. Similar to Visa, MasterCard was owned by financial institutions until its IPO in 2006. In 2002, MasterCard moved from a member association to a private share company and began making filings with the SEC.[8] MasterCard is the second-largest card network but the IPO has commonly been cited as a catalyst for the company.

MasterCard's performance since IPO has been phenomenal. MasterCard's annual ROE has been in excess of 40 percent from calendar 2009 through 2015. Key drivers of growth since the IPO include: [9]

- M&A activity
- Focus on new markets—e-commerce, mobile, prepaid (which helps the underbanked)
- Broadened focus—not just on the large players but also the small and midsize issuers
- Able to have more of a negotiating process with issuing and acquiring banks since they are no longer owners
- A better relationship with vendors, who no longer feel they are being overcharged
- Promoting debit and not just credit cards

An impetus for the IPO for both Visa and MasterCard was a litany of antitrust lawsuits brought by merchants who felt that MasterCard, Visa, and major banks were colluding on the cost of interchange. The IPO helped to change the ownership structure, which was being closely scrutinized, and reducing bank ownership. MasterCard management also attributed the IPO with the ability to compete more effectively following a rapidly evolving and dynamic environment as the payments industry underwent significant changes since mid-2000.

Key Takeaways from the Visa and MasterCard Examples

Both the Visa and MasterCard examples are interesting templates for FinTech companies today in that a bank partnership model was effective as they grew, but then once it got to a certain size it transitioned to a more traditional ownership structure. Both structures helped the company compete and thrive during different stages of the corporate lifecycle. Additionally, the IPOs of both Visa and MasterCard created profits for a number of banks as both were owned by banks at the time of their IPO.

CORE VENDORS

FinTech companies important to community banks are core vendors. Three of the largest core vendors are FiServ, FIS, and Jack Henry. Each company has a unique history that provides context for FinTech companies focused on providing technology services to banks, particularly those focused on serving community banks.

FiServ

FiServ Inc. is a global financial services technology provider based in Brookfield, Wisconsin. FiServ was created in 1984 as the result of a merger between two smaller pioneer bank technology firms, First Data Processing and Sunshine State Systems. FiServ operated as a privately held company for two years before going public in 1986 as a $70 million data processing business serving large financial institutions. FiServ's IPO occurred on September 25, 1986, at a price of $1.10 per share under the ticker symbol FISV.

After operating profitably for several years, FiServ began an aggressive corporate strategy of acquiring smaller firms to increase their capabilities and customer offerings. FiServ's first major acquisition came in 1994 when it bought out Citicorp Information Resources, a division of Citi Group. This strategic move expanded FiServ into the commercial banking space and greatly increased its customer base. FiServ also was certified with the

ISO 9000 standard of quality in 1994, which ensured that the company was meeting both the needs of customers and regulatory requirements related to their suite of products.

FiServ continued its aggressive strategy into 1995 with the acquisition of Information Technology Inc. The acquisition of ITI made FiServ the leader in client/server solutions and would prompt the launch of Fiserv.com later in the year. On the heels of this tremendous growth, FiServ announced it had surpassed $1 billion in revenue in 1998, firmly establishing itself at the forefront of bank technology solutions.

The company's largest acquisition to date occurred in 2007 when it bought CheckFree Corporation for $4.4 billion in cash. This massive transaction gave FiServ electronic billing and payment capabilities to offer to their clients, which have proliferated across the banking industry.

In 2008, FiServ launched its first mobile banking system, which created banking access in text message, web browser, and app form. FiServ's latest innovation, PopMoney, launched in 2012 and enables banks to offer instant person-to-person transfers and payments to their customers.

Thus, through acquisitions and innovation, FiServ has been on the leading edge of the introduction of many of the new services being offered by FinTech startups today. In 2016, FiServ generates over $5 billion in revenue annually, has more than 170 patents issued or pending, and has seen double-digit EPS growth every year for the past 30 years.

Per its website, FiServ defines itself as a financial services technology provider, but is fundamentally very different from the disruptive FinTech companies that have popped up in the past few years. Given that FiServ has been in operation since 1984, it has gained the scale needed to be at the forefront of the FinTech industry as a leading player.

While many FinTech startups look to disrupt the business models of banks, established FinTechs like FiServ attempt to facilitate innovation in banks and lead them through a dynamic technological landscape. FiServ CEO Jeff Yabuki articulated this role in Fiserv's recent annual shareholders' meeting in May:

> *The big difference is we don't view ourselves as being disruptors to our clients. We view ourselves as being enablers. And so by investing in innovation, by investing in technologies that deliver new experiences, we believe that we will equip our clients, the banking industry, the billers, and frankly even our end consumers to be able to perform even better versus some of the FinTech alternatives that are out there. So we view ourselves as partners, not as disruptors.*[10]

As previously mentioned, FiServ experienced tremendous growth beginning in 1994 through its aggressive strategy of acquiring emerging companies and leveraging these companies' innovations to better serve their clients. FiServ's largest deal to date, its acquisition of CheckFree Corporation, was lauded as the deal that would "bury independent, pure-play options for banks' back offices" and sent shockwaves across the bank technology industry.[11] Both companies mutually benefited from the transaction as FiServ gained access to CheckFree's electronic bill-pay technology and CheckFree could showcase their product on a larger platform while both gained access to each other's extensive client book. One analyst took on a less positive view of the deal, stating, "After years of ... failing to emulate chief competitor Metavante in growing organically its own payment processing business, Fiserv has finally reverted to its primary skill—using its stock as currency to grow the company by acquisition."[12] While this may be true, the strategy has served FiServ well as evidenced by the steady growth of its EPS and revenue as well as the consistently favorable performance of its equity in the market.

In conclusion, as one of the earliest FinTech pioneers, FiServ is in a position where it does not have to disrupt the industry to make a name for itself as many FinTech startups are forced to do. Rather, FiServ can willingly act as strategic partner and facilitator with banks to help them improve their processes in order to better serve their customers through sleeker platforms, new innovations, and enhanced security measures. Furthermore, FiServ has clearly benefited from its strategy of acquiring emerging FinTech companies through leveraging their technologies rather than trying to build new technology in-house. While this has created a corporate structure that makes FiServ look more like a large holding company made up of many different smaller entities, the strategy has allowed FiServ to offer a diverse suite of products to banks of all sizes and the customers of these banks.

FIS™

FIS is a large global provider of bank and payments technology based in Jacksonville, Florida. FIS was founded in 1968 as a data processing company based in Arkansas called Systematics. In 1990, Systematics was acquired by Alltel and rebranded as Alltel Information Services. Alltel Information Services was acquired by Fidelity National Financial in 2003 and again renamed, this time as Fidelity Information Services.

Since its most recent incarnation as FIS, the company has experienced tremendous growth through a combination of strategic acquisitions and organic growth from within. As a result of this growth, FIS has become the world's largest global provider of banking and payments technology and a member of both the Fortune 500 and the S&P 500. FIS offers a large suite of products and services designed to serve the entire scope of the banking industry from smaller community banks to large investment banks spanning the globe.

FIS's growth strategy in the past ten years has been aided by its willingness to acquire and merge with other companies to increase capabilities and market share. FIS began to gain the scale to establish itself as an industry leader in bank technology when it merged with Certegy in 2006. With the merger, Certegy was meant to be the surviving entity, but changed its name to Fidelity Information Services and relocated to Jacksonville, Florida, leaving FIS as the de facto surviving entity. The newly formed FIS could now offer payment processing services, as Certegy was an industry leader in check verification and credit card processing. FIS began trading on the New York Stock Exchange in 2006 after completing the merger with Certegy. The combined company became Fidelity National Information Services and traded under the ticker symbol FIS.

FIS's next big move came in 2009 when it acquired its chief competitor, Metavante Technologies Inc., for around $3 billion. The move was beneficial for both companies as FIS could capitalize off of Metavante's strong U.S. footprint and Metavante could leverage FIS's global presence to present its products to a wider customer base. The deal sent shockwaves throughout the FinTech industry, catching many off guard as Metavante was not considered to be an acquisition target since it held a very large market share in competing with FIS. Bob Hunt of TowerGroup commented on the massive implications of the deal:

> I did not foresee a deal between these two companies because they're both so big in the market. You always think of [FIS and Metavante] as the two survivors. This is probably the most significant acquisition we've seen over the last 10 years.[13]

Hunt would go on to observe that with the acquisition, FIS would now serve around 50 of the top 100 banks in the deposit processing space. For FIS, the most attractive factor in expanding its business through the acquisition of Metavante was the ability to leverage Metavante's extensive payment processing network, which had been in use in banks worldwide, whereas FIS's payment processing network was more confined to domestic banks. Further, in observing the effects of the acquisition on the bank technology industry, Bob Meara of Celent commented that "this will bring FIS up to roughly the same scale as FiServ, leaving OSI [Open Solutions] and Jack Henry trailing by quite a distance."[14]

Most recently, FIS acquired SunGard, which at the time was one of the world's leading providers of enterprise banking and capital market solutions. The deal closed in November 2015, giving FIS both expanded and newfound capabilities in providing tech solutions in the capital markets and investment banks. Gary Norcross, CEO of FIS, commented on the deal, stating that he favored "acquisitions that fit two veins: those offering us a new product or service in one of our existing markets, or those that allow us to break into an adjacent market, or in a perfect scenario, both. SunGard was that perfect scenario—it broke us into the asset management space and extended our wealth capabilities." The deal contributed to FIS's creating a complete and holistic suite of technology solutions for banks and other financial institutions. The SunGard acquisition, along with the strategic acquisitions of Certegy and Metavante, has brought FIS to the scale that they enjoy today as a leading global provider of bank technology.

Not only has FIS been able to grow its business to nearly $9 billion in revenue through strategic acquisitions and mergers, it has also benefited from a plan to foster organic growth from within its organization. FIS focuses on two facets to this plan for growth—growing its base business by keeping clients in step with technological innovation and reinvesting revenue into research and development—which when coupled with its acquisition strategy come together to create an all-encompassing strategic growth plan.[15]

FIS has addressed the first part of this plan, growing its base business, by staying in touch with the rapidly evolving technological world and effectively introducing their clients to potentially disruptive technologies such as blockchain and cloud computing in an effort to give existing clients new capabilities to more efficiently serve their customers. The second part of FIS's plan for organic growth has been implemented through FIS's 6 percent investment of revenue back into the company's research and development department. This investment has funded various centers of research with different focuses in FIS offices around the globe. For example, the FIS office in San Francisco specializes in exploring the ways in which mobile capabilities are impacting banks, offices in New York are exploring how the acquisition of SunGard could shape capital markets in the future, and FIS in Bangalore is extensively studying global financial inclusion. These research hubs will allow FIS to more effectively respond to innovation and disruption in the bank technology industry and grow its business into unchartered territory. While acquisitions and mergers have contributed to the rapid growth of FIS's business, the company's plan for growth from within is set to foster sustained and steady growth in a rapidly evolving technological environment.

In conclusion, FIS has benefited from its positioning itself as a technological partner to banks of all sizes spanning the globe. FIS's equity shares have performed well in the public market over the past five years, outpacing the S&P 500 by nearly 100 basis points in price change.[16] As a FinTech giant, FIS does not have to rely on disrupting the financial services industry to generate scale and revenue as a FinTech startup would, but rather can help banks leverage technological innovations in the financial landscape and provide tech solutions that will help banks grow their business and more efficiently serve their customers.

Jack Henry

Jack Henry & Associates is a financial services technology provider dedicated to "enabling our customers to process financial transactions, automate their businesses and succeed in an increasingly competitive marketplace."[17] Jack Henry & Associates was founded in 1976 in Monett, Missouri, by Jack Henry and Jerry Hall and has kept its corporate headquarters in Monett since its founding. After bringing in $9,360 in 1977, Jack Henry steadily grew its business before going public in October 1985 with an initial offering of 1.5 million shares on the NASDAQ exchange.

Jack Henry entered the outsourcing business in 1992 and continued to develop bank software and refine its processes through the 1990s, establishing itself as an industry leader in bank technology. In 2000, Jack Henry made its first big acquisition with the purchase of the Symitar brand and its Episys core processor. The company fully immersed itself in the acquisition game in 2004 when it announced an official targeted acquisition strategy. Jack Henry began acquiring companies with clients outside of its traditional core client group, allowing it to expand into financial institutions of varying types and charter sizes.

In 2006, the company officially launched the three distinct brands that operate under the Jack Henry umbrella: JH Banking, Symitar, and Profit Stars. These three brands employ different core competencies from one another and serve various types and sizes of financial institutions. Together, these three brands helped Jack Henry & Associates bring in a reported $1.3 billion in revenue in 2015.

JH Banking evolved out of Jack Henry's original business model of providing banks with software and tech solutions to enable its customers to efficiently and effectively process transactions. JH Banking currently serves around 1,300 mid-tier banks, which equates to around 20 percent of these banks that have between $1 and $30 billion in assets.[18] The brand offers three distinct core processors that enable banks to execute their business strategies: SilverLake System, CIF 20/20, and Core Director. Furthermore, through constant surveys and questionnaires, JH Banking offers exceptional customer service measures to gain a competitive advantage. This allows JH Banking to refine their processes internally by keeping in touch with their client base, leading to enhanced growth from within the company. The internal growth strategy by providing exceptional customer service has served JH Banking well, as evidenced by its market share in U.S. community, mid-tier banks.

In its 2000 acquisition of Symitar Systems Inc., Jack Henry gained the second of its three distinct brands. Symitar was founded as a private company in 1984 and operated as such before being acquired by Jack Henry in 2000. At the time of the acquisition, Symitar was, and still is, recognized as an industry leader in core data processing and tech solutions for U.S. credit unions. The advantages and growth opportunities for Jack Henry were twofold in acquiring Symitar. First, Symitar's core offering and platform, Episys, was in high use and demand in credit unions throughout the United States and the acquisition allowed Jack Henry to offer Episys to clients through Symitar. Second, in acquiring Symitar, Jack Henry was able to expand its business into U.S. credit unions, a space in which it had not previously operated. Jack Henry continued to build the Symitar brand in 2002 with the acquisition of CU Solutions Inc. and its Cruise processing system.

With Episys and Cruise in its portfolio of offerings for clients, Symitar has become the recognized leader of tech solutions for U.S. credit unions. Today, Episys is utilized in over 650 U.S. credit unions and 40 percent of U.S. credit unions with assets in excess of $1 billion. Cruise is currently being deployed in 180 small U.S. credit unions.[19] Thus, Jack Henry created and has grown the Symitar brand through strategic targeted acquisitions, as opposed to the organic, in-house growth that has fueled JH Banking.

The third bank technology brand operating under the Jack Henry & Associates umbrella is ProfitStars, an overall provider of tech solutions for financial institutions of all sizes and types. ProfitStars combines the legacy background enjoyed by Jack Henry with innovative breakthroughs in six performance groups: financial performance, retail delivery, imaging, payment solutions, information security/risk management, and online/mobile.[20]

ProfitStars can support any core processing system that a bank may utilize, making it an attractive option for many financial institutions. ProfitStars was launched by Jack Henry in 2006 as a result of a series of acquisitions that enhanced the company's capabilities. It was not launched as a standalone company as the result of an acquisition like Symitar, but rather was a conglomeration of FinTech companies Jack Henry had acquired that offered a diverse suite of products and services. Thus, Jack Henry grew its business through ProfitStars with a combination of organic growth and targeted acquisitions. Today, ProfitStars serves more than 10,500 clients nationwide and is recognized as an industry leader in financial services technology.

Jack Henry has clearly benefited from a combination of its targeted acquisition strategy and sustained organic growth from within its organization. Given the strong record of its equity performance and consistently outstanding customer reviews, one can infer that Jack Henry has carved out its niche in the FinTech space as a dependable technology solutions provider.

Key Takeaways

These companies are examples of companies that are focused not on directly competing with banks but rather on providing technology services and solutions that can serve to improve efficiency, profitability, and regulatory compliance of the existing banks. Each company has used a combination of acquisition and organic growth strategies to grow and remain at the forefront of FinTech trends.

NOTES

1. Sources for this section:
   http://www.engineersgarage.com/invention-stories/atm-history.
   https://www.bloomberg.com/view/articles/2013-03-27/how-the-atm-revolutionized-the-banking-business.
   http://www.theatlantic.com/technology/archive/2015/03/a-brief-history-of-the-atm/388547/.
2. "ABA Survey: More Consumers Turning to Mobile Banking," *American Bankers Association*, August 11, 2015, http://www.aba.com/Press/Pages/081115MobileBankingSurvey.aspx.
3. "Internet Is Top Banking Model," *eMarketer*, September 28, 2009, http://www.emarketer.com/Article/Internet-Top-Banking-Method/1007295.
4. "Automated Teller Machines per 100,000 Adults," *The World Bank*, http://data.worldbank.org/indicator/FB.ATM.TOTL.P5.
5. Orcun Kaya, "High Frequency Trading Reaching the Limits," Deutsche Bank Research, May 24, 2016, https://www.dbresearch.com/.
6. M. Mitchell Waldrop, "The Trillion-Dollar Vision of Dee Hock, *Fast Company*, October 31, 1996, http://www.fastcompany.com/27333/trillion-dollar-vision-dee-hock.
7. "History of Visa: Our Journey," Visa.com, https://usa.visa.com/about-visa/our_business/history-of-visa.html.
8. Linda Punch, "MasterCard, Five Years After the IPO, Digital Transactions," May 1, 2011, http://www.digitaltransactions.net/news/story/MasterCard_-Five-Years-After-the-IPO.
9. Ibid.
10. FISV—Fiserv Inc., Annual Shareholders Meeting, May 18, 2016.
11. Glenn Fest, "Merger Mania: Fiserv–CheckFree Deal Shakes Up Industry," *American Banker*, September 1, 2007, accessed June 30, 2016.
12. Nancy Feig, "FiServ Acquisition of Checkfree Expands Its Core Offering," *InformationWeek*, August 17, 2007, accessed June 30, 2016.
13. Maria Bruno-Britz, "Combined FIS/Metavante Merger to Be a Game Changer," *Information Week*, April 2, 2009, accessed July 1, 2016.
14. Ibid.
15. FIS Investor Presentation (May 2016), SNL.com, accessed July 1, /2016.
16. SNL.com, accessed July 1, 2016.
17. Jackhenry.com, accessed July 5, 2016.
18. Jackhenrybanking.com, accessed July 5, 2016.
19. Symitar.com, accessed July 5, 2016.
20. Profitstars.com, accessed July 5, 2016.

Section Two of this book presents background and key trends in promi-nent FinTech niches for those community bankers interested in pursuing FinTech opportunities. For Fintech entrepreneurs, we provide key insights into each niche, as well as examples of recent successful startups. The niches presented include: **Bank Technology** (Chapter 4), **Alternative Lending** (Chapter 5), **Payments** (Chapter 6), including blockchain technology, **Wealth Management** (Chapter 7), including robo-advisory, and **Insurance Technology** (Chapter 8).

State of Community Banks Embracing FinTech Today

INTRODUCTION

FinTech is an increasingly important topic for bankers seeking to navigate complex and difficult market conditions. This chapter provides an overview of financial performance trends in the U.S. banking industry. Additionally, key FinTech trends that are developing and expected to impact the industry are discussed. At the end of this chapter, we provide two case studies on Simple and Banno, which are two FinTech companies that illustrate the ability to utilize technology as a growth strategy.

OVERVIEW OF U.S. COMMUNITY BANK INDUSTRY TRENDS

While the following discussion uses data and examples primarily for the U.S. banking industry, certain broad themes noted in the discussion are present in other markets. For example, banking is a relatively mature industry globally. Many banks around the world are experiencing market conditions similar to those impacting U.S. banks, such as competition from non-bank providers and FinTech companies, margin pressure from historically low interest rates, and increasing regulatory complexity. Additionally, banks worldwide are searching for ways to remain relevant in a highly competitive and mature banking industry where enhanced efficiency and increased scale, along with strong customer service, are key factors in success.

In the United States, there are nearly 6,000 community banks with 52,000 locations (including commercial banks, thrifts, and savings institutions). Community banks constitute the vast majority of U.S. banks (approximately 90% of U.S. banks have assets below $1 billion).[1] Collectively, community banks have a significant economic impact, holding $3.9 trillion in assets, employing over 700,000 people, and providing the majority of small business and agricultural loans in the United States.[2]

Many community banks have survived by having a local focus, engaging with their community, and being more accessible in order to make timelier decisions for customers. This focus on service and timeliness often resonates with customers, particularly commercial customers, and has helped a number to survive. In the Federal Reserve's 2015 Small Business Credit Survey, small banks (75%) outscored credit unions (56%), large banks (51%), and online lenders (15%) in lender satisfaction (defined as the share satisfied with the lender minus the share dissatisfied).[3]

The mature and highly competitive nature of the banking industry often rewards efficiencies and economies of scale, though, and there has been a consistent theme of bank consolidation, particularly among community banks, in the last 25 years. As illustrated in Figure 4.1, the total number of banks has consistently declined over the past 25 years (a 3–4% annual decline). The reduction in the number of banks has been most profound among the smallest banks, particularly those having assets less than $100 million, potentially illustrating the importance of scale and efficiency. FDIC research has "found that most of the economies of scale for community banks are realized by the time they reach $100 million in assets."[4]

For those surviving community banks, performance has lagged in recent periods. The median community bank ROA and ROE in 2015 were 0.92 and 8.33 percent, respectively, which represented an improvement from the depths of the financial crisis, but was still well below pre–financial crisis levels.[5] The two largest factors negatively impacting profitability,

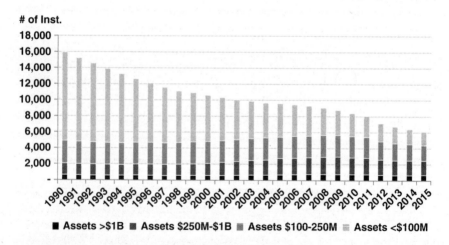

FIGURE 4.1 Overview of U.S. Banks and Thrifts
Source: S&P Global Market Intelligence

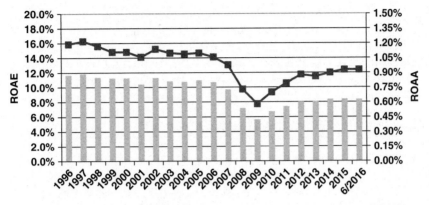

Median Return on Avg. Equity (ROAE) **Median Return on Avg. Assets (ROAA)**

* *6/2016 represents annualized YTD figure*

FIGURE 4.2 Community Bank Profitability Trends
Source: S&P Global Market Intelligence

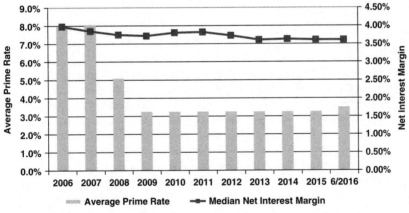

Average Prime Rate **Median Net Interest Margin**

* *6/2016 represents annualized YTD figure*

FIGURE 4.3 Net Interest Income Trends
Source: S&P Global Market Intelligence

according to a 2015 survey by *Bank Director*, were regulatory compliance (64% of bankers surveyed) and interest rates (70% of bankers surveyed).[6] (See Figure 4.2.)

Community banks tend to rely to a greater extent on spread-related revenues than larger banks and thus were particularly vulnerable to margin compression. As shown in Figure 4.3, net interest margins (NIMs) were at their lowest level over the examined 10-year historical period. One key factor impacting NIMs is the Federal Reserve's post–financial crisis zero-interest-rate policy (ZIRP), which has resulted in ongoing compression of asset yields while funding costs essentially have reached a floor. In December 2015, the Federal Reserve ended ZIRP and announced the first increase in the target fed funds rate since 2006, but rates remain at historically low levels.

BANKS AND FINTECH INCREASINGLY INTERSECT

In response to these challenging market conditions, financial institutions, and community banks specifically, have continually adopted new electronic products and technology. Despite their perceived reputation as laggards in technology adoption and innovation, the financial services industry is the most technologically intense sector today as measured by IT spending relative to revenue. Banks spend more globally on IT, an average of 5–9 percent of revenues annually, than the 3.3 and 2.6 percent of the insurance and airline industries.[7]

Even in the current adverse revenue growth environment where banks are looking to temper costs in any way possible, IT spending is yet to be subject to cost-cutting measures. Analysts with consulting firm Ovum see no end in this spending pattern, as they predict that IT spending in banks will increase 5 percent annually to $158 billion in 2019 (up from $131 billion in 2015).[8] Top spending initiatives are planned in the areas of security, analytics, and digital banking (an umbrella term for online and mobile), according to industry research.

While there are a number of FinTech trends and innovations that could potentially impact the banking sector significantly, we highlight a few prominent FinTech trends that we foresee impacting community banks. This discussion largely focuses on those technologies that seek to lower expenses and enhance efficiency as opposed to enhancing revenue. In later chapters we discuss in greater detail other FinTech niches that are more focused on generating greater revenues such as alternative lending, payments, robo-advisory, blockchain, and insurance.

SERVING MORE CUSTOMERS DIGITALLY

As technological advances continue to penetrate the banking industry, small community banks need to continue to upgrade their processes and communication systems in order to more effectively serve small businesses and consumers in an evolving environment. To do so, community banks will increasingly relying on a model that makes widespread use of ATMs, the Internet, mobile apps, data analytics, and algorithm-driven decision making, enabling them to deliver services to customers in a streamlined and efficient manner.

This shift is understandable since servicing customers through online or mobile interactions is vastly cheaper than servicing customers through traditional in-person branch visits. According to a research study conducted by Diebold and Forrester, branch networks make up approximately 47 percent of banks' operating costs, and 54 percent of that branch expenditure goes to staffing.[9] For perspective, the cost of an ATM or computer-sourced transaction is less than 10 percent of the cost of using a branch, paper order, or using a teller.[10]

Opportunities to leverage technology further are still prevalent for many banks as personnel expenses from operating a vast branch network still comprise the largest expense area for most banks. In *Bank Director's 2015 Growth Strategy Survey*, 75 percent of bankers indicated that they plan to invest in more technology within their branch network.[11]

Bankers should be able to leverage FinTech without sacrificing their service element. Customers increasingly prefer digital interactions over traditional in-person visits and those transactions are less costly for the bank. Online banking surpassed branch transactions as the preferred banking method for the first time in 2009 and the gap has only continued to widen.[12] In a 2015 survey by the American Bankers Association, banking online was the most preferred banking method at 32 percent of customers while branch banking had trended down and was only preferred by 17 percent of customers.[13] The number of people preferring mobile was also growing at 12 percent of customers a significantly smaller proportion five years earlier. In a 2015 survey of Bank CIOs, nearly one-third of CIOs expected a 20 percent or more increase in spending on branch technology.[14]

Beyond lowering costs, forward-thinking banks will be able to leverage technology in other areas to enhance profitability. Given the significant amount of data created in banking and other digital channels, banks will be able to analyze data to customize marketing and outreach to customers, analyze credit performance, enhance underwriting, and manage risks. Later in this book, we discuss FinTech innovations that may help banks enhance revenues and certain FinTech innovations may offer benefits in multiple areas (revenues, expenses, risk/compliance, etc.).

More Bank FinTech Partnerships (Including Bank-Sponsored FinTech Accelerators)

More partnerships between banks and FinTech companies are likely to develop. To illustrate the potential power of partnerships between FinTech and traditional banks, two of the largest successes in FinTech history, Visa and MasterCard (discussed in greater detail in Chapter 3), essentially developed through a partnership model with a number of banks.

The most basic advantage of a strategic partnership will be the new-found ability of a bank to leverage the innovations and personnel driving the startup while the startup gains access to the resources and customer base of the bank. In a sense, this levels the playing field on both sides—community banks gain access to some of the same technological solutions as larger banks while smaller FinTech startups gain access to some of the same resources as their larger competitors. We talk more about the pros and cons of these partnerships in Chapter 9 and how a bank should structure a potential framework to assess FinTech partnerships.

Another reason we believe partnerships will be more common is acquisitions of FinTech companies by traditional incumbents (either large or small) are difficult to execute. There are several significant obstacles to the merger of a bank and a FinTech company, including goodwill creation, culture clashes, and valuation differentials between the bank and the FinTech company. We discuss each of these obstacles in more depth in Chapter 11.

One of the most proactive responses from banks seeking to partner with FinTech companies has been the creation of corporate accelerators of varying sizes to fund, mentor, and grow early-stage FinTech startups. Corporate accelerators, by definition, are short-term programs designed to fuel rapid growth in a competitive environment sponsored by companies whose main business does not involve funding startups. The sponsoring company will typically provide stipends, mentorship, and introductions in return for an equity stake in the startup. The application process is normally highly competitive and the winners among the startups working in the accelerator are provided with some amount of funding to continue to grow their business.[15] Participating in a bank-sponsored accelerator is an attractive option for FinTech startups, but also provides benefits for the sponsoring bank and can serve as an excellent source of added value if managed and sustained correctly.

The advantages of participating in a bank-sponsored accelerator are numerous for a FinTech startup, which explains the highly competitive application process. A FinTech startup gains access to the bank's data capabilities, customers, and business connections. This can help grow its business. If deemed successful at the end of the program, a FinTech startup can also reap the benefits of a large funding round from the bank to continue its growth.

For a bank, the advantages of sponsoring an accelerator program may not be as obvious, but can be just as beneficial. In sponsoring a FinTech accelerator, a bank is able to stay ahead of the pack or at least keep pace in terms of technology offerings for its customers and back-office process technology. The service offerings from a FinTech company can help fill the innovation gap that often confounds more traditional banks. A bank can also take an equity stake in one or more startup companies and those equity stakes have the potential to become very valuable. Given the in-house nature of the accelerator programs, a bank can also leverage the innovations seen firsthand in their accelerator program by acquiring a startup or hiring the talent behind the startup.

The structures of these accelerators are as varied and wide ranging as their participants, but there seems to be a pattern to most of them to ensure the creation of an environment conducive to rapid growth in a short period of time. Most accelerator programs include several participating startups in each round, last between three and six months, and offer mentorship, capital, and office space during the program. The winner is awarded a round of funding at the conclusion of the program in return for an equity stake in the company.

This foray into sponsoring accelerators has not been restricted to banks of any certain size, as there are examples of both large national banks and small community banks creating and sponsoring FinTech accelerators. Even the central bank of the United Kingdom, the Bank of England, recently announced plans to launch a FinTech accelerator in an effort to "offer firms the chance to demonstrate their solutions for real issues facing us as policy-makers, together with the valuable 'first client' reference that comes with it," according to Bank of England Governor Mark Carney.[16] In the United States, large systemically important banks such as Citi, Wells Fargo, and JP Morgan have all launched accelerators in an effort to get out in front of FinTech disruption by improving internal processes and customer experience. Many of the accelerators sponsored by the larger banks give a specific focus or project to each class of innovators, offering the bank a different perspective on issues faced in today's ever-evolving financial world. For example, JP Morgan's FinLab, which recently announced its nine winners and granted them $250,000 in capital, chose to focus on financial shocks as the challenge topic for its first class of participants.[17]

Small community banks are also getting in on the FinTech accelerator action with the most notable example being Eastern Labs, a project started by Eastern Bank of Boston to foster innovative FinTech growth within the bank. Eastern Labs follows a more open-ended model, leaving its application process open at all times and constantly bringing in new startups. First National Bank of Omaha put a more interesting spin on the accelerator model by hosting a yearly "hackathon" in which 15 teams of three people compete over 48 hours to come up with a tech-based financial services product from scratch. The winning team of this flash accelerator goes home with $7,500 and a chance to bring their innovative talents to the bank as a full-time employee.[18] Thus, banks of all sizes are using different forms of accelerators to further innovation within the industry and give themselves a leg up on competing banks.

Cybersecurity Spending and Innovation Increase

As banks focused on remaining profitable and, ultimately, solvent during the recession, auxiliary services and emerging issues such as cybersecurity were often secondary considerations as resources were focused on resolving and identifying credit issues and problem assets. A combination of the improving economy since the recession and growing concerns about cybersecurity have forced community banks to allocate a larger portion of their IT spending and resources to security. Community bank CIOs and technology officers are increasingly aware of the constant threats of hackers, spammers, purveyors of malware, and others looking to inflict harm upon the network and central processes of banks. Protecting data becomes increasingly vital as more customer interactions occur online. FinTech services are being created to protect against cybersecurity threats.

The Role of Core Processors in Innovation Evolves

Because many smaller community banks have limited financial resources, they increasingly use outsourcing and third-party providers to contain operating costs and gain access to technologies and services that help them compete but would otherwise be cost prohibitive.[19] As we discussed in greater detail in Chapter 3, core processors have often assisted community banks with their technology needs. A recent survey of banks noted that only 4 percent of banks utilized their core provider for core processing only. The majority use their core provider for technology offerings such as mobile banking (71%) and remote deposit capture/mobile bill pay (75%). This dependence upon core providers can be problematic for community bankers especially when it comes to enhancing technology offerings and innovating. For example, 81 percent of CTOs and CIOs indicate that their core processor is slow to respond, 30 percent reported that they had pulled back on an innovative product due to the core being slow to respond, and 11 percent continued on in spite of negative pushback from the core.[20] As banks increasingly look to innovate, one would expect to see either the core processors evolve and become more responsive to innovation and develop or acquire more FinTech companies or bankers developing more technological expertise to facilitate innovation and be less reliant on their core providers.

EVOLVING REGULATORY OVERSIGHT OF FINTECH

There are unique regulatory considerations for FinTech companies and their technological innovations for the banking sector. Considerations have included regulating FinTech companies as stringently as community banks are regulated, establishing a unique FinTech charter that is less stringent and more accommodating for innovation, and creating a regulatory sandbox to allow traditional financial institutions and FinTech companies to partner and work together on fostering innovations.

From a regulatory perspective, FinTech offers the opportunity for expanding financial services to the unbanked and underbanked as well as ways for traditional financial institutions to enhance efficiency and profitability. This in turn helps improve the capitalization, safety, and soundness of the banking industry and the broader economy. However, it also presents several complex regulatory challenges as new innovations potentially develop outside of, or push the boundaries of, existing regulations.

This push-and-pull from regulation as it relates to technology and innovation is not unique to the financial services industry. Throughout history many technological innovations have needed light oversight initially to nurture their development. It is hard to imagine the airline or automotive industry developing to current levels had the first airplanes been faced with the same requirements that newly manufactured planes encounter today. The OCC appears to have taken the lead among the bank regulators in terms of establishing a framework for bank regulators to monitor FinTech, although there are still more questions than answers.

Case Studies

Despite the challenges facing the industry and the potential promises of FinTech to provide bank technology solutions, many bankers are primarily focusing on traditional growth strategies to improve profitability. According to the *2015 Growth Strategy Survey*, the top growth strategies were organic loan origination (82%), bank acquisitions (41%), de novo branches (22%), investments in fee-based businesses such as insurance or trust (21%), or branch acquisitions (17%).[21] Leveraging FinTech was not noted as a potential growth strategy and mobile banking was only ranked as #4 on ways to improve fee income. The following case studies of two FinTech companies, Simple and Banno, illustrate the ability to utilize FinTech as a growth strategy for both community bankers and FinTech entrepreneurs.

Simple

Simple, a FinTech company, was started in 2009. It created a digital interface for banking through web and mobile apps. Without physical branches, Simple was able to attract customers through digital bank offerings at significantly lower costs than traditional brick-and-mortar banks and was later acquired by a traditional bank, Banco Bilbao Vizcaya Argentaria (BBVA), five years after inception (in 2014). Simple's revenue was generated through interchange fees as well as interest on customer deposits. Simple's corporate history provides a number of interesting lessons for both bankers and FinTech entrepreneurs as they explore ways to work together to attract customers. Table 4.1 provides an overview of Simple's history from inception to exiting through a sale to a traditional bank.

Simple's history provides key takeaways for both bankers and FinTech entrepreneurs, three of which are outlined in the following.

Top Three Takeaways for Bankers

1. Digital banking provides a template for account growth absent a traditional branch-banking model.

   ■ In roughly four years and with total funding of $15 million, Simple's deposit accounts grew to 100,000 in all U.S. states with zero branches and had another 250,000 invite requests.
   ■ Research and development is fairly well understood in other corporate fields. Should bankers incorporate a similar mindset with their digital bank platform?
   ■ Would bank management and stakeholders be happy with investing $15 million over a four-year period for a digital banking platform that can generate and service deposit accounts at a comparable level?

2. Investing in digital bank offerings can generate shareholder value.

   ■ Simple's customer acquisition costs were $150 per customer ($15 million invested divided by 100,000 customers), which were below traditional bank customer acquisition costs ($250 to $450 per customer).[22]
   ■ Once developed, the digital banking platform is scalable and customer acquisition and account servicing costs should be lower than the traditional bank retail model. Consider that Simple added 100,000 accounts in 2013 with a minimal capital raise ($2 million).

3. It is possible for digital banking to compete on customer service and not just interest rates.

   ■ Simple differed from prior digital bank offerings in that it attracted depositors absent offering higher interest rates.

TABLE 4.1 Simple's Significant Corporate Events

Year	Significant Corporate Events
2009	In mid-July, the email that started Simple was sent by one of the founders, who posed the question of starting a "really boring, simple bank" that could accomplish the four key tasks of a bank as he saw it: (1) hold money; (2) electronic payments and transfers; (3) lend cash for a risk-adjusted return; and (4) the opposite of 3 = borrowing Simple's seed fundraising round was completed in November ($190,000 invested)
2010	Simple began taking invite requests to bank with them from customers Roughly 20,000 invite requests as of August Developed staff and certain partnerships Series A round ($2.9 million invested in September)
2011	Additional partnerships were formed By midyear, beta testing of products began with the first Simple debit cards issued to employees/directors 50,000 customers had requested an invitation by May Name and logo change from BankSimple to Simple Late 2011, Simple began inviting first non-employee customers Series B round ($10 million invested in August)
2012	Released a number of products, including iOS mobile banking application, photo check deposit, Reports (which allows for trend analysis of customer financial data, and Goals (a money-saving/budgeting application)
2013	Released Android mobile application, Instant (allows for instant money transfers across Simple customer accounts) Experienced relatively rapid customer growth—20,000 customers in January, 40,000 customers by midyear, and 100,000 customers by year-end Processed $1.7 billion in debit card transactions in 2013 Series C round ($2.2 million invested in June)
2014	Simple sold to BBVA for $117 million

■ A Deloitte survey of bank customers released in 2013 indicated that a digital banking plan that provides a limited level of in-person services in exchange for reduced fees was the most popular option among customers.[23]

Top Three Takeaways for FinTech Entrepreneurs

1. The importance of partnerships.

   - Almost at the outset, Simple developed a number of partnerships that enabled it to scale up quickly and focus on improving its digital bank platform and customer experience. For perspective, consider the partnerships Simple developed:
     - FDIC Insurance on Deposits (product)—The Bancorp Bank (partner)
     - ATM Network—Allpoint
     - Debit Cards and Payments—Visa
     - Core Processing—TxVia
     - Attach image, PDF, or text file to transactions—Dropbox
     - Mobile Payments—Braintree/Venmo Touch
     - Funding/Capital—several venture capital funds

2. Venture capital interest is high and will likely grow following the BBVA deal, particularly if banks follow BBVA's lead and show interest in doing FinTech investments/acquisitions.

   - Consider the returns implied: approximately $15 million invested in Simple across funding rounds. Simple ultimately sold for $117 million, which implies the following:
     - Internal rate of return: 91%
     - Cash-on-cash: 7.7×
     - Return on investment: 665%
     - Customers acquired at cost of $150 and sold for approximately $1,170

3. Find a niche early as it is difficult to match all services provided by traditional banks.

   - Simple demonstrated the ability to generate deposit customers through a digital platform, but never offered other products such as lending, credit cards, insurance, wealth management, etc.

Banno

Banno, a FinTech company, was founded in Iowa in 2006. It is an example of leveraging big data and using data analytics to enhance offerings to customers and ultimately bank profitability. Additionally, Banno serves as an interesting example of the role that core processors could ultimately play as FinTech evolves since it was subsequently acquired in 2014 by one of the larger core processors, Jack Henry.

Originally, Banno provided technology and advertising services for non-financial companies, but began focusing solely on banks as it developed a niche in that area. Banno's FinTech product developments prior to acquisition included:

- Grip, a mobile banking tool with account aggregations, merchant details, ATM search, photo receipt upload, billpay, and remote deposit capture.
- Kernel, a system that segments online visitors and delivers tailored advertisements specific to their interest.

Table 4.2 provides an overview of Banno's history and significant corporate milestones.[24]

TABLE 4.2 Banno's Significant Corporate Events

Year	Significant Corporate Events
2006–2009	Originally, Banno performed technology and advertising services for larger nonfinancial companies Raised capital of $500,000 from local Iowa real estate developers at the beginning of 2008 In 2009, T8 Design (precursor to Banno) pivoted when revenues from services to banks outpaced other professional services
2009–2013	Began selling a product that lets banks offer customers a way to customize debit cards with photos, evolved later to be named Cre8 My Card Renamed company Banno in 2008 and was reported at that time to have approximately 60 programmers, sales, and IT staff; $4 million in revenue; and 400 bank customers Debuted Grip, which offers mobile personal financial management, at FinovateFall in 2011 In September 2012, the Iowa Economic Development Authority matched a $1 million private loan from one of Banno's lenders for an additional $2 million total funding Debuted Kernel, which delivers tailored advertisements that are product specific based on their customers' interest across several electronic channels at FinovateSpring in 2013
March 2014	Jack Henry, a global leader in payment technology and solutions, acquired Banno for $28 million in cash Pricing multiples were not disclosed but Banno was reported to have revenues of $848,000 and a net loss of $1.1 million for the four-month period from acquisition date to June 30, 2014 (based upon JKHY's Form 10-K for FY ended 6/14) This implies a price/annualized revenue multiple of 11×

Key Takeaways for Bankers and FinTech Entrepreneurs   Banno's corporate history provides lessons for both bankers and FinTech entrepreneurs.

1. As FinTech continues to evolve, Banno provides a solid example of the benefits from combining technology, marketing, and financial services expertise. As banks look to leverage data for growth purposes, we should expect to see similar innovations that combine data analytics and technology.

   ■ Kernel offers a way for banks to maintain and enhance their customer relationships in a digital environment. Historically, these types of banking activities have largely occurred offline. Products like Kernel should continue to attract interest from bankers.

2. Banno's ability to operate and exit successfully from a nontraditional market is encouraging for other FinTech startups and rural community banks.

   ■ Banno was able to successfully attract talent, capital, and financial services customers while operating from Iowa.
   ■ Given the significant amount of capital and resources required to grow FinTech companies, Banno's template of establishing operations in a lower-cost market and utilizing local funding incentives (such as the use of the Iowa Economic Development Authority) could be a nice path to follow.
   ■ Strengths of partnerships are typically huge for FinTech startups but may have been more important for Banno given its location. Banno's partners included Jack Henry and Deluxe Financial Services, two larger players.

CONCLUSION

As FinTech disruption continues to spread across the financial landscape, banks of all sizes—from the Bank of England to local community banks—are beginning to craft their responses and prepare either to embrace future innovations as an improvement to their business models or attempt to shield their business models from potential disruption.

Some community banks have embraced FinTech through accelerators. Others are still exploring their relationship with FinTech. At the *Crossroads: Banking and Fintech Conference* (Atlanta, May 2016), many community bankers expressed the exploratory nature of their use of FinTech going forward. William Easterlin, president and CEO of Queensborough National Bank & Trust Co. in Louisville, Georgia, remarked, "I don't need technology that is going to help me make more loans. I need something that is going to help me make the loans I'm already making more efficiently."[25] According to several bankers at the conference, FinTech is expected to serve an auxiliary role to existing business models by helping update and optimize outdated processes. Bankers were also concerned about keeping up with the fast-moving technological environment. Mr. Easterlin went on to say, "We do it (include tech in customer offerings) because I'm afraid if we don't we'll be left two or three generations behind in technology."[26]

Community banks will have to embrace at least some aspects of Fin-Tech disruption to avoid being left clinging to outdated processes and an antiquated interface. It may not be prudent or feasible for every community bank to fund an accelerator or host an all-night hackathon; however, adopting a framework and strategic plan for assessing FinTech innovations that result from the "FinTech reformation" (coined by Bank of England Governor Mark Carney) will ensure that community banks are able to survive and thrive in the coming years.[27] Ostensibly, the most likely outcome of technology adoption by community banks will be strategic partnerships with similarly aligned FinTech startups, which will benefit both organizations. We discuss key considerations related to partnerships in Chapter 9.

NOTES

1. "Community Bank Facts," http://www.icba.org/go-local/why-go-local/stats-facts, accessed January 11, 2017.
2. Ibid.
3. "2015 Small Business Credit Survey: Report on Employer Firms," *United States Federal Reserve System*, Washington, DC, 2016, https://www.clevelandfed.org/community-development/small-business/about-the-joint-small-business-credit-survey/2015-joint-small-business-credit-survey.aspx.
4. Stefan Jacewitz and Paul Kupiec, "Community Bank Efficiency and Economies of Scale," *FDIC*, December 2012, https://www.fdic.gov/regulations/resources/cbi/report/cbi-eff.pdf (published under the FDIC Community Banking Initiative).
5. The discussion of trends in the community banking industry focuses on banks, savings banks, and savings and loan associations located in the United States having assets between $100 million and $5 billion at year-end 2015, excluding those with unusual loan portfolio and revenue composition. The screens applied yielded 4,128 banks meeting this criterion. The data was analyzed by Mercer Capital and sourced from S&P Global Market Intelligence.
6. Emily McCormick, "2015 Growth Strategy Survey," *Bank Director*, August 2015, http://www.bankdirector.com/download_file/view_inline/4268.
7. "Breakthrough IT Banking," *McKinsey Report*, June 22, 2016.
8. "Retail Banking Technology," *Ovum.com*, http://www.ovum.com/retail-banking-technology/, accessed June 22, 2016.

9. Jonathan Camhi, "The Next Generation of Bank Branch Employees," *Information Week*, http://www.banktech.com/channels/the-next-generation-of-bank-branch-employees/d/d-id/1298073, accessed April 21, 2015.

10. "Robert H. Smith, "Banking's Big Challenge: Breaking Away from the Branch Model," *American Banker*, October 14, 2014, http://www.americanbanker.com/bankthink/banking-big-challenge-breaking-away-from-the-branch-model-1043727-1.html.

11. Emily McCormick, "2015 Growth Strategy Survey," *Bank Director*, August 2015, http://www.bankdirector.com/download_file/view_inline/4268.

12. "ABA Survey: Consumers Prefer Banking Online," http://www.mediapost.com/publications/article/113969/survey-consumers-prefer-banking-online.html?edition, September 21, 2009.

13. "ABA Survey: Consumers Turn to Mobile Banking," http://www.aba.com/Press/Pages/081115MobileBankingSurvey.aspx, August 11, 2015.

14. Harry Terris, "Banks to Spend More on Tech in 2016, Especially Security," *American Banks*, October 15, 2015, http://www.americanbanker.com/news/bank-technology/banks-to-spend-more-on-tech-in-2016-especially-security-1077200-1.html, accessed June 22, 2016.

15. Florian Heinemann, "What Are Corporate Accelerators?" *Massachusetts Institute of Technology*, August 7, 2015, https://www.florianheinemann.com/assets/ThesisFlorianHeinemannCorporateAccelerators.pdf, accessed June 23, 2016.

16. Giulio Prisco, "Bank of England Launches Fintech Accelerator," *Bitcoin Magazine*, June 21, 2016, https://bitcoinmagazine.com/articles/bank-of-england-launches-fintech-accelerator-partners-with-pwc-on-distributed-ledger-project-1466522623, accessed June 23, 2016.

17. Paul Vigna, "Winners Named in J.P. Morgan's First Fintech Competition," *Wall Street Journal*, June 12, 2015, http://blogs.wsj.com/moneybeat/2015/06/12/winners-named-in-j-p-morgans-first-fintech-competition/, accessed June 24, 2016.

18. Cole Epley, "Hackathons like First National Bank's Popular among Tech Giants, Financial Institutions Seeking Innovation," *Omaha World-Herald*, September 28, 2015, http://www.omaha.com/money/hackathons-like-first-national-bank-s-popular-among-tech-giants/article_a20db660-3e0f-57c9-beae-f0a28fb42e2e.html, accessed June 24, 2015.

19. Jonathan Camhi, "2014 Forecast: Many Community Banks to Increase IT Investment Next Year," *Bank Tech*, December 27, 2013, http://www.banktech.com/management-strategies/2014-forecast-many-community-banks-to-in/240165037, accessed January 24, 2014.

20. Emily McCormick, "2016 Technology Survey," *Bank Director*, August 29, 2016, http://www.bankdirector.com/files/4714/7189/2505/2016_Technology_Survey_Report.pdf.

21. Emily McCormick, "2015 Growth Strategy Survey," *Bank Director*, August 2015, http://www.bankdirector.com/download_file/view_inline/4268.

22. Victoria Finkle, "Free Checking Isn't Cheap for Banks," *American Banker*, December 9, 2011, http://www.americanbanker.com/issues/176_238/checking-account-free-checking-debit-fees-1044756-1.html.

23. Deloitte Center for Financial Services, "Retail Bank Pricing—Resetting Customer Expectations," *Deloitte*, February 12, 2013, https://www2.deloitte .com/content/dam/Deloitte/global/Documents/Financial-Services/dttl-fsi-us-consulting-Retail-Bank-PricingPOV-02122013.pdf.

24. *Sources:* Various articles mentioning Banno, SNL Financial, and JKHY filings, including www.finovate.com, "Wade Arnold: Coder in the Cornfield," *American Banker*, http://www.americanbanker.com/btn/26_1/banno-s-wade-arnold-coder-in-the-iowa-cornfields-1055363-1.html.

25. Robert Barba, "Are FinTech and Community Banks a Perfect Match?" *American Banker*, April 22, 2016, http://www.americanbanker.com/news/bank-technology/are-fintech-and-community-banks-a-perfect-match-1080629-1 .html, accessed June 23, 2016.

26. Ibid.

27. Giulio Prisco, "Bank of England Launches Fintech Accelerator," *Bitcoin*, June 21, 2016, https://bitcoinmagazine.com/articles/bank-of-england-launches-fin tech-accelerator-partners-with-pwc-on-distributed-ledger-project-1466522623, accessed June 23, 2016.

CHAPTER 5

The Alternative Lending Niche

Providing loans to borrowers is at the center of services that banks offer to customers and a key driver of bank health and profitability. Lending is also a key element to assess when determining the value of a bank as trends related to the loan portfolio such as growth outlook, credit quality, concentration risks, yields, and margins can all significantly impact profitability, health, and valuation of a bank. An assessment of the loan portfolio is even more critical for community banks, which are more dependent upon spread income than their larger brethren.

While lending is vital to community banks, community banks face intense competition from both larger banks and non-bank lenders—several of which utilize alternative lending models that rely heavily on technology and FinTech innovations. Consequently, developing digital lending operations is paramount for community banks. Many are successfully developing online loan platforms to either enhance the efficiency and profitability of their existing lending operations or expand into new alternative lending models. To understand the growth of non-bank lenders in recent history and provide a deeper perspective on the market share being lost to these non-bank lenders, let's take a closer look at the rise of non-bank lenders in the mortgage and consumer lending markets and analyze alternative lending trends that we expect will impact banks for years to come.

THE MORTGAGE MARKET

Before the peak of the housing market in 2006, mortgage lenders relaxed lending requirements and developed new loan products, which expanded who qualified for mortgages. As the housing market collapsed and the Great Recession ensued, the value of securities tied to U.S. real estate declined and the performance of a number of companies in the banking and mortgage industry weakened. Consistent with weaker economic conditions, credit availability contracted, consumers faced tougher requirements to qualify for home mortgages, home prices and homeowner's equity declined, and foreclosures increased. This led to significant volatility among mortgage originators (both banks and non-banks) and contractions in the total level of mortgage originations. Of the 20 largest mortgage originators in 2006, only five were still in operation in 2011 and the level of funded mortgage loans declined from $2.6 trillion in 2006 to $1.5 trillion in 2011.

As shown in Table 5.1, six of the top 10 and 15 of the top 20 mortgage originators were gone by 2011 through a combination of failure,

TABLE 5.1 2006 Top Mortgage Originators

2006 Rank	Company	2006 Funded Loans ($000)
1	Countrywide Home Loans (CA)	175,303,594
2	Wells Fargo Bank NA (SD)	164,470,884
3	Washington Mutual Bank (NV)	106,208,510
4	Bank of America NA (NC)	88,924,401
5	JPMorgan Chase Bank NA (OH)	68,735,060
6	National City Bank (OH)	63,615,098
7	American Home Mortgage Inc. (NY)	54,662,352
8	SunTrust Mortgage Inc. (VA)	45,013,141
9	Wachovia Mortgage FSB (NV)	43,522,561
10	New Century Mortgage Corp. (CA)	41,964,905
11	IndyMac Bank FSB (CA)	39,297,385
12	Countrywide Bank FSB (CO)	36,362,199
13	CitiMortgage Inc. (MO)	35,208,105
14	Fremont Investment & Loan (CA)	32,490,599
15	GreenPoint Mrtg Fndg Inc. (CA)	30,822,359
16	WMC Mortgage Corp. (CA)	29,137,964
17	HomeComings Financial LLC (MN)	28,323,169
18	MetLife Home Loans (TX)	28,104,550
19	Option One Mortgage Corp. (CA)	25,437,753
20	First Magnus Financial Corp. (AZ)	24,932,294
	Total for Institutions in Market	2,599,435,491

Source: SNL Financial originally sourced to the Home Mortgage Disclosure Act data compiled annually by the Federal Financial Institutions Examination Council

mergers, or exiting the business. The highlighted companies represent those that survived.

Following the financial crisis, market conditions improved and historically low interest rates persist, leading to relatively high mortgage origination volumes. Mortgage banking is a highly cyclical industry with demand for mortgage originations driven by a variety of factors, including home sales, housing market conditions, economic conditions, mortgage rates, and refinancing prospects. The profitability of individual companies can also be highly cyclical and depend on a number of factors, including volume, interest rate spreads, and efficiency. In recent years, mortgage originations have benefited from higher refinancing activity from low interest rates and increased eligibility from a combination of an improving economy, increasing home prices, and the government's Home Affordability Refinance Program (HARP).[1]

The upheaval in the mortgage market and improved market conditions created an opening for non-bank alternative lenders. A number of these non-bank lenders utilize technology more heavily in their operations and their less-regulated status provides them with certain regulatory and compliance efficiencies. Table 5.2 details the top mortgage originators in 2014 and highlights two companies within the top 10 that rely upon technology more heavily in their origination process than many mortgage groups of traditional banks.

THE CONSUMER LENDING MARKET

Because loans are made but deposits are not handled, non-bank lenders, like finance companies that supply credit to businesses and consumers, are often categorized as non-depository institutions. These institutions acquire funds to make loans largely by selling securities or insurance policies to the public. Consumer finance companies make loans to consumers who want to finance purchases from household items to cars, make home improvements, and refinance small debts. As financial intermediaries, finance companies compete with banks, savings institutions, and credit unions.

To illustrate the growth of non-bank lenders like finance companies in the consumer lending segment, see Table 5.3, which highlights the uptick in market share of finance companies in consumer lending (more than 20% in the last five years compared to ~13% in 1995).[2]

Non-bank lenders are taking mortgage and consumer lending market share from traditional banks in recent years. One driver of this trend is that banks have been slower to adopt more innovative and technology-driven

TABLE 5.2 2014 Top Mortgage Originators

2014 Rank	Company	Type	2014 Funded Loans ($000)
1	Wells Fargo Bank NA (SD)	Comm'l Bank	111,131,648
2	Quicken Loans Inc. (MI)	Mortgage Bank	55,816,267
3	JPMorgan Chase Bank NA (OH)	Comm'l Bank	55,669,805
4	Bank of America NA (NC)	Comm'l Bank	42,523,994
5	Citibank NA (SD)	Comm'l Bank	22,727,601
6	Flagstar Bank FSB (MI)	Thrift	19,711,131
7	U.S. Bank NA (OH)	Comm'l Bank	18,732,061
8	PNC Bank NA (DE)	Comm'l Bank	15,042,892
9	loanDepot.com LLC (CA)	Mortgage Bank	13,074,091
10	Stearns Lending LLC (CA)	Mortgage Bank	12,156,504
11	USAA FSB (TX)	Thrift	11,860,567
12	Freedom Mortgage Corp. (NJ)	Mortgage Bank	11,610,890
13	Nationstar Mortgage LLC (TX)	Mortgage Bank	10,930,968
14	PrimeLending (TX)	Mortgage Bank	10,294,720
15	Guaranteed Rate Inc. (IL)	Mortgage Bank	9,778,832
16	MUFG Union Bank NA (NY)	Comm'l Bank	9,356,228
17	Walker & Dunlop LLC (MD)	Mortgage Bank	9,296,504
18	First Repub Bank (CA)	Bank	9,100,858
19	United Shore Finl Svcs LLC (MI)	Mortgage Bank	8,829,114
20	Branch Banking & Trust Co. (NC)	Comm'l Bank	8,771,827
	Total for Institutions in Market		1,382,303,081

Source: SNL Financial originally sourced to the Home Mortgage Disclosure Act data compiled annually by the Federal Financial Institutions Examination Council

loan products, which has created an opending for non-bank lenders that leverage technology effectively. As a result, community banks have become more dependent on real estate loans, particularly commercial real estate (we discussed this in greater detail in Chapter 2). The growth of alternative lending and digital lending affords banks some opportunities to recapture market share lost in other non–real estate loan segments, which could improve loan portfolio diversification and growth opportunities for many community banks.

TABLE 5.3 Major Holders of Consumer Credit Outstanding ($Billions)

	2011	2012	2013	2014	2015	% Change 2014–2015
Depository institutions	$1,192.6	$1,218.6	$1,271.6	$1,343.1	$1,439.2	7.2%
Finance companies	687.6	679.8	679.1	684.1	683.4	−0.1%
Credit unions	223.0	243.6	265.6	302.8	341.7	12.8%
Federal government	484.7	616.8	729.8	840.9	945.6	12.5%
Nonprofit and educational institutions	74.5	65.6	59.3	53.6	47.2	−11.9%
Nonfinancial business	47.4	49.2	43.5	43.0	42.2	−1.9%
Pools of securitized assets	46.2	50.0	48.6	49.8	47.5	−4.6%
Total*	$2,755.4	$2,922.9	$3,098.8	$3,317.2	$3,546.8	6.9%
Finance Cos. % of Total	24.95%	23.26%	21.91%	20.62%	19.27%	−1.4%

*May not sum to total
Source: Federal Reserve Consumer Credit Statistical Release (G. 19), February 2016

Trends in Lending

To help community banks stay in front of the technology wave, we discuss two key trends that we expect to have a long-term impact on lending.

Alternative Lending and Leveraging Technology for Lending Will Continue to Grow

In the wake of the financial crisis and subsequent recession, many banks reduced their risk profile by ratcheting up their lending requirements, forcing many consumers to look elsewhere for loans. Banks turned away the same subprime borrowers that many had freely lent to in the years leading up to the crisis. This created a lending gap full of underserved potential borrowers. Concurrent with this contraction in the credit cycle, alternative online lending pioneers with peer-to-peer models such as Lending Club and OnDeck began to pop up across the financial landscape, giving borrowers and subprime borrowers accessible options outside of traditional retail banks.

As the supply of credit continued to decrease, more alternative online lending startups, including peer-to-peer lenders, began to adopt new technology that would automate the credit screening process and match borrowers and lenders. This created a perfect environment for the widespread proliferation of alternative online lending platforms.

As these alternative lenders emerged, differences between alternative lending platforms and traditional retail banks became evident and include the following:

- **Peer-to-Peer Lending Models.** Alternative lenders use online platforms to directly match lenders and borrowers in a marketplace style environment. However, there is also a partner bank often involved in a number of peer-to-peer lending models that serves as an intermediary between the lending platform and the borrowers and investors. Often the partner bank will actually issue the loan to the borrower once the borrower meets the criteria of the lending platform and an investor is found and then sell the loan back to the lending platform.
- **Alternative Screening Methods.** Alternative lenders leverage metrics beyond credit scores used by traditional lenders to more accurately assess the creditworthiness of borrowers.
- **Faster, Sleeker Processes.** In most alternative lending platforms, the onboarding of borrowers is automated, allowing for faster access to funds.
- **Quicker and Automated Underwriting.** Automated screening processes are able to cut out much of the adverse selection issues encountered by banks and can ensure the (relative) creditworthiness of borrowers.
- **Increased Accessibility to Funds.** More widespread sources of lending offering less stringent credit requirements allow alternative lenders the ability to provide funding to a broader spectrum of borrowers.
- **Reduced Costs.** An improved understanding of borrower risk may lower the margins by which intermediaries make profit, leading to a lower cost to obtain a loan for borrowers and higher returns for lenders.
- **Enhanced Customer Experience.** Streamlined, automated processes create an improved customer-oriented environment.

As the alternative lending models grew, venture capital funding increased. Table 5.4 details some of the largest venture capital fundraising rounds of U.S.-based alternative lending platforms in 2015 and the first half of 2016.

Being successful in banking—particularly lending—is akin to tennis at the beginner level, where the player who makes the fewest mistakes usually has the best results. In the context of the convergence of financial services and technology, lenders that use technology to take costs out of the system

TABLE 5.4 Selection of Largest Alternative Lending Funding of 2015 to Mid-2016 in the United States

Period	Company	Amount ($M)	Company Description
Q3 2015	SoFI (Social Finance)	$1,000.00	Alternative (Marketplace) lender—student loan focus
Q2 2015	Avant	$400.00	Personal loan and line of credit provider that lowers the barriers and cost of borrowing
Q3 2015	Avant	$339.00	Alternative lender—consumer focus
Q3 2015	Avant	$325.00	Alternative lender—consumer focus
Q4 2015	Pave	$300.00	Alternative (Marketplace) lender—peer-to-peer
Q2 2015	Affirm	$275.00	Offers more flexible installment loans at the point of sale focused on Millennials
Q4 2015	Earnest	$275.00	Alternative (Marketplace) lender— personal and student loans
Q1 2016	CommonBond	$275.00	Alternative lender—student loans/ peer-to-peer
Q1 2015	SoFI	$200.00	Marketplace for student loan refinancing and other loans
Q2 2016	Mosaic	$200.00	Marketplace lender for residential solar projects
Q2 2016	Avant	$188.00	Online alternative lender free of origination fees
Q2 2015	Prosper	$165.00	Online peer-to-peer lending service in which people invest in each other
Q1 2015	CommonBond	$150.00	Student loan marketplace lender
Q4 2015	Kabbage	$135.00	Alternative lender—small business focus
Q2 2015	Bond Street	$110.00	Online small business lender

Source: Mercer Capital Quarterly FinTech Newsletters from Q1 2015 through Q2 2016, "Alternative Lending Will Become More Tested"

and perform more efficiently can yield the best results. However, avoiding mistakes is still vital regardless of whether loans are originated in a digital or traditional environment.

For example, Lending Club was founded in 2007 just before the financial crisis. Through a combination of perfect timing, housing an innovative product, and several rounds of funding, Lending Club became the leading player in alternative lending platforms. After garnering nearly $400 million worth of funding through 2014, Lending Club went public on December 11, 2014, with an IPO of $24.72 per share, well above the anticipated $15 per share.[3] This gave Lending Club a market valuation of nearly $9 billion, which was above the market cap of the 15th largest bank in the United States. This was a testament to the strength of the alternative lending industry at the time. After closing at an all-time high of $27.90 per share on December 17, 2014, Lending Club's price has gone on a steady decline with a low coming on May 13, 2016, when the stock closed at just $3.51 per share. While the stock recovered some in mid-to-late 2016, it still remained well below $10 per share.

So what caused one of the darlings of the FinTech industry to undergo an 87 percent decrease in price in a little under a year and a half? The answer lies in a variety of internal and external issues. Perhaps the most glaring of these issues was the scandal of 2016, resulting in the firing of their CEO due to potential conflicts of interest regarding undisclosed investments he had made in funds related to Lending Club's operation. Also, dates on loan documents during that CEO's tenure were changed to satisfy an institutional investor's requirements. This warranted the departure of their CEO in the eyes of the board and resulted in the tailspin of the stock price after the firing.

Another large public online lender, OnDeck, saw its stock price decline as a result of internal issues following its IPO. OnDeck was founded in 2007 with a focus on providing loans to small businesses. In its first quarter 2016 conference call, management explained a reduction in loan volume as a result of tighter credit standards, raising questions about the quality of the loans made. This suspicion about loan quality was deepened when management went on to say that only 15–20 percent of the company's loans were being sold on the secondary market, compared to the originally reported number of 35–40 percent.[4]

While internal issues drove the declines of both companies, Lending Club[5] and OnDeck have also seen their stock price drop as a result of some broader questions that investors have about the alternative lending industry as a whole.

First, investors are beginning to question whether online lenders are sufficiently protected from competition. With their large marketing budgets and established infrastructures, it is possible that traditional banks will cut out smaller lenders upon entering the online lending scene. Banks are beginning to explore the online lending environment, as many small banks are forming strategic partnerships with online lenders or developing their own online lending platforms in efforts to increase loan volumes. A widespread entrance of banks into the online lending space could pose a threat to alternative lending platforms that specialize in online lending.

A potential onslaught of regulation is also complicating the environment for non-bank online lenders. Online lenders will have to survive increasing legislation and regulatory burdens, which will undoubtedly come with high compliance costs. These companies do not have the massive compliance departments of banks and may have to reimagine their entire business model if the regulatory environment becomes too restrictive.

Finally, and perhaps most importantly, is the question of whether alternative lending platforms can survive a contractionary credit cycle. Lending Club was an infant company at the time of the financial crisis and was largely unaffected by the intense economic downturn. If Lending Club and OnDeck are experiencing this much difficulty in a time of steady consumer demand for credit, then the outcome of a fall in demand for credit and higher credit and funding costs from weaker economic conditions could be disastrous for them and other alternative lending platforms.

Thus, a variety of internal and external factors have led to a tumultuous 2016 for Lending Club and OnDeck, both of which are widely thought to be representatives of the alternative lending industry at large. Whether these companies are able to recover remains to be seen and will certainly test the resiliency of the alternative lending platform industry going forward.

GOVERNMENT REGULATION OF ALTERNATIVE LENDING PLATFORMS

While there has not been much concrete legislation or regulations enacted to date, regulatory bodies are beginning to publish their expectations for industry behavior.[6] In March 2016, the OCC released a report on the effect of technology within the banking system, specifically calling for collaboration between banks and online lenders in order to capitalize on each other's respective advantages. The OCC called for what they termed to be "responsible innovation" of technology within the banking sector while also laying out a plan to foster this responsible innovation and improve the banking sector altogether.[7] This gave online lenders a regulatory framework going forward to ensure that they stay within the bounds of the OCC. The U.S. Department of the Treasury released a whitepaper titled "Opportunities and Challenges in Online Marketplace Lending" in May 2016, further adding to the eventful month for the online lending space.[8] The OCC whitepaper gives a broad overview of the industry before making several recommendations for online lenders going forward in terms of what potential regulation might look like. Other regulatory bodies have released publications commenting on alternative lending platforms, giving the industry a heads-up that they may be subject to more regulation in coming days.

One of the more interesting recent developments from the alternative lending industry is some online marketplace lenders actually calling for regulation, as they believe it would be advantageous for their business models. The creation of a specialized FinTech charter for online lenders by the OCC would allow alternative lending platforms to preempt some state chartering processes and, perhaps more importantly, collect FDIC-insured deposits to provide funding for their loans. A bank charter either through an acquisition or a newly created specialized charter could streamline the online lending process even further by cutting out third-party sources of funding, an idea that has become increasingly attractive to online lenders. In the case of online lenders, constructive regulation could actually make their business models more efficient, rather than act as a deterrent to their growth and profitability.

CONCLUSION

In tennis, a common question is, "How would yesterday's superstars compete against the stars of today?" Fans like myself are then left to wonder how John McEnroe would have fared against Rafael Nadal or Novak Djokovic. While this is merely a dream for most tennis fans, we may get to see this type of competition take place in banking, particularly in lending, where a 100-year-old community bank will increasingly compete with rising FinTech companies for customers.

There is no way to accurately project the trajectory of the alternative lending industry moving forward. We do not yet know how traditional banks will respond. Additionally, loans originated by innovative, alternative lenders have still not experienced a full credit cycle. However, there are several potential outcomes that seem likely assuming a manageable credit environment and reasonable regulation. The potential outcomes include: disruption of traditional intermediaries by alternative lending platforms, alternative lending platforms serving banks in an auxiliary capacity, and alternative lending platforms acting as wakeup calls for banks to implement and invest in digital lending technology.

First, alternative lending models may move further upstream in the market to cause mass disruption to the traditional intermediaries. Alternative lenders are able to operate with sleeker, more efficient technology than traditional banks and are not, at present, weighed down by the capital requirements and regulatory/compliance costs that banks are. Of course, if alternative lenders are to move more into the mainstream, they will be subjected to some of the same regulatory scrutiny as retail banks.

Alternative lending platforms may ultimately begin to look more like retail banks in this scenario and could undermine the vast market share of lending that banks currently enjoy.

Second, alternative lending platforms could begin to complement retail banks and serve an auxiliary role in their lending operations in the form of strategic partnerships. In this scenario, retail banks will be able to capitalize on lending to higher risk borrowers that alternative lenders often rely on. As alternative lenders become more associated with traditional banks, they will gain greater consumer trust. This will enable them to expand their lending base into lower-risk borrowers. In a partnership with an online lender, retail banks can serve high-risk customers while earning origination revenue from these customers without assuming all of the risk. To mitigate the risk, the bank may sell the underlying loan to another investor rather than the primary loan and credit risk remaining with the alternative lender. In this scenario, the expansion of credit brought by alternative lenders could continue without disrupting the traditional structure of the bank industry.

Finally, alternative lending platforms could serve as agents of change within the traditional retail bank lending model, as banks realize the potential disruptive effects and efficiencies of online lenders. As banks begin to adopt and mimic the technology associated with digital lenders, their processes are sped up and made more efficient through more accurate underwriting and faster access to funds. With their scale advantages and preexisting customer relationships, banks could force out digital lenders by essentially offering services that mirror online lenders. This scenario would allow traditional retail banks to maintain their dominance in the lending market while simultaneously improving the process and infrastructure of traditional lending.

NOTES

1. "MBA Mortgage Finance Forecast," December 18, 2015, https://www.mba.org/Documents/Research/Mortgage%20Finance%20Forecast%20Dec%202015.pdf.
2. "Consumer Credit," Federal Reserve, http://www.federalreserve.gov/releases/g19/, accessed February 5, 2016.
3. PYMNTS, "Is the Great Contraction Coming Soon to Alt Lending?" *PYMNTS*, June 14, 2016, http://www.pymnts.com/news/2016/is-the-great-contraction-coming-soon-to-alt-lending/.
4. Jay Jenkins, "The $1.3 Billion Problem with On Deck Capital and Lending Club," *The Motley Fool*, May 9, 2016, http://www.fool.com/investing/general/2016/05/09/the-13-billion-problem-with-on-deck-capital-and-le.aspx.
5. Matt Egan, "LendingClub's Fall from Grace from Rock Star Status," *CNN Money*, May 17, 2016, http://money.cnn.com/2016/05/17/investing/lendingclub-stock-doj-probe/.

6. Colin Wilhelm, "Regulatory Road Likely to Get Bumpier for Alternative Lenders," *American Banker*, May 15, 2015, http://www.americanbanker.com/news/marketplace-lending/regulatory-road-likely-to-get-bumpier-for-alternative-lenders-1074363-1.html?pg=1.
7. Travis P. Nelson, "OCC's White Paper Addresses Responsiveness to FinTech Innovation," *Global Regulatory Enforcement Law Blog*, April 1, 2016, https://www.globalregulatoryenforcementlawblog.com/2016/04/articles/uncategorized/occs-white-paper-addresses-responsiveness-to-FinTech-innovation/.
8. "Opportunities and Challenges in Online Marketplace Lending," *U.S. Department of the Treasury*, May 10, 2016, https://www.treasury.gov/connect/blog/Documents/Opportunities_and_Challenges_in_Online_Marketplace_Lending_white_paper.pdf.

CHAPTER 6

The Payments Niche

The means and methods by which people pay for goods and services has continually evolved throughout history—from commodity-bartering economies to the proliferation of modern fiat money to checks to credit and debit cards. Today, this evolution continues with mobile apps and online platforms increasingly being used and streamlining payments processes to create a more efficient economy. In this chapter, we take a closer look at emerging payment trends and FinTech innovations, including retailer-specific mobile apps that allow customers to order and pay from their mobile devices, mobile wallets that hold card and account information to allow mobile payments to be made virtually anywhere, solutions that allow merchants to accept these mobile payments, and mobile apps offering direct peer-to-peer payments. Additionally, we take a closer look at blockchain technology, the FinTech innovation behind emerging digital currencies, and identify potential areas where blockchain could impact financial and payment services. While this chapter does not cover all of the emerging FinTech payments solutions, it does address the core competencies of the space and takes into account some of the main players and emerging trends in the industry.

TRENDS TO WATCH

Movement to a Cashless Society

In the United States, according to a recent article, cash remains king as it was used in 32 percent of all transactions, the highest of any payment method.[1] Cash was particularly strong in small transactions (payments under $10) where it was used 66 percent of the time. However, we seem to be moving toward a more cashless system as cash's lead over other payment methods has declined from 40 percent in 2012 as usage of both debit and credit cards continues to inch higher. According to the *2016 UPS Pulse of the Online*

Shopper survey,[2] consumers for the first time bought more of their purchases on the web than in stores (51% in 2016 compared to 48% in 2015 and 47% in 2014) with Millennials accounting for the bulk of those online shoppers (54%). In addition, cryptocurrencies such as bitcoin (discussed at length later in this chapter) and mobile payment options like Apple Pay are working hard to become more accepted. Globally, mobile payments are becoming more common. A MasterCard survey found that more than 70 percent of respondents were ready to use their smartphone to make payments in the Middle East and Africa compared to only 38 percent in Europe.[3]

As a cashless society continues to emerge, banks are increasingly facing competition from upstart FinTech companies that are innovating in the payments niche. While many banks were able to partner with Visa and MasterCard as society transitioned from cash to cards, it remains to be seen whether banks will remain squarely in the payments loop as payments continue to evolve to digital (online and mobile).

To better understand trends in the payments niche, we provide case studies of innovative FinTech companies (Square, Gyft, Check, and Stripe) in the payments niche. The payment innovations discussed are leveraging mobile connectivity to make payments easier for consumers, even for small transactions. Many of the current innovations in payment solutions are not disrupting the existing process, but modifying and refining the existing front-end process (i.e., interaction between customer and merchant).

FinTech Payment Company Case Studies

Square Square is a mobile payment solution provider founded in 2009 by Twitter CEO Jack Dorsey and Jim McKelvey. Square has placed itself at the forefront of the point-of-sale (POS) segment of the mobile payments industry by offering software and hardware solutions for merchants to accept credit and debit card transactions on their iOS or Android devices. Square's first and flagship product, the Square Reader, plugs into a merchant's mobile device and houses a card reader through which consumers swipe their cards.

Square's other main payments hardware device, Square Stand, was introduced in 2013 and offers a more complete POS system by providing a larger card reader and rotatable mount for various models of iPads to sit on. This allows consumers to tip and sign for purchases through Square Register, the payments software behind the Reader and Stand. Square also offers a peer-to-peer money-transfer service, small business financing service, and payroll support service. Square's fee-based business model is primarily predicated on a flat fee of 2.75 percent per credit card swipe. A Square Stand can be purchased for $99 while a Square Reader is offered for free on Square.com (however, a contactless Square Reader does cost $49). Square is free of monthly fees and setup costs, and funds deducted off the service fees are deposited into the merchant's bank account within one-to-two days. Attracted by this clear pricing and fast deposit model, small businesses and merchants such as food trucks, independent retailers, and salons make up Square's largest customer base.

Square IPO'd at $9 per share in November 2015, in what many considered to be the most high-profile FinTech IPO of 2015.[4] The stock has generally underperformed market expectations since its IPO, as its price had dropped to $8.75 by January 2016.[5] Although the stock price has recovered somewhat on the heels of the company's announcement that it is further expanding its operations into European markets (trading at $10.22 as of 8/3/16), it is still being outpaced by broader markets thus far in 2016. The stagnation of Square's stock price reflects a number of underlying issues but two significant obstacles facing the company is that it is not yet profitable and it lost a significant partner in October 2016 when its relationship with Starbucks ended.[6] When the partnership was announced in 2013, it was seen as a huge coup for the payments startup to land a corporate whale like Starbucks. With the success of the Starbucks app, the coffee giant and Square parted ways, leaving Square to primarily rely on small businesses in efforts to turn a profit.

Despite these issues, Square has continued to grow (as measured by the number of merchants and processing volume) and, as previously mentioned, is gearing up to further expand in European markets. Going forward, it will be interesting to see whether Square will mature into a leader in the payments industry or become another example of a FinTech company with a revolutionary idea that did not have the business model to generate profits sufficient to support it.

Gyft   Gyft is a mobile gift card app that allows customers to buy, store, send, and redeem gift cards conveniently from their mobile device. Gyft's mobile applications allow users to upload and check mobile gift card balances, earn rewards points for using a gift card, purchase with bitcoin or PayPal, and purchase and send gift cards electronically to friends or family.

Table 6.1 provides an overview of Gyft since its founding as well as a timeline related to key milestones achieved.[7]

Gyft Key Takeaways

1. When developing a FinTech innovation, have a clear, validated idea that adds value to both end-user and partner/provider (in this case retailers).

   ▪ Targeted a large sector of the payments segment, gift card industry that totaled approximately $100 billion that could be disrupted technologically.

TABLE 6.1   Gyft's Significant Corporate Events

Timeline	Significant Corporate Events
2012	Company founded in January and originally focused on developing an iPhone app that allowed users to buy, give, and share gift cards Received first round of seed funding of $1.3M from South African investor in June Announced integration with Apple's Passbook, including over 200 different retail gift cards Received second round of seed funding of $1.3M in September following being a finalist at TechCrunch Disrupt SF
2013	Expanded application to web and Android Reported to have around 200,000-plus gift cards with $10M uploaded to platform and offering over 300 retail cards Received $5M of Series A funding (September) Introduced features like re-gifting, bitcoin support, and a registry option
2014	Tried to expand internationally and introduced a card-swapping option Announced its new mobile gift card solution (Gyft Cloud) for small-to-midsized businesses Partnered with Clover, a First Data subsidiary company that offers an innovative all-in-one POS payment and business solution for small-to-midsized businesses
July 30, 2014	First Data, a global leader in payment technology and solutions, announces deal to acquire Gyft Exact details of the transaction have not been disclosed

- Value to consumer—Offered a solution to consumers who often forgot or lost cards with dollars going unused.
- Value to retailer—Offered a solution to retailers who often have unused legacy gift cards and no idea where the cards reside, which is a problem because a 2010 law prevented retailers from booking gift card sales as revenue until the cards are redeemed (value to retailer).
- Value to both—Took concept of managing mobile payments for gift cards for individual companies and developed a multichannel space for consumers and businesses.
- Retailers can target messaging to consumers regarding incentives or promotions and also send reminders to use a forgotten/unused card.

2. In a competitive FinTech niche (like payments), attempt to differentiate your strategy from competitors.

   ▪ Gyft launched in a very competitive space in 2010 and there were a number of other competitors attempting to disrupt the gift card industry—most notably a few who were attempting to promote social gifting experiences.
   ▪ Gyft differentiated itself from those competitors by working with existing retailers and users, and focused on digitizing the existing gift card network/experience on mobile rather than significantly changing user behavior.

3. Focus on mobile and digital appeared successful in the FinTech payments niche.

   ▪ Gyft was able to grow both consumer and retailer adoption related to digitizing offline gift cards to mobile.
   ▪ Will this avenue work in other areas of payments or was the gift card industry unique?

4. Disruptive FinTech startups continue to value partnerships and this may lead to acquisitions by partners.

   ▪ Gyft joins the list of recent FinTech startups (Check, Simple, Banno, etc.) who were ultimately acquired by those existing companies that they initially sought to disrupt.
   ▪ Given the significant amount of capital and resources required to grow the user base of FinTech startups where heavily regulated markets and institutions are common, growing the user/activity base to a level to achieve enough scale to attract more capital or profits to propel future growth may be more difficult than in other sectors.
   ▪ Additionally, the importance of partnership in the FinTech sector seems to lend itself to transactions similar to Gyft, where a larger, more established partner acquires the startup as it gains traction.
   ▪ Consider the following quote from Gyft's Founder, Vinny Lingham:

     > *We have been building this relationship for a while.... We started the company with a mission to digitize and transform the plastic gift card space.... But as we were going through the process it was a lot more complicated than it seemed. Onboarding merchants was a real grind.... We don't see this as an exit. We see this as a continuation of what we're already doing, but with a lot more resources.*[8]

Check Check offers a mobile application that provides an efficient and secure way for consumers to access bills and money from their smartphones. The mobile application has more than 10 million users and allows users to monitor bank accounts and credit cards, send reminders regarding bill and low funds, and automatically pay bills.

Check provides an example of the emerging trends toward a cashless and checkless world as it bridged the intersection between personal finance and a disruptive bill pay capability that is basically free for the consumer. Table 6.2 provides an overview of Check since its founding, as well as a timeline related to key milestones achieved by Check.[9]

TABLE 6.2 Check's Significant Corporate Events

Timeline	Significant Corporate Events
2007	Initially founded as a web company named Pageonce to solve a problem that one of the founders found extremely frustrating: remembering usernames and passwords to online accounts
2008	Launched "Internet assistant" to help users manage online lives after a private beta period where it collected 20,000 users and built support for more than 60,000 account types. As users began to use product, Check discovered that 50% of users had linked financial accounts. Therefore, they began to focus more on being an aggregator of personal financial data and putting all the information onto one page.
	As user growth slowed, Check pivoted from focusing on building web platform to focusing on mobile application; Pageonce Personal Assistant Mobile Application was one of original 100 applications available when the iPhone App Store launched
	Angel round ($1.5 million invested in January 2008)
2009	Mobile application hit 1 million users and was in the top 20 in iPhone store for 2009
	Revenue model was focused on advertising in free applications and charging for a premium version
	Series A round ($6.5 million invested in December)
2011	Sophistication of application increased to where application could track bank accounts, credit cards, investment and travel plans, monitor bills and manage money; raised capital to become the "wallet of the future"; launched mobile bill pay feature
	Unknown ($15 million invested in May 2011)
2013	Changed name from Pageonce to Check; 8 million users and payments volume of approximately $1.5 million per month
	Started allowing users to set up mobile person-to-person payments
	Series C round ($24 million in September 2013)
2014	10+ million users and $500 million in payments processed per year
	Check sold to Intuit for $360 million (total funding since inception $47 million)

Check Key Takeaways

1. It is important to maintain flexibility and openness to pivot if needed.
   - Check pivoted from desktop "Internet assistant" application to mobile personal financial application and then, more specifically, to mobile payments.
     - The pivot grew out of slowing user growth on desktop application, as well as recognition of potential growth in mobile and ultimately mobile payments.
     - Even had an unsuccessful attempt at a Facebook application before successfully opening mobile application in iPhone store.

2. When developing a FinTech strategy, focus on consumer trends/desires and your core beliefs regarding where the market is headed.
   - Check's pivot was consistent with their belief that mobile adoption would increase for financial services.
     - This turned out to be consistent with consumer trends and shift from offline to online and mobile.
     - For perspective, mobile payments currently represent a fraction of in-store purchases but the percentage rose 103 percent in the United States between 2010 and 2013.[10]
     - U.S. Consumers were expected to pay more than 14.7 million bills in 2013 with online and mobile payments accounting for more than half.[11]

3. Check was another successful exit for FinTech venture capital investors and demonstrates the potential for value creation and enhanced returns from investments in FinTech startups.
   - Approximately $47 million invested in Check starting with Angel round in 2008. Check ultimately sold for $360 million in 2014, which implies the following:
     - Internal rate of return: 88%
     - Cash-on-cash: 7.7×
     - Return on investment: 666%
   - Significantly higher than 11.5% median IRR for 2009 Vintage U.S. VC Funds (with asset size between $250 and $500 million) as reported by PitchBook.

Stripe Stripe attempts to improve Internet commerce by making it easier to process transactions and manage an online business. The company provides fraud prevention and the technical banking infrastructure required to operate online payment systems accounts (Table 6.3).

TABLE 6.3 Stripe's Significant Corporate Events

Timeline	Significant Corporate Events
2010–2011	Two seed rounds, one undisclosed and another at $2M (Y Combinator alum) Stripe launched in 2011 Software allows companies to take online payments securely and is noted for being relatively easy to use and customizable
2012	Raised $18M in a Series A in February (reported $100M valuation) and $20M in a Series B in July (reported $500M valuation) Acquired chat and task-management application kickoff
2014	Raised $80M in January (reported $1.75B valuation) and $70M in December (reported $3.5B valuation) Announced support for bitcoin transactions
2015	Raised $90M in a Series C (reported $5BN valuation) in July Announced Visa partnership to help expand further internationally Unveiled Stripe Relay, tools for retailers to help them build native buying experiences within other apps like Twitter; intended to improve the buying experience by not requiring users to jump through multiple websites

First, it's really simple for a business to get started using Stripe, and second, it's easy for developers to customize Stripe's technology for their own needs—which is super-important because not all online businesses have the same needs.
                    —Business Insider Research Analyst John Heggestuen[12]

Stripe Key Takeaways

1. Despite larger and mature incumbents in the payments space, niches still exist to exploit.

   ▪ Payments is an industry that has existed in some form for thousands of years, but evolving customer expectations and preferences (transitioning to more mobile and online commerce) continue to create opportunities for savvy companies and entrepreneurs.

2. Focus on the headaches when considering FinTech innovations.

   ▪ Stripe's Relay product clearly targets the elimination of certain headaches that customers and retailers have with trying to sell items online.

■ For example, Stripe's "buy" buttons reduce headaches experienced by both retailers (who advertise products on social media) and consumers (who have to click through to multiple sites to buy).

3. When developing an innovation in certain FinTech niches, ease of use and ability to customize may require flexibility and fading into the background.

■ Building "buy" buttons that work in other apps/sites and allowing companies to customize their payment options are examples of ways Stripe competes by allowing the user (i.e., retailer) to have tremendous flexibility.

4. Again, FinTech partnerships prove to be vital.

■ Stripe has partnered with a number of companies, including traditional financial services companies (such as AmEx, Visa), as well as nonfinancials (such as developing "buy" buttons for Pinterest, Facebook, and Twitter).

Retailer-Specific Mobile Payment Apps and Loyalty Programs

One potential result of a more cashless world is banks losing greater control over the customer experience. As banks increasingly fight to remain relevant in payments, banks may begin partnering with merchants to drive usage of merchant-specific cards and other solutions to gain their share of the digital wallet. To better understand merchant-specific wallets, loyalty programs, and emerging trends in this area, we discuss two of the more prominent examples—the offerings of Starbucks and Walmart.

The Starbucks App   The Starbucks app, available on iPhone and Android operating systems, has emerged as one of the most functional and well-regarded mobile payments systems in the retail industry. This status has been achieved through the app's consumer-friendly interface, as well as the capability of each Starbucks location to efficiently process in-store orders and mobile orders from the app. When setting up the mobile app, customers link their debit or credit card to the app and add funds to create a balance in the app. Upon arrival at the store, customers who have ordered their coffee via the app are automatically given a unique barcode through their device to scan at the register when they pick up their order. With the scan, the funds are transferred out of the app and to the store, rendering the transaction complete. The app also links any purchases made to the customer's loyalty rewards account, in which points can be accumulated and put toward free refills, drinks, and sandwiches.

Much of the success and widespread adoption of the Starbucks app can be attributed to the efficient infrastructure of Starbucks' locations that allows baristas to fill mobile orders quickly and consistently without sacrificing a quality in-store experience for the traditional customer. The app served as a key driver of a 9 percent increase in sales for the company in fiscal 2015 in its Americas division, with more than 1 million users leveraging the app in December 2015 alone.[13] Perhaps the most impressive metric stemming from the app lies in the fact that 10 percent of all orders come from the app in Starbucks' most high-volume locations.[14] As one of the most well-established and user-friendly mobile payment apps in the retail industry, the Starbucks app should continue to turn rising levels of mobile usage among consumers into tangible growth for its company.

Walmart Pay   As one of the bellwethers of the retail industry, Walmart's move into the mobile payments space should come as no surprise. However, despite its status as a retail juggernaut worldwide, Walmart's expansion into mobile payments came somewhat late when compared to other retail leaders that have adopted Apple Pay or developed their own mobile payment systems.

In June 2016, Walmart rolled out "Walmart Pay" in all of its stores, giving its customers the ability to pay for items at checkout by simply taking a picture of a barcode with their mobile device. Walmart Pay is available on any phone that can download the Walmart app and is only accessible through the Walmart app. It entails a fairly simple setup process. Users enter credit or debit card information into the app to begin the process and from there may begin to make purchases. At checkout, the user indicates to the cashier or self-checkout kiosk that he or she would like to use Walmart Pay. A QR code (barcode) is then generated at the point of sale terminal and the user takes a picture of this barcode on a code-reading camera accessed through the app. The user then confirms his purchase through the app, the transaction is completed, and a receipt is sent to the user via email.

The process of actually using the app to pay for purchases has received mixed reviews from consumers, as some find it to be cumbersome and less streamlined than simply paying with a card. Nonetheless, Walmart Pay fills a need for many Walmart customers who either don't own a completely payment capable smartphone or would be more inclined to share payment information with Walmart than Apple or Google.

DIGITAL CURRENCIES AND BLOCKCHAIN TECHNOLOGY

Blockchain originated as the underlying technology that powered bitcoin, the most prolific worldwide cryptocurrency system. While bitcoin's future remains uncertain and difficult to predict, it is possible that blockchain technology becomes the most valuable contribution to emerge from bitcoin.

The use of blockchain allows bitcoin users to exchange the currency through a decentralized system that lends itself to digital integrity and previously unseen levels of openness. Despite bitcoin's perhaps undeserved reputation as the chief facilitator of the online black market as a result of being the currency used by illegal online bazaar Silk Road, blockchain has emerged as a legitimate tech solution for financial institutions that could potentially change the entire landscape of the industry.[15] Banks, insurers, and other traditional incumbents have begun exploring the possibilities of the use of blockchain as it pertains to making their processes faster and more efficient. Essentially, traditional incumbents are trying to test the ability of the blockchain and a distributed ledger to enhance efficiency in a variety of processes.

To sum, blockchain technology is viewed by many as the most applicable component of bitcoin to the traditional financial system and has created a view among traditional players that while bitcoin has been a revolutionary cultural concept and has some application to the system, the real value of bitcoin lies in its proliferation of blockchain as a feasible tech solution that could disrupt and improve the financial ecosystem.

What Is Blockchain?

Blockchain is a digital, distributed transaction ledger that continuously updates its extensive list of data records by holding data in chronological blocks and adding these blocks to an existing chain of blocks with the anonymous approval of the other members of the chain through time-stamping and corresponding information. Once entered into a blockchain, information can never be altered or erased, ensuring a transparent and accurate record of transactions and information available to many. Given the fact that every node (computer) in the system has a copy of the blockchain, users can quickly detect any discrepancy that may be a sign of potential fraud or hacking attempts. Figure 6.1 presents a visual picture of how blockchain works.

The key characteristics of blockchain are listed here.

- **Reliability.** Given that blockchain operates through a wide circle of participants without a single centralized location, there is no one point of failure. This allows the system to continuously run without fear of a shutdown or interruption.
- **Transparency.** All transactions are visible to all members of the blockchain, increasing trust and auditability.
- **Immutability.** It is more difficult to make changes to the blockchain without detection than traditional payment systems, increasing confidence in transactions.

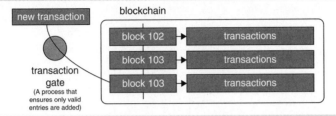

A blockchain is a database shared by every participant in a given system. The blockchain stores the complete transaction history of a cryptocurrency or other record-keeping system.

Transactions aren't recognized until they are added to the blockchain. Tampering is immediately evident, and the blockchain is safe as record because everyone has a copy. The source of discrepancies is also immediately obvious.

FIGURE 6.1 How Blockchain Works
Source: ZD Net | Used with permission of ZDNET.com. Copyright © 2017. All rights reserved

- **Irrevocability.** The permanent and fixed nature of the blockchain makes it possible for transactions to become binding and final.

Consistent with the potential applications and excitement around blockchain technology, venture capital investment into companies providing blockchain services has soared from only $3 million in 2011 to nearly $475 million in 2015. In total, investors have poured nearly a billion dollars into over 120 startups operating on every continent except Antarctica. Before 2015, investors focused mainly on the digital payments through the bitcoin side of blockchain investment, but have recently shifted toward a preference for startups that provide blockchain software and infrastructure.

In terms of investment by functionality, funders have segmented the industry into three distinct groups: applications and solutions, middleware, and infrastructure. The segment that has received the most funding from investors has been applications and solutions. These companies provide and operate bitcoin wallets as alternative payment solutions utilizing blockchain and include startups such as ribbit.me, Circle, and Shocard.

Similar to the growing excitement for FinTech applications in the payments area that we discussed earlier in this chapter, there has also been increased interest in startups that provide blockchain services to companies, whether it be software for companies to build their own blockchain applications or the blockchain infrastructure itself. Providers of software to build blockchain-capable applications have become known as middleware companies. Some of the most prominent middleware startups are Blockcypher and Factom. The infrastructure segment includes companies that provide a

TABLE 6.4 Largest Payments, Bitcoin, and Blockchain Funding in 2015–2016

Period	Company	Amount ($M)	Company Description
Q3 2015	AvidXchange	$225	Payment solutions (Automated Billpay & A/P)
Q1 2015	21 Inc.	$116	Stealth bitcoin startup
Q1 2015	Zuora	$115	Cloud-based subscription billing services
Q1 2015	Coinbase	$75	Cryptocurrency wallet and exchange
Q2 2015	Yapstone	$60	Online electronic payments processing platform for online marketplaces
Q2 2015	ZenPayroll	$60	Cloud-based comprehensive payroll service making processing payroll for business simple
Q1 2015	Raise Marketplace	$56	Marketplace for buying and selling giftcards
Q1 2015	Bill.com	$50	Small and Medium Business invoicing and payments platform
Q2 2015	Circle	$50	Bitcoin-based digital service to store, send, and receive money
Q3 2015	Shift Payments	$50	Debit card with universal currency access
Q3 2015	Payoneer	$50	International money transfers
Q2 2015	WePay	$40	Provides marketplaces, crowdfunding sites, and other platform businesses a payments platform
Q2 2016	Remitly	$39	International payment service allowing customers to make international transfers from United States
Q2 2016	Simplee	$38	Software platform for health-care payments and billing
Q1 2015	Ripple Labs	$30	Open source payment network

Source: Mercer Capital Quarterly FinTech Newsletters from Q1 2015 through Q2 2016

blockchain infrastructure to build secure platforms for their clients, such as successful startup Ripple.

Table 6.4 provides an overview of the largest recent venture fundings in both blockchain and payments companies.

Potential Applications of Blockchain Moving Forward

Payment Solutions The payment solutions industry is ripe for potential applications of blockchain to increase efficiency, transparency, and accuracy. Blockchain could facilitate low-cost micropayments processed without fees, which may open up new business models such as a newspaper website charging by articles read rather than a monthly subscription. Electronic signature and digital transaction management could remove barriers in the car buying and leasing processes by integrating proof of concept with blockchain to record contracts. Furthermore, the settlement process in travel, retail, and hospitality loyalty programs could be vastly improved, as blockchain could handle a more organized and efficient treatment of loyalty points and update these points in real time. BTC Smart Meters, a South African utilities company, is already integrating blockchain into the way its customers pay for utilities by accepting bitcoin as a form of digital payment supported by blockchain capabilities.

Financial Services Beyond payments applications, blockchain technology has a number of far-reaching and potentially disruptive applications for financial institutions if adopted. Not only are massive public blockchain companies being discussed as possibilities for transaction support, but permissioned (private) blockchain companies could give institutions the capability to run a blockchain within only their organization. Blockchain could also eliminate the need for central authorities to certify ownership and clear transactions, as the information would be widely available on a massive securities exchange blockchain. Nearly instantaneous settlement of securities transactions would be made possible by blockchain and the traditional t + 3 settlement window could be reduced to t + "whatever regulatory bodies deem acceptable," which would lower the cost to trade as less capital will be tied up in the settlement process. NASDAQ is already testing the use of blockchain in its NASDAQ Private Market, a marketplace for pre-IPO trading of private companies. NASDAQ Linq, as the blockchain product has been named, has already drawn praise for the way it has increased efficiency and speed in the clearance and settlement of trades. With the introduction of Linq, NASDAQ is on the leading of edge of what could become a widespread introduction of blockchain into the financial services industry.[16]

Blockchain technology also has a number of horizontal applications that could impact all industries, not just financial services. While not all-inclusive, a few primary potential applications of blockchain in other industries include the following:

- **Smart Contracts.** Blockchain will be able to create agreements represented as software that can automatically trigger an action under certain conditions, such as when a payment is made or missed.

- **Automated Auditing.** Blockchain can allow for automated third-party verification by a distributed network to ensure that transactions are accurate and complete.
- **Cybersecurity.** The nature of blockchain enables the immediate detection of data manipulation and verifies the integrity of IT systems.

There are broad potential future applications of blockchain, including:

- Digital asset management
- eVoting
- Smart contracts and self-executing wills
- Digital notary
- Registration and title of goods beyond cars and homes
- Money tracking for government tax-funded projects
- Secure cloud storage across multiple platforms

Government Regulation of Blockchain

Given that blockchain technology is still rapidly evolving, governments worldwide have been left in somewhat of a holding pattern as it pertains to the regulation of blockchain companies. Perhaps the biggest obstacle facing governmental agencies and other regulatory bodies is that given the global nature of the technology and the sheer volume of regulation it could be subject to, the capabilities and potential uses of blockchain could be greatly constrained if it were to come under excess regulation by a vast cross-section of international agencies. Still, conversations about regulation among governments and regulatory bodies are becoming more prevalent as blockchain penetrates the financial industry, although the outcomes of these conversations are often inconclusive.

The European Securities and Market Authority (ESMA) released a paper in June 2016 stating that it had still not established a concrete opinion on the regulation of blockchains or their potential to disrupt the financial industry.[17] Their position argues that it is still too early to tell whether governments will be able to regulate blockchain in an efficient way that has minimal effect on the use of the technology. The ESMA does concede that blockchain could boost efficiency, reduce intermediation, and foster transparency in securities transactions, but states that scaling, international governance, and security issues still make the future of blockchain too uncertain to have a regulatory or legal opinion.

Regulation of blockchain in the United States is in an even more juvenile stage as the government is just beginning to recognize it as a legitimate disruptor. Members of Congress recently met with representatives from the industry to discuss its potential and gain a better understanding of blockchain.[18] This meeting was meant to serve as a briefing for members of Congress and showed that the United States is becoming more proactive in taking steps toward regulating blockchain. However, there is still a great deal of debate as to whether this regulation should take place at the state or federal level, as some states have taken the lead in regulation while others are waiting to see if the federal government will handle the arduous process. At *The Blockchain and Distributed Ledger Technology Conference* in April 2016, a panel made up of FDIC regulators and state securities commission representatives reasoned that regulation would remain at the state level, as most of the companies interested in blockchain technology are small, heavily localized companies.[19] Thus, while governments and regulatory agencies both domestic and abroad are making some headway in figuring out a strategy to regulate blockchains, concrete pieces of legislation seriously affecting the industry are still a long ways off.

Digital Currency Case Study

In order to provide perspective on FinTech companies emerging in the digital currency space, let's take a look at Coinbase, a mobile bitcoin wallet provider that allows customers to buy, store, and accept bitcoin currency from the web or their mobile device.

Coinbase Coinbase's mobile application allows users to store bitcoins in customer's wallets or vaults for zero fees, purchase/sell bitcoins, and check and manage accounts. For better perspective on Coinbase's operations, consider the following quotes related to Coinbase:

> *Coinbase, headquartered in San Francisco, has become one of the most prominent businesses, allowing people to buy and store bitcoins and developing deals with merchants to help them carry out bitcoin transactions.*
>
> **—*Time*[20]**

> *Finally, bitcoin is being recognized as a great vehicle for banking. It is clear that not only can bitcoin be used for remittances and stored value, but also for banking efficiency and credit-card transactions.*
>
> **—Tim Draper of DFJ[21]**

> *A lot of these companies, they want to invest in category leaders, and we made a convincing case that that was us.*
>
> **—Brian Armstrong, CEO of Coinbase[22]**

Table 6.5 provides an overview of Coinbase since its founding as well as a timeline related to key milestones achieved by the company.[23]

TABLE 6.5   Coinbase's Significant Corporate Events

Timeline	Significant Corporate Events
2012	June: company founded by Brian Armstrong and Fred Eshram September: received $600,000 in seed funding from Y Combinator, Funders Club, and other individual investors
2013	May: raised Series A funding of $6.1 million from Ribbit Capital, Union Square Ventures, Red Swan Ventures, among other investors December: raised Series B funding of $25 million from Andreessen Horowitz, Union Square Ventures, QueensBridge Venture Partners, Ribbit Capital, and other individual investors
2014	May: acquired Kippt, a collaborative bookmarking system for professional networks that allows users to collect and share content August: acquired Blockr.io, a popular explorer for the blockchain, or the distributed public ledger that keeps track of all bitcoin transactions September: Coinbase expands into Europe
2015	January: raised Series C funding of $75 million from New York Stock Exchange, Valor Capital Group, DFJ, BBVA Ventures, and other investors January: Coinbase becomes first regulated bitcoin exchange in the United States

Coinbase Key Takeaways

1. Bitcoin and blockchain have implications beyond payment processing.

   - Bitcoin is more than just a new way to make purchases. It is a protocol for exchanging value over the Internet without an intermediary.
   - Anywhere a transaction between two parties has traditionally required third-party validation, bitcoin or blockchain may be applicable, including the execution of contracts, the transfer of property, and identity management.

2. Wall Street is beginning to take bitcoin seriously.

   - NYSE's entrance into the bitcoin space through its investment in Coinbase is a signal that more moderate consumers and investors may be warming to the idea of a decentralized currency.
   - With further adoption, businesses and individuals are seeing the opportunities for increased ease and greater accessibility within international financial markets.
   - The cost of transacting, through avoiding typical banking channels and other payment processing middlemen, is significantly lower.

3. Focus on mobile and digital appears successful in this segment of the payments industry.

- Coinbase intends to use its new capital to grow its employee base while focusing on improving its mobile product as it eyes entry into developing markets.
- Mobile use may be even more critical in emerging markets, especially where computer access is limited.

CONCLUSION

With society continuing to move toward a more cashless system, banks will increasingly face competition from upstart FinTech companies such as the companies profiled in this chapter. Additionally, banks will increasingly have customers who use retailer-specific applications and loyalty programs, which may ultimately threaten many banks' present role within the payments loop. As these trends continue to emerge, banks need to determine how they can best partner and innovate in order to stay relevant and maintain revenue from facilitating payments.

In addition to the continued transition to a more cashless society and the emergence of retailer-specific apps, blockchain technology could have a significant impact the financial services industry. Banks, exchanges, and other intermediaries are beginning to explore various uses of blockchain to improve speed, efficiency, and transparency in an increasingly complex and dense financial environment. While the use of blockchain is starting to proliferate across the financial landscape, some looming questions in the short and long term remain that will determine whether blockchain truly does restructure the entire system or become an afterthought fondly looked back upon as a peculiar fad 20 years in the future.

The most immediate crux regarding the adoption of blockchain by financial institutions is the question of whether to acquire software that enables the incumbents to build their own blockchain in house, or outsource this task to a startup with expertise and create a strategic partnership moving forward. Some institutions are already taking the lead in answering this question, the most notable being the partnership between digital distributed ledger provider R3 and over 40 of the world's leading financial institutions, including BNP Paribas, Barclays, Goldman Sachs, Credit Suisse, JP Morgan, UBS, and Wells Fargo, in what has become known as the R3 Consortium.[24] These partnerships have edged the financial landscape closer to total global interconnectivity between institutions, exchanges, brokers, custodial entities, and all other parties in a transaction. This will greatly reduce intermediation in the financial landscape and cut down on the cost of doing business for providers of financial services. On the other hand, some institutions are attempting to build their own blockchain system in-house, such as NAS-DAQ's Linq. In the short term, this question of whether to partner with providers of blockchain infrastructure or attempt to design a blockchain infrastructure looms the largest over financial institutions just beginning to dip their toes into the deep pool of blockchain technology.

The most pressing long-term issue for blockchain adoption is the treatment of the technology by governments and regulatory bodies, which at present is unclear. As mentioned earlier, the global nature of blockchain could create an environment of undue regulatory restraint on the capabilities of the technology, as legislation and regulation could close in on blockchain from multiple governments and regulatory agencies spanning the globe with little coordination between the agencies. Despite the potential for this adverse environment, governments and regulatory agencies appear to be behind the curve in regard to blockchain, although it could improve their operations through innovations such as eVoting and improved recordkeeping. Most governing bodies are still grappling with key questions such as what exactly is blockchain and should it be regulated at a federal or local level. As officials and regulators work through these initial queries, blockchain will continue to evolve, leading to more headaches for those attempting to dictate what companies can and cannot do with blockchain and, as a result, to an even longer period of time before widespread legislation is seen in regard to the technology.

In closing, with large institutions rapidly adopting blockchain technology and regulatory bodies scratching their heads and dragging their feet, an environment ripe for innovation and change within the financial landscape has been created. Blockchain startups and financial institutions have been able to get out in front of legislation and basically operate with limited oversight as they attempt to increase speed, efficiency, and transparency within the financial ecosystem. While it is still far too early to make an observation on any widespread effect of blockchain on the financial landscape, the recognition and early adoption by institutions of blockchain as a legitimate technological solution coupled with an evolving regulatory environment has created the potential for blockchain to act as a highly disruptive technology that could enact seismic change in the entire financial ecosystem.

NOTES

1. Patrick Gillespie, "Cash Is Still King for Americans," *Money.cnn.com*, November 4, 2016, http://money.cnn.com/2016/11/04/news/economy/cash-is-king-san-francisco-fed/index.html?iid=ob_homepage_deskrecommended_pool.

2. Available online at https://solvers.ups.com/assets/2016_UPS_Pulse_of_the_ Online_Shopper.pdf.

3. "'Give Us Even More Digital Services,' Consumers Across the Globe Say," *MasterCard Press Release*, September 27, 2016, http://newsroom.mastercard .com/press-releases/give-us-even-more-digital-services-consumers-across-the- globe-say/.

4. Telios Demos and Corrie Driebusch, "Square's $9-a-Share Price Deals Blow to IPO Market," *Wall Street Journal*, November 19, 2015, http://www.wsj.com/ articles/square-ipo-prices-at-9-a-share-below-11-to-13-range-1447893733.

5. Leena Rao, "Square Falls Below Its IPO Price," *Fortune*, January 20, 2016, http://fortune.com/2016/01/20/square-stock-price/.

6. Matt Weinberger, "The Big Starbucks Deal Was a Disaster for Square," *Business Insider*, October 14, 2015, http://www.businessinsider.com/starbucks-deal- with-square-is-over-a-bust-2015-10.

7. *Sources:* Techcrunch.com; check company website; numerous articles, including:

Sarah Perez, "First Data Acquires Mobile Gift Card Platform Gift," *Tech- Crunch*, July 30, 2014, https://techcrunch.com/2014/07/30/first-data-acquires- mobile-gift-card-platform-gyft/.

Michael Carney, "Payments Giant First Data Acquires Gyft in an Effort to Bring Digital Gift Cards to the Masses," *Pando*, July 30, 2014, https:// pando.com/2014/07/30/payments-giant-first-data-acquires-gyft-in-an-effort- to-bring-digital-gift-cards-to-the-masses/.

"Gyft Announces Launch of First Cloud-based Mobile Gift Card Solution for Small to Mid-Sized Businesses," Reuters, April 8, 2014.

"Digital Gift Card Platform Gyft Raises $5M," Vato.com.

Sarah Perez, "Digital Gift Card Platform Gyft Raises $5 Million Series A," *TechCrunch* September 25, 2013, https://techcrunch.com/2013/09/25/digital- gift-card-platform-gyft-raises-5-million-series-a/.

Sarah Perez, "Gyft Brings Gift Cards Over 200 Retailers to Apple's Pass- book," *TechCrunch*, September 24, 2012, https://techcrunch.com/2012/09/24/ gyft-brings-gift-cards-from-over-200-retailers-to-apples-passbook/.

8. Michael Carney, "Payments Giant First Data Acquires Gyft in an Effort to Bring Digital Gift Cards to the Masses," *PandoDaily*, July 30, 2014, https:// pando.com/2014/07/30/payments-giant-first-data-acquires-gyft-in-an-effort- to-bring-digital-gift-cards-to-the-masses/.

9. *Sources:* Techcrunch.com; check company website; numerous articles, including:

Chris Morrison, "PageOnce Raises $1.5M for Online Personal Assistant," *VentureBeat*, January 9, 2008, http://venturebeat.com/2008/01/09/pageonce- raises-15m-for-online-personal-assistant/.

Mark Hendrickson, "One-Stop Accounts Manager PageOnce Launches," *TechCrunch*, January 1, 2008, https://techcrunch.com/2008/06/02/one-stop- account-manager-pageonce-launches/.

Anthony Ha, "Mobile Personal Assistant Pageonce Raises $6.5M," *Venture- Beat*, December 9, 2009, http://venturebeat.com/2009/12/09/mobile-personal- assistant-pageonce-raises-6-5m/.

Tom Taulli, "Pageonce Changes Its Name and Gets Ready for the Mobile Payments Revolution," *Forbes*, May 6, 2013, http://www.forbes.com/sites/tomtaulli/2013/05/06/pageonce-changes-its-name-and-gets-ready-for-the-mobile-payments-revolution/#309b0f6a71c3.

Olga Kharif, "Check Raises $24 Million to Bolster Mobile Bill Payment Service," *Bloomberg*, September 4, 2013, https://www.bloomberg.com/news/articles/2013-09-04/check-raises-24-million-to-bolster-mobile-bill-payment-service.

Reuters, "Intuit to Buy Check Inc. for $360 million," *Reuters: Technology News*, May 27, 2014, http://www.reuters.com/article/us-intuit-acquisition-idUSKBN0E71RT20140527.

10. Karim Ahmad and Gerard du Toit, "Banks Should Act Now on Mobile Payments," *American Banker*, May 19, 2014, http://www.americanbanker.com/bankthink/banks-should-act-now-on-mobile-payments-1067543-1.html.

11. Reuters, "Intuit to Buy Check Inc. for $360 Million," *Reuters: Technology News*, May 27, 2014, http://www.reuters.com/article/us-intuit-acquisition-idUSKBN0E71RT20140527.

12. Matt Weinberger, "Here's the Next Key Challenge for Stripe, the Hot Payment Startup Whose Valuation Keeps Soaring," *Business Insider*, May 21, 2015, http://www.businessinsider.com/stripe-valuation-hitting-5-billion-as-payments-market-heats-up-2015-5.

13. Ashraf Eassa, "Starbucks Is Winning Mobile Payments, But Others Are Not Far Behind," November 28, 2016, http://www.fool.com/investing/general/2016/02/03/starbucks-is-winning-mobile-payments-and-its-not-e.aspx.

14. Ibid.

15. David Schatsky, Craig Muraskin, "Beyond Bitcoin: Blockchain Is Coming to Disrupt Your Industry," *Deloitte University Press*, December 7, 2015, https://dupress.deloitte.com/dup-us-en/focus/signals-for-strategists/trends-blockchain-bitcoin-security-transparency.html.

16. Pete Rizzo, "Hands On with Linq, Nasdaq's Private Markets Blockchain Project," *CoinDesk*, November 21, 2015, http://www.coindesk.com/hands-on-with-linq-nasdaqs-private-markets-blockchain-project/.

17. "ESMA Assesses Usefulness of Distributed Ledger Technologies," *ESMA*, June 2, 2016, https://www.esma.europa.eu/press-news/esma-news/esma-assesses-usefulness-distributed-ledger-technologies.

18. Pete Rizzo, "U.S. Congress Reps Receive Blockchain Briefing at Capitol Hill Event," *CoinDesk*, May 27, 2016, http://www.coindesk.com/capitol-hill-blockchain-briefing/.

19. Michael del Castillo, "Regulators: Federal Preemption of State Blockchain Laws Unlikely," *CoinDesk*, April 13, 2016, http://www.coindesk.com/federal-state-blockchain-laws/.

20. Victor Luckerson, "Top 10 Exciting Startups," *Time*, December 4, 2013, http://business.time.com/2013/12/04/business/slide/top-10-exciting-startups/.

21. Paul Vigna and Michael J. Casey, "Coinbase Raises $75 Million in Funding Round," *Wall Street Journal*, January 20, 2015, http://www.wsj.com/articles/coinbase-raises-75-million-in-funding-round-1421762403.

22. Pete Rizzo, "Megabank Joins Coinbase's Record $75 Million Funding Round," *CoinDesk*, January 20, 2015, http://www.coindesk.com/coinbases-75-million-series-c/.

23. *Sources:* Techcrunch.com; Coinbase; numerous articles, including:
    John Biggs, "Up Close with Coinbase Exchange," *Techcrunch*, January 28, 2015, https://techcrunch.com/2015/01/28/up-close-with-coinbase-exchange/.
    "Coinbase Raises $75 Million Funding Round," http://www.wsj.com/articles/coinbase-raises-75-million-in-funding-round-1421762403.
    "Coinbase Confirms $75M Raise from DFJ, NYSE, Strategic Banking Partners," http://techcrunch.com/2015/01/20/coinbase-confirms-75m-raise-from-dfj-nyse-strategic-banking-partners/.

24. Garrick Hileman, "State of Blockchain Q1 2016: Blockchain Funding Overtakes Bitcoin," *CoinDesk*, May 11, 2016, http://www.coindesk.com/state-of-blockchain-q1-2016/.

CHAPTER 7

The Wealth Management Niche

INTRODUCTION

Wealth management services have traditionally been offered by a variety of financial institutions, including banks, RIAs (registered investment advisors), and insurers. Historically, wealth managers have focused primarily on clients with a high net worth and ample capital available to invest. The services provided by a wealth manager can vary from assisting with analyzing and advising on potential investments and portfolio allocations to strategic advisory services such as advice on tax-efficient wealth transfer strategies and retirement planning.

Banking and wealth management have intersected with a number of banks offering trust and wealth management services to customers through their trust and wealth management divisions. In the twelve months ended June 30, 2016, community banks (banks with assets between $100 million and $5 billion) collectively had $1.5 billion in fiduciary-related revenues compared to $8.3 billion in fiduciary income for the Big Banks (banks with assets greater than $5 billion).

Despite the wealth management offering of a number of community banks, this is an area where community banks have historically underperformed the Big Banks.[1] Income from fiduciary activities comprised approximately 14 percent of non-interest income for the Big Banks compared to only 8 percent of non-interest income for community banks. Approximately 75 percent of the community banks reported no fiduciary-related income compared to ~35 percent of the Big Banks. Additionally, the majority of community bank trust departments are below $500 million in assets under management, which presents a significant challenge to remain consistently profitable.

Of those banks that did report wealth management revenues, the average assets under management was smaller for community banks compared to the Big Banks and fiduciary income approximated comprised a lower percentage of fiduciary assets under management, implying lower fee schedules. The overall contribution to profitability from wealth management services was lower among the community banks compared to the Big Banks, reflecting the lower AUM and fees as a proportion of assets (i.e., lower fee schedule).

Given the importance of wealth management services to traditional banks and the underperformance of community banks in this area historically, it is important for bankers to track emerging trends within wealth management and ascertain whether opportunities exist to improve performance and enhance profitability and value. Several trends have emerged in wealth management recently. As the wealth management industry continues to evolve, technology is increasingly intersecting with traditional advisory services and the traditional role of the advisor is beginning to shift. Managers have increasingly focused on a greater proportion of the population and shifted their focus from the high net worth to the mass affluent. Regulations for both non-bank advisors and banks offering wealth management services have increased and impacted the industry, including the significant changes to wealth management in the United States following the implementation of the Department of Labor's (DOL) Fiduciary Rule (financial advisory firms have until January 2018 to become compliant). Greater transparency has also allowed customers to compare product offerings more easily. Lastly, there has been a general trend toward investors preferring passive strategies for a variety of reasons ranging from lower cost to economic uncertainty.

FinTech innovation within wealth management has also developed consistent with these trends. FinTech innovations are helping improve access to wealth management tools for a broader population segment, increase transparency, lower regulatory and compliance costs, and deliver robo-advisory services with investment strategies that are more passive. These changes present community banks with a potential opportunity to reinvigorate their wealth management offerings or to expand their service offerings to include wealth management. For those currently offering wealth management services but seeing limited profitability from their offerings, FinTech and the development of robo-advisory could help provide a way to enhance the profitability and growth prospects of their existing team. For those not offering wealth management services, the evolution of wealth management could offer opportunities to selectively begin offering this service and certain FinTech offerings may be attractive. Similar to other traditional incumbents exploring FinTech opportunities, banks are presented with strategic options ranging from building their own robo-advisory to buying a robo-advisory, partnering with an existing robo-advisory, or not offering wealth management services. We suspect that partnerships will be the preferred route for those that choose to offer wealth management services although one might expect to eventually see acquisitions and internal builds among larger banks that have the scale to justify the higher costs of those strategies.

Despite the potential for FinTech innovation within wealth management, significant uncertainty still exists regarding whether these innovations will displace traditional wealth management business models. An example of industry evolution due to technological innovation is the online brokerage industry. It provides an excellent case study for the interaction among wealth management, technology, regulation, and customer adoption of new technology products.

THE EVOLUTION OF THE ONLINE BROKERAGE INDUSTRY

The discount broker traces its roots to 1975 when the Securities Act Amendments of 1975 abolished fixed-rate brokerage commissions on May 1 (May Day). At the time of implementation, many industry participants and other pundits predicted commission revenue would shrivel for the industry as commission rates declined. Initial pricing at Charles Schwab & Co. (Schwab) was $70 or about half what a full-service broker would then charge to execute a trade for several hundred shares prior to May Day.

The opposite happened, though. As commission rates declined, more investors were empowered (or intrigued) to trade themselves without the support of a full-service broker such as those then found at Merrill Lynch, Bache Securities, and the like. Trading volume grew significantly following the abolishment of fixed-rate brokerage and offset steady declines in the costs of commissions per trade. For consumers, the evolution of discount brokerage served to expand access to trading markets and empowered them to trade more independently. For example, the average daily share volume in April 2016 on the NYSE was 1.2 billion shares compared to 20.3 million shares in April 1975, representing an 11 percent compound annual growth rate in daily average share volume over that 41-year period. Today, online brokers advertise equity trades in the $7 to $10 range.

This evolution of discount brokerage is a unique example in the history of FinTech that provides guideposts regarding how future FinTech niches and companies may evolve. The change in regulation in May 1975 ushered in new players to provide discount brokerage services and also fostered changes in the incumbents as they ultimately began to offer similar services. This combination of newer, early-stage companies and older, traditional incumbents and technology development ultimately led to increased innovation in the sector.

By the early 2000s, key larger established industry participants included firms that were founded in the 1970s and early 1980s, including Schwab (founded in 1971), TD Ameritrade Holding Corporation (TD Ameritrade, founded in 1971), E*TRADE Financial Corporation (E*TRADE, founded in 1982), and Interactive Brokers Group Inc. (Interactive, founded in 1978). Additionally, hundreds of other financial services companies with significantly longer corporate histories adapted to some extent and currently offer online brokerage services. For example, Fidelity Investments (Fidelity, founded in 1946) offers online equity trades for $7.95 and Merrill Lynch (founded in 1914) via Merrill Edge is presently offering $6.95 online equity and ETF trades or 30 commission-free online equity or ETF trades subject to certain limitations.

As the discount brokerage industry has continued to evolve, companies in it have diversified beyond low-cost equity trade execution services by expanding into banking, investment advisory, and trade execution for ETFs, options, futures, and other products. Services offered from discount brokerages immediately following May Day were initially limited to price quotes and trade execution. The initial revenue model entailed commission income and net interest income earned on customers' net credit cash positions. Diversification efforts first entailed offering more bank-like products, which eventually led to bank acquisitions and formations by some firms. For example, E*TRADE acquired Telebanc Financial Corporation in 2000 to create the first pure-play Internet company that combined brokerage and banking within one company. Schwab also subsequently chartered Schwab Bank in 2003 to provide customers with FDIC-insured deposits, loans, and other banking products. TD Ameritrade does not own a bank; rather, the company has a formal agreement that establishes credit rates for customer funds that are swept to Toronto Dominion Bank—thereby obtaining most of the same benefits without having to hold the amount of capital that a wholly owned bank would require.

More recent diversification efforts by the industry have included the introduction of managed accounts, access to sell-side research, enhanced trading platforms for active traders, and a growing partnership with independent *registered investment advisors*. Many RIAs have fled traditional brokerage operations to start their own firm or partner with an existing firm whereby services are provided for a fee. Independent RIA assets approximate $2.2 trillion and a number of online brokers actively seek to attract RIAs to their platform. As of September 2015, the Advisor Services group at Schwab accounted for $1.2 trillion of $2.4 trillion of client assets.

Expansion notwithstanding, the online brokerage industry is mature, which has resulted in periodic bouts of M&A as industry leaders have acquired to expand product offerings and increase the number of customers. M&A activity during the 1990s and early 2000s was largely geared to acquiring accounts and gaining economies of scale. The legacy predecessor company to TD Ameritrade was particularly active in acquiring online and discount brokers before combining with TD Waterhouse USA. Although Schwab did not pioneer online brokerage, Schwab built its online operation from its sizable discount brokerage operation. Fidelity did so by leveraging its mutual fund business.

While industry participants have diversified revenues over the past decade, the key revenue drivers for online brokers are customer accounts, customer assets, daily average revenue trades (DARTs), and the spread on client deposits and free credit balances. Also, the trading mix (e.g., the number of options) also influences revenues. Several of these revenue drivers are influenced by the condition of capital markets and trading activity. The performance of the U.S. economy in terms of the level and trend in corporate profits, employment, and U.S. monetary policy, which impacts investors' view of equities and other financial assets, are all important factors influencing trading activity and market conditions. Monetary policy also impacts the spread between the yield banks and other financial intermediaries earn on interest-earning assets and the cost of funds for deposits and borrowings used to finance the assets.

In the last few years, the Federal Reserve's zero-interest-rate policy (ZIRP), in which short-term rates are maintained near zero, has negatively impacted spread revenues for discount brokers and other financial institutions. In its 2015 annual report, Schwab management noted that the then-seven years of ZIRP had caused Schwab to waive $4.0 billion of money market management fees during 2009–2014 so that clients would not receive negative yields to cover the cost of offering the funds.[2] Schwab also noted that client assets had grown 120 percent since the onset of ZIRP while revenues had only grown 24 percent largely due to the rate environment as its spread was 1.60 percent in 2015 compared to 3.84 percent in 2008.[3] During this period, client assets more than doubled to $2.5 trillion from $1.1 trillion, yet it took until the end of 2013 for revenues to return to the 2008 level.[4]

The other key activity driver is market volatility, which has been lacking in recent years. According to *Bloomberg*, U.S. equity trading volume averaged approximately 7 billion shares per day in 2015, up slightly from 2013 and 2014 levels, yet well below the approximately 10 billion shares per day posted in 2009.[5]

THE RISE OF ROBO-ADVISORS

Robo-advisory has the potential to significantly impact traditional wealth management. It represents a FinTech niche that is similar to the transition from full-service traditional brokers to discount online brokers.

Robo-advisors were noted by the CFA Institute as the FinTech innovation most likely to have the greatest impact on the financial services industry in the short term (one year) and medium term (five years).[6] Robo-advisory has gained traction in the past several years as a niche within the FinTech industry offering online wealth management tools powered by sophisticated algorithms that can help investors manage their portfolios at low costs and with minimal need for human contact or advice. Technological advances making this business model possible, coupled with a loss of consumer trust in the wealth management industry in the wake of the financial crisis, have created a favorable environment for the growth of robo-advisory startups meant to disrupt financial advisories, RIAs, and wealth managers. This growth is forcing traditional incumbents to explore their treatment of the robo-advisory model in an effort to determine their response to the disruption of the industry.

While there are a number of reasons for the success of robo-advisors attracting and retaining clients thus far, we highlight a few primary reasons.

- **Low Cost.** Automated, algorithm-driven decision making greatly lowers the cost of financial advice and portfolio management.
- **Accessible.** As a result of the lowered cost of financial advice, advanced investment strategies are more accessible to a wider customer base.
- **Personalized Strategies.** Sophisticated algorithms and computer systems create personalized investment strategies that are highly tailored to the specific needs of individual investors.
- **Transparent.** Through online platforms and mobile apps, clients are able to view information about their portfolios and enjoy visibility in regard to the way their money is being managed.
- **Convenient.** Portfolio information and management becomes available on-demand through online platforms and mobile apps.

Consistent with the rise in consumer demand for robo-advisory, investor interest has grown steadily. While robo-advisory has not drawn the levels of investment seen in other niches (such as online lending platforms), venture capital funding of robo-advisories has skyrocketed from almost nonexistent levels 10 years ago to hundreds of millions of dollars invested annually the past few years. The year 2016 saw several notable rounds of investment not only into some of the industry's largest and most mature players (including rounds of $100 million for Betterment and $75 million for Personal Capital), but also for innovative startups just getting off the ground (such as SigFig and Vestmark).

Table 7.1 provides an overview of the fee schedules, assets under management, and account opening minimums for several of the larger robo-advisors. The robo-advisors are separated into three tiers. Tier I consists

TABLE 7.1 Comparison of Key Metrics of Selected Robo-Advisory Services

Tier I	AUM ($B)	Fee Structure	Account Minimum
Betterment	$4	0.35% annual fee on <$10k, 0.25% on $10k to $100k, 0.15% on $100k+	$0
WealthFront	$3	0.25% on all accounts	$500
Personal Capital	$2	0.89% annually on <$1MM, 0.79% on $3MM, 0.69% on $5MM, 0.59% on <$10MM, 0.49% on >$10MM	$25,000

Tier II	AUM ($B)	Fee Structure	Account Minimum
FutureAdvisor	$1	0.5% annual fee of assets managed	$0
SigFig	$0	No fee on first $10k, 0.25% annual fee on accounts over $10k	$2,000

Tier III	AUM ($B)	Fee Structure	Account Minimum
Vanguard Personal Advisor	$31	0.30% annually	$50,000
Schwab Intelligent Portfolio	$5	No fees for account management and service	$5,000

Source: Mercer Capital Research, company websites, as of June 2016

of early robo-advisory firms that have positioned themselves at the top of the industry. Tier II consists of more recent robo-advisory startups that are experiencing rapid growth and are ripe for partnership. Tier III consists of robo-advisory services of traditional players that have decided to build and run their own technology in-house. As shown in Table 7.1, account opening sizes and fee schedules are lower than many traditional wealth management firms. The strategic challenge for a number of the FinTech startups in Tiers I and II is generating enough AUM and scale to produce revenue sufficient to maintain the significantly lower fee schedules. This can be challenging since the cost to acquire a new customer can be significant and each of these startups has required significant venture capital funding to develop. For example, each of these companies has raised over $100 million of venture capital funding since inception.

Key Potential Effects of Robo-Advisory

We see four potential effects of robo-advisors entering the financial services landscape.

1. **The Democratization of Wealth Management.** As a result of the low costs of robo-advisory services, new investors have been able to gain access to sophisticated investment strategies that in the past have only been available to high-net-worth, accredited investors.
2. **Holistic Financial Life Management.** As more people have access to financial advice through robo-advisors, traditional financial advisors are being forced to move away from return-driven goals for clients and pivot toward offering a more complete picture of a client's financial wellbeing as clients save for milestones such as retirement, a child's education, and a new house. This phenomenon has increased the differentiation pressure on traditional financial advisors and RIAs, as robo-advisors can offer a holistic snapshot in a manner that is comprehensive and easy to understand
3. **Drivers of the Changing Role of the Traditional Financial Advisor.** The potential shift away from return-driven goals could leave the role of the traditional financial advisor in limbo. This raises the question of what traditional wealth managers will look like going forward. One potential answer is traditional financial advisors will tackle more complex issues, such as tax and estate planning, and leave the more programmed decision making to robo-advisors.
4. **Build, Buy, Partner, or Wait and See.** We discuss each strategic option in more depth in the following section.

Build, Buy, Partner, or Wait and See

Perhaps even more so than other FinTech industry niches, robo-advisory is well positioned for mergers, acquisitions, and partnerships. As mentioned earlier, traditional incumbents are being forced to determine what they want their future relationship with robo-advisors to look like as the role of the financial advisor changes. This quandary leaves incumbents with four options: attempt to build their own robo-advisory platform in-house, buy out a startup and incorporate its technology into their investment strategies, create a business-to-business partnership with a startup, or sit out the robo-advisory wave and continue to operate as usual.

Of these options, we are seeing a rise in incumbents acquiring robo-advisory expertise. Large firms that have followed this strategy include Invesco's acquisition of Jemstep, Goldman Sachs' acquisition of Honest

Dollar, BlackRock's acquisition of Future Advisor, and Ally's acquisition of TradeKing.

Other incumbents have elected to be more direct and build their own robo-advisory services in-house. Schwab's Intelligent Portfolio service launched in March 2015 and was on the leading edge of traditional players building and offering their own robo-advisory services. Two months later, Vanguard launched its internally built robo-advisor, named Personal Advisor, which has already become quite large and manages $31 billion in assets. Furthermore, Morgan Stanley, TD Ameritrade, and Fidelity have all announced plans to release their own homegrown robo-advisories in the future.

The partnership strategy has also popped up among traditional incumbents. Partnerships allow traditional incumbents to gain access to a broader array of products to offer their customers without acquiring a robo-advisor. In May 2016, UBS's Wealth Management Americas group announced a major partnership with startup SigFig in which SigFig will design and customize digital tools for UBS advisors to offer their clients.[7] In exchange, UBS made an equity investment in SigFig, showing the confidence UBS has in SigFig's ability to create an innovative platform. Also, FutureAdvisor, operating under the auspices of BlackRock, announced partnerships with RBC, BBVA Compass, and LPL in 2016 to offer these institutions' clients more affordable and automated investment advice, as the institutions continue to explore the idea of building their own robo-advisory service. Personal Capital, a robo-advisor started in 2009, announced a partnership with AlliancePartners to offer its digital wealth management platform to approximately 200 community banks. As seen in the actions of these incumbents, partnering with a startup is becoming an increasingly attractive option, as it allows the incumbent to give robo-advisory a test drive without wholly committing to the idea yet.

Lastly, we have also seen traditional incumbents elect to ignore the robo-advisory trend altogether. Raymond James indicated that they would not be offering or launching a robo-advisory platform to compete with its advisors. Raymond James noted that their core business is serving financial advisors and a robo-advisory solution that offers wealth management solutions directly to consumers does not fit their business model. They did indicate that they are looking to expand technology and other services to help their investment advisors but noted that robo-advisory is not a solution that they plan to launch presently.[8]

Thus, there are a number of strategic options with varying degrees of commitment by which traditional incumbents can either enter the robo-advisory field or elect to stay on the sideline near-term. The question of whether to build, buy, partner, or wait and see will become increasingly asked and may extend from large incumbents to smaller RIAs, banks, and wealth managers as robo-advisories continue to pop up across the financial landscape and consumers increasingly desire these products.

For those financial institutions considering strategic options as it relates to robo-advisory, we take a closer look at two of the announced robo-advisory transactions—BlackRock/Future Advisor and Ally/TradeKing—in greater detail.

BlackRock's Acquisition of Future Advisor[9]

BlackRock's acquisition of robo-advisory startup FutureAdvisor for an undisclosed amount in August 2015 is perhaps the most notable example of a robo-advisor acquisition strategy. The acquisition showed the increased staying power of robo-advisors, as BlackRock is the world's largest asset manager. FutureAdvisor provides investors with a low-cost index investing service that diversifies their portfolio in a personalized and holistic manner based on the individual investor's age, needs, and risk tolerance.[10] A series of algorithms automatically rebalance investors' accounts, constantly look for tax savings, and manage multiple accounts for investors. Assets are held by Fidelity or TD Ameritrade in the investor's name, to assuage investors' fears concerning safety and accessibility of funds.

FutureAdvisor was founded by Jon Xu and Bo Lu, former Microsoft employees, in early 2010. Significant funding rounds included a first round of seed funding ($1 million in early 2010), another seed funding round and a $5 million Series A issue in 2012, and a Series B issue of $15.5 million in 2014. As previously noted, following BlackRock's acquisition announcement in August 2015, FutureAdvisor announced several significant partnerships (BBVA Compass, RBC, and LPL) to offer low-cost investment advice to each entity's clients.

Bo-Lu, a co-founder of Future Advisor, referred to the acquisition as a "watershed moment, not just as an entity but for the broader financial services industry as a whole." To better understand the mindset of BlackRock, consider two quotes from members of BlackRock.

> *Over the next several years, no matter what you think about digital advice, you would be pressed to argue that it won't be more popular versus less popular five to ten years from now.*
> **—Rob Goldstein, head of BlackRock's Tech Division**[11]

> *More Americans are responsible for investing for the important life goals, whether that is retirement, education, etc. We think that a broad cross section of that market may be slightly under-served. We believe that is the mass-affluent or those who don't want to seek out a traditional advice model.*
> **—Frank Porcelli, head of BlackRock's U.S. Wealth Advisory business**[12]

The acquisition confirmed the increased staying power of automated investment advice. BlackRock is the world's largest asset manager and the acquisition of FutureAdvisor signaled BlackRock's intent to stay ahead of the robo-advisory curve. In addition, FutureAdvisor's partnership with LPL, BBVA Compass, and RBC prompted other banks to follow suit, including UBS's partnership with FinTech startup SigFig and Morgan Stanley's effort to build its own robo-advisor.

After the acquisition, FutureAdvisor was able to evolve into a "startup within a huge company," according to founder Jon Xu. The company still held onto the creative culture and environment of a tech startup, but now has the resources and tools of asset management giant BlackRock at its disposal.

The acquisition also reinforced the trend toward a model based on convenience for the consumer rooted in the automated processes. The evolution of financial advising and wealth management will hinge on whether the knowledge and personal attention of a human can add enough value to outweigh the benefits of convenience fostered by automation.

Ally's Acquisition of TradeKing[13]

In April 2016, Ally Financial Inc., a bank holding company that provides a variety of financial services, including auto financing, corporate financing, and insurance, announced an acquisition of TradeKing for a total purchase price of $275 million. TradeKing is a discount online brokerage firm that provides trading tools to self-directed investors. TradeKing initially offered some of the lowest cost stock trade commissions (at ~$5 share on equity trades) and was also one of the earlier online brokers to integrate social networking and an online community where customers could discuss trading analysis and strategies. Interestingly, Ally noted that it was not interested in offering traditional advisor-led investment services but was interested in digital offerings such as robo-advisors, and robo-advisory was cited as a primary consideration for Ally's interest in TradeKing. In 2014, TradeKing formed TradeKing Advisors, which offers robo-advisory services for a minimum investment of $500.

The acquisition reflected creative thinking in the banking industry as bank M&A is typically primarily about cost savings and secondarily about expansion into new markets. Revenue synergies are touted periodically in bank acquisitions but they tend to be secondary considerations for investors and bank managers/directors. The TradeKing acquisition represents a shift in this mindset as the potential benefits from the transaction will largely be in the form of revenue synergies as Ally leverages TradeKing's brokerage platform and attempts to achieve greater revenues by offering trading and wealth management services to its existing customer base. Convenience for Ally's customers was clearly top of mind as evidenced by the following quotes from the CEO of both TradeKing and Ally around the time of announcement:

> *Banking and brokerage should be together so you can save and invest—and easily move money between the two.*
> —**Don Montonaro, CEO TradeKing**[14]

> *We have a good composition of customers across all demographic segments, from affluent boomers to millennials . . . . Our customers have been happy with our deposit products, but are asking for more from the online bank.*
> —**Diane Morais, Ally Bank, CEO**[15]

The Regulatory Environment for Robo-Advisory in the United States

The regulatory environment for robo-advisors is on the minds of banks and other traditional incumbents seeking to expand into the robo-advisory niche. Robo-advisors have not been subjected to a great deal of regulatory scrutiny from government agencies and other bodies, despite the rapid growth of robo-advisory services. However, the regulatory environment surrounding robo-advisors is starting to take shape, as agencies begin to recognize the potential for disruption that robo-advisory firms hold. This shift in the regulatory landscape represents a major risk in regard to the widespread proliferation of robo-advisors and has been gradually gaining steam. The first signs of movement toward regulation occurred in May 2015, with a joint release by the SEC and FINRA warning investors of the potential pitfalls and limitations of robo-advisors.[16] In this release, regulators conceded that while robo-advisories have some very obvious benefits, investors should be wary of ambiguous fee structures, programmed assumptions made by the algorithms, misleading investor questionnaires, misaligned investment strategies, and potential for the loss of personal information. The alert not only informed consumers of the potential dangers of robo-advisories, but also gave robo-advisory firms an idea of what concrete regulation may look like in the future and how they should be preparing for impending regulation.

Perhaps the most pressing question in regard to the regulation of robo-advisors is whether automated investment advice platforms have the capacity to act in a fiduciary manner. In short, a fiduciary, as it pertains to wealth management and financial advisory, is a trustee who acts in the best interest of his clients, free of conflicts of interest, and without taking unfair advantage of his client's trust. Can a computer replicate this standard of trust? This is the key question that regulators are trying to resolve in the wake of the Department of Labor's requirement (the DOL's Fiduciary Rule) that all advice in regard to retirement investment must be held to this fiduciary standard.

In March 2016, FINRA released another report outlining its findings on the potential shortcomings of robo-advisors for investors and, although not explicitly stated, the body implies that robo-advisors may not be able to uphold a fiduciary standard: "Investors should be aware that conflicts of interest can exist even with digital investment advice, and that the advice they receive depends on the investment approach and underlying assumptions used in the digital tool."[17] The Massachusetts State Securities Division echoed this sentiment in an April 2016 release, harshly stating that robo-advisories fail to conduct proper due diligence on their clients and "specifically decline to act in their clients' best interests."[18] Robo-advisors seeking to register their firms in Massachusetts will from now on be held to this fiduciary standard and be examined on a case-by-case basis.

Thus, while legislation and regulation specifically targeting robo-advisors is not yet widespread, conversations are beginning to take place about whether robo-advisors can act in a fiduciary manner and whether automated investment advice has the necessary human element to qualify its standard of advice as being fiduciary.

CONCLUSION

The proliferation of robo-advisory services across the financial landscape carries many potential outcomes for the wealth management industry and traditional players in the space like banks. Up to this point, the initial success in attracting assets by robo-advisors indicates that there exists a broad base of customers that demand holistic financial management and online investment and portfolio management platforms with the ability for programmed decision making. While we cannot predict the future, one possibility sees large incumbents continuing to snatch up and leverage the capabilities of robo-advisor startups, leaving only the largest and most established online robo-advisory platforms able to continue to operate on their own. Smaller wealth management firms and RIAs may look to partner with robo-advisor platforms as well or return to focusing exclusively on high-net-worth clients and offering more personalized services.

Beyond robo-advisory, FinTech innovation within wealth management may also broaden access to wealth management tools, increase transparency, and lower regulatory and compliance costs. These changes present community banks with the chance to enhance their wealth management and trust divisions or to develop one that leverages FinTech innovations.

Similar to other traditional incumbents exploring FinTech opportunities, banks are presented with strategic options ranging from building their own robo-advisory, buying a robo-advisory, partnering with an existing robo-advisory, or not offering wealth management services. While we suspect that partnerships will be the more preferred route, one might expect to eventually see acquisitions and internal builds among larger banks that have enough scale to justify the higher costs of those strategies.

For large incumbents, the trend of acquiring robo-advisory startups and adopting the technology behind robo-advisory through other means is already well underway. As previously mentioned, some of the industry's largest players such as Goldman Sachs and BlackRock have acquired smaller robo-advisory startups and are integrating these startups' capabilities into their online platforms. Partnerships and in-house builds are also occurring across the financial landscape as financial institutions begin to recognize not only this evolving consumer preference, but also the efficiency that programmed portfolio management decision making can bring. As incumbents continue to integrate robo-advisory capabilities into their wealth management and financial advisory divisions through acquisitions, partnerships, and in-house buildouts, they will continue to gain scale and increase their already massive presence within the financial ecosystem.

In the frenzied wake of traditional institutions' acquiring or partnering with robo-advisory startups, startups operating on their own will likely begin to fade as they join with more established players in efforts to gain better access to funding or a larger platform to promote their products. As the technology behind robo-advisors becomes more accessible, the importance of scale will likely increase, leaving many smaller startups with no choice but to sell to or be acquired by a larger player. This mass consolidation of the market could then leave only the most established and largest robo-advisors, such as Wealthfront, Betterment, and Personal Capital, able to stand alone and continue to operate independently.

Finally, as large institutions can more readily offer low-cost, automated investment advice and portfolio management services, smaller wealth management firms and divisions of banks and RIAs may be forced to move into more specialized areas, such as intergenerational wealth transfer and tax planning. Smaller firms will also have to focus on retaining high-net-worth clients that represent the largest section of their customer base, as greatly lowered costs may lure clients toward working exclusively with large institutions offering robo-advisory services. Unless small wealth management firms and RIAs can respond to changes in customer preference by adopting some aspects of robo-advisory services, there is the potential for their business model and role within the financial landscape to be greatly disrupted. While it still remains to be seen whether high-net-worth clients will begin to move away from traditional, people-centric firms, the proliferation of robo-advisors has certainly created the potential for it. Large institutions can now leverage robo-advisory services to offer a complete snapshot of a client's financial status in a clear and transparent manner through online platforms driven by algorithm-based, programmed decision making.

While all of these outcomes are certainly possible, there are still a number of factors that could inhibit the continued proliferation of robo-advisors, including government regulation and a renewed investor realization of the value of investment advice and portfolio management that includes a human element. Although the days of completely relying on robo-advisory for all of our financial advisory and wealth management needs are still a long way off (if they ever come at all), robo-advisors have made inroads into the financial landscape and have shown just how innovative and disruptive the technology can be. However, it may only serve as a complementary piece to the financial landscape rather than one that overhauls the entire system.

NOTES

1. Data in this paragraph based upon Mercer Capital research of data obtained from S&P Global Intelligence.
2. Schwab 2015 Annual Report, https://aboutschwab.com/images/uploads/inline/Schwab_AR2015.pdf.
3. Ibid.
4. Ibid.
5. Michael P. Regan, "Trading Is a Volume Business Again," *Bloomberg*, December 29, 2015, https://www.bloomberg.com/gadfly/articles/2015-12-29/e-trade-and-schwab-benefit-as-stock-trading-volume-rises.
6. "CFA Institute Survey Indicates Substantial Impact of Robo-Advisers on Investment Management," *CFA Institute*, May 6, 2016, https://www.cfainstitute.org/about/press/release/Pages/05062016_129708.aspx.
7. "UBS and SigFig to Form Strategic Alliance for Wealth Management Technology Development," *Business Wire*, May 16, 2016, http://www.businesswire.com/news/home/20160516005979/en/UBS-SigFig-Form-Strategic-Alliance-Wealth-Management.
8. Jeff Benjamin, "Raymond James Won't Launch Robo-Adviser to Compete with Independents," *Investment News*, October 20, 2015, http://www.investmentnews.com/article/20151020/FREE/151029999/raymond-james-wont-launch-robo-adviser-to-compete-with-independents.
9. *Sources:* Financialadvising.com, "Jon Xu Interview."Forbes.com, "BlackRock to Buy FutureAdvisor, Signaling Robo-Advice Is Here to Stay," Financialplanning.com, "FutureAdvisor Co-founder: Risk, Robos and Hyperpersonalization."
10. *Source:* Crunchbase; Forbes.com, "BlackRock to Buy FutureAdvisor, Signaling Robo-Advice Is Here to Stay," *Forbes*, August 26, 2015.

11. Samantha Sharf, "BlackRock to Buy FutureAdvisor, Signaling Robo-Advice Is Here to Stay," *Forbes*, August 26, 2015, http://www.forbes.com/sites/samanthasharf/2015/08/26/blackrock-to-buy-futureadvisor-signaling-robo-advice-is-here-to-stay/#ef9253322947.
12. Ibid.
13. *Sources for Case Study:* Techcrunch; S&P Global Market Intelligence; various articles, including: Theresa W. Carey, "Ally, Fidelity to Launch Robo-Advisory Services," Digital Investor; TradeKing website; and Bloomberg Business.
14. Theresa W. Carey, "Ally, Fidelity to Launch Robo-Advisory Services," *Barron's*, April 23, 2016, http://www.barrons.com/articles/ally-fidelity-to-launch-robo-advisory-services-1461385575.
15. Ibid.
16. Melanie Waddell, "SEC, FINRA Issue Robo-Advisor Warning," *ThinkAdvisor*, May 15, 2016, http://www.thinkadvisor.com/2015/05/11/sec-finra-issue-robo-advisor-warning?slreturn=1477518245.
17. Melanie Waddell, "FINRA Warns BDs to Follow Robo-Advice Rules," *ThinkAdvisor*, March 17, 2016, http://www.thinkadvisor.com/2016/03/17/finra-warns-bds-to-follow-robo-advice-rules.
18. Melanie Waddell, "Massachusetts to Scrutinize Robo-Advisors on Fiduciary Duties," *ThinkAdvisor*, April 1, 2016, http://www.thinkadvisor.com/2016/04/01/massachusetts-to-scrutinize-robo-advisors-on-fiduc.

CHAPTER 8

InsurTech and the Future of Insurance[1]

The stalwart foundations on which the insurance industry has established itself are, for the first time, under siege. Disruptive forces are challenging historical conventions in ways that would rid the industry of its value proposition, among them shifts in customer expectations, transformations in the macro-economy and culture, and the emergence of new types of risk altogether. These trends and the introduction of innovative "InsurTech" technologies have accelerated the pace of change and appear likely to continue to do so. As the dust begins to settle, obvious gaps in the value chain have materialized where new InsurTech competitors from both inside and outside the industry are looking to capitalize.

While InsurTech presents new sources of potential competition, the insurance industry has historically been highly competitive and legacy providers have largely endured trends, cycles, and changes in the industry. The insurance industry today is relatively fragmented as it can be broken into the following key players: insurance carriers that price and under-write risk and manage investments, insurance agencies and brokerages that are intermediaries and earn commission/fee-based income, and the insureds who pay premiums and insure against risk. Of the $1.5 trillion in premiums written in the United States in 2014, they were roughly split between property and casualty insurance (auto, home, commercial lines, workers compensation, marine, and financial/mortgage) and life and health insurance (annuities, life, accident/health, and other insurance).[2] Similar to banking, the insurance industry is impacted by cycles. The underwriting cycle results in premiums rising and falling as supply and demand ebb and flow over the cycle. Factors impacting insurance pricing and their level of volatility during the cycle include different lines of business as well as account sizes.

Banks have also been an enduring legacy player in the insurance space, often setting up or partnering with a broker or brokerage and offering insurance products to customers.[3] In the twelve months ended June 30, 2016, community banks collectively had approximately $615 million in insurance-related revenues (includes F&C annuities and sales, insurance and reinsurance underwriting, and insurance commissions and fees) and these insurance revenues comprised only 3.4 percent of non-interest income. Approximately 50 percent of the community banks reported insurance revenues, which was higher than some other non-interest income services offered, like wealth management, where only 25 percent of banks reported wealth management revenues. However, the contributions to earnings were significantly smaller with the average bank that reported insurance revenues reporting approximately $300,000 of revenues (compared to over $1 million contribution to revenue on average for those banks offering wealth management). Similar to wealth management, though, community banks underperformed the Big Banks in insurance revenues and offerings. Approximately 75 percent of the Big Banks reported insurance revenues and the average contribution to revenue for those Big Banks that reported insurance revenue was significantly higher than the community banks.

As a key player, banks are also taking notice of the looming changes and trends in the sector that might impact their insurance business lines. Thus far, a number of the legacy insurance industry players, including banks, have lacked the sense of urgency required to attack InsurTech trends in a way that will not only mitigate their harmful consequences, but position them to be beneficial—in other words, turn disruptors into enablers. This has likely occurred because many legacy players have held steadfast to a set of assumptions that formed barriers to entry in the past and thus shielded them from disruption. However, in the context of fresh sources of capital, novel risk-transfer options, heightened connectivity of devices, and unforeseen challenges rising from the growing sharing economy, it is clear that disruptive forces are at work. As the legacy models of underwriting and distribution become increasingly vulnerable, insurance industry players cannot continue to observe; they must adapt.

INTRODUCTION TO INSURTECH

After spending many years ignored, the insurance subset of FinTech, InsurTech, is finally firmly in the spotlight. Many technology firms and investors are anxious to gain traction in the market as a slew of startups have arisen and continue to garner heavy financial support. Investment in the insurance technology sector in 2015 reached $2.65 billion, per CB Insights, a trifold increase over 2014. It is obvious why insurance is so appealing from a growth perspective; the global insurance industry reaps premium revenues of $5 trillion annually and records assets under management of nearly $15 trillion.[4]

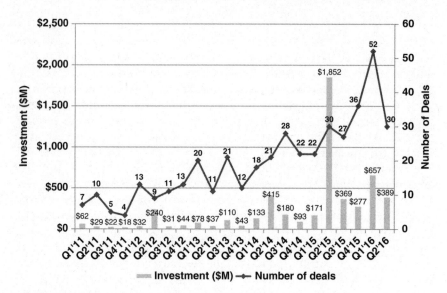

FIGURE 8.1   InsurTech Financing Trend
Source: CB Insights

An industry of such immense market size that has changed very little over the course of history presents a prime opportunity for nimble and inventive new players (both new technology companies as well as banks looking to grow non-interest income from InsurTech offerings). But seemingly, legacy players have been slow to jump on the InsurTech bandwagon. (See Figure 8.1.)

Technology spending in the global insurance industry is currently estimated to be approximately $189 billion and this figure is expected to jump to $205 billion by 2019.[5] But what is important is that this does not represent an increase in technology spending as a percentage of premiums.

Currently, only 3.8 percent of insurance companies' direct premiums written are directed to information technology spending and, according to a report from letstalkpayments.com, this fraction has in fact declined over the last four years.[6] Instead, the spending of incumbent insurance industry players has concentrated around advances in efficiency and productivity. These are incremental improvements, rather than disruptive changes, like revolutions in the customer experience or ventures into alternative business models. To enact these types of changes, existing players will need to position themselves to benefit from the same innovation that could potentially be disruptive, either by partnering with or acquiring InsurTech organizations or developing identical capabilities internally.

Regardless of what role extant insurance industry players take in it, the surge in financing and M&A activity in the InsurTech space will continue into the foreseeable future. Technology and innovation have propelled forward countless other industries in recent years, from banking to healthcare, and now it is insurance's turn.

TECHNOLOGY TRENDS IN INSURANCE

Established Customer Relationships with Traditional Insurance Providers Are Being Challenged by Disruptors

One assumption of incumbent insurance industry players being challenged by InsurTech innovation is the belief that established customer connections to carriers will withstand pressure from attempts at wide-scale interruption. However, the historically strained relationship between carriers and their detached customers is a point along the insurance value chain that is particularly vulnerable to disruption in our view, thanks to shifting consumer expectations and the arrival of blockchain technology. The high brand recognition and extensive agency networks of established carriers can no longer be successfully leveraged by incumbent players as they weather reputational storms and attempt to connect with a coming generation very different from those that preceded it.

By nature, insurance is often only purchased begrudgingly. Relations between insurers and customers are often distant, contact infrequent and even intermediated, almost intentionally so as to not bother the reluctant purchaser. Only recently have consumers begun to view comprehensive insurance coverage and guidance as an expectation of their carrier. They now desire personalized products, unrestricted access and assistance, and frequent and tangible benefits. Further worsening matters is the increasing propensity of consumers to quickly adopt change.

The logical result of these environmental conditions is the advent of alternative risk-transfer mechanisms that circumvent insurer interaction altogether. Peer-to-peer (P2P) insurance networks are one such model that poses perhaps the gravest risk of disruption to traditional insurers. Given the Millennial generation's affinity for technology and thirst for transparency, it is no surprise they are wary of legacy insurers. These customers will welcome the arrival of innovative P2P networks that pool likeminded groups of individuals and incentivize risk-reducing practices with the potential refund benefits offered by mutual insurance companies, all through convenient mobile applications. These services enable precise policy personalization and promise easier use, lower expenses, and improved customer experience.

Though brilliant in theory, the peer-to-peer concept was not entirely practical until recently. The development of blockchain technology, which allows for the recording of online transactions on a secure public ledger, could bring P2P models to fruition much more quickly than anticipated, just as the technology may propel the banking and financial services industries forward. Smart contracts powered by blockchain could provide a solution to claims management dilemmas for both customers and insurers by validating the payment of only legitimate claims. The blockchain infrastructure would keep costs down for P2P InsurTech startups and would also empower them to attack the trust problem that has plagued the industry.

Instead of assuming that consumer familiarity and brand loyalty will preclude disruption from industry entrants, incumbent insurers need to make efforts to fundamentally change their customer relationships as continuous customer engagement quickly replaces price as the primary purchasing criterion. They must begin to provide added value to the insured not just by settling claims, but in becoming part of the customers' everyday lives and shifting the nature of their services from reactive to preventative and proactive. Insurers will need to strategically position innovative technologies as enablers to do so. By using social media as a catalyst for efficient communication, for example, legacy insurers can expand the number of touchpoints with their insured and in the process begin to strengthen the now-threatened customer relationships they have long relied upon.

The Agency Distribution Model Faces Pressure

As transparency into insurance products increases and differentiated providers begin to offer more innovative purchasing alternatives, the expertise and sales acumen provided by the agency distribution model will be challenged. The delivery of comprehensive services that rid insurance of its mystery is not contingent on the broker distribution model. Rather, these new models purport to capture the added value historically supplied by brokers and do so at a fraction of the cost.

The vested interests of agencies have largely stifled attempts at industry overhaul historically, but this trend is not likely to continue to withstand the mounting cost pressures. On the property and casualty (P&C) side alone, carriers issued $54.9 billion in net commissions and brokerage fees in 2015.[7] Similar to the costs of operating an extensive branch network on the banking side, acquisition, marketing, and distribution costs that the broker model entails are significant and increasingly being challenged as many insurance products become commoditized and competitors further leverage technology. Additionally, consumers, and particularly the Millennial generation, are increasingly valuing speed and simplicity of use over established conventions and connections with legacy insurance brokers. It is important to note that disruptions to the established agency model will not just affect agencies, however. For years, insurance carriers have relied on connections to brokers to encourage customer loyalty. As a result, new forms of intermediaries or direct-to-consumer channels threaten to undermine the client relationships of agencies as well.

Because so many distinct models have emerged, it is not known which specific forms of disruption pose the greatest risk to intermediaries at this point in time. One familiar brand of disruptor, aggregator websites, can hardly be considered innovative. Price comparison websites of this nature have existed for decades across various industries, though they are now proliferating more rapidly and differentiating themselves by supplementing pricing information with expertise of coverage intricacies and in some cases by actually becoming brokers themselves.

The agency model is more severely threatened by the introduction of innovative forms of insurance policies that require alternative distribution methods. One early example is an insurance policy tailored to the specific needs of very particular groups of individuals. Many such niche markets are underserved and a new form of intermediary, the "social broker," has emerged to incite community engagement to form the groups and negotiate favorable pricing terms on their behalf. Because social brokers do not ultimately act as actual brokers, they do not inflate costs for consumers. Accompanying the rise of the sharing economy, on-demand insurance and pay-per-use insurance have originated as dynamic models that do not necessitate brokers whatsoever, and the peer-to-peer insurance networks that were discussed earlier might also eliminate the traditional role of brokers.

The expansion of these innovative forms of "microinsurance" exhibits the shift in consumers' expectations of insurance, a new ideology that no longer holds the added value of brokers as imperative. However, this fundamental attitude change need not spell disaster for legacy insurers; rather, it presents major opportunities to diversify distribution channels and drive growth if proactively attacked. This can be done through two routes: strategically partnering with emerging InsurTech firms or developing internal equivalents. The exponential increase in funding in the InsurTech space illustrated above is mostly comprised of venture capital investments. While there have been a few notable corporate partnerships with startup firms, there is likely to be an increasing trend of insurers establishing connections with startups they believe will impact the industry, morphing the disruptors into enablers. The overall implications of InsurTech on the insurance industry are largely tied to how collaborative (or competitive) these relationships prove to be.

Regardless of methodology, insurers laden with legacy systems will be especially challenged to expand their digital distribution capabilities to decrease reliance on the agency model. A renewed focus on analytics, segmentation, and targeting will be required for insurers to turn the disruptive forces of technology in their favor. One potential scenario could see brokers continuing to play a role, albeit a limited one. In this outcome, the agency/broker model would focus on providing complex offerings while online direct distribution outlets market the more standardized products.

Data Analytics Will Increasingly Impact Insurance

Information is more readily available than ever before and will increasingly impact the ability of traditional insurers and new, emerging insurers to assess and price risk. Connected devices that constitute the Internet of Things (IoT) are empowering innovative carriers to leverage detailed customer knowledge to create personalized policies. According to the International Data Corporation, worldwide spending on the IoT is expected to double to $1.3 trillion by 2019.[8] No longer enjoying exclusive access to data, insurers need to move first to attempt to monetize the abundance of data using predictive modeling and sophisticated underwriting techniques.

The data revolution is first striking the auto insurance industry. In addition to the potential for self-driving cars to radically change the auto and auto insurance industries, telematics technology that tracks things like average rate of speed and number of sharp breaks is affording carriers the ability to differentiate between high- and low-risk drivers and personalize their coverage accordingly. IoT connectivity is growing so rapidly that it will not be long before similar behavior-tracking technologies reach other arenas of insurance, like property and health insurance. "Smart" homes and wearable fitness devices will soon transmit information that will allow for personalized policy issuance. InsurTech startups and even other types of technology firms are primed to exploit these innovations by implementing risk-transfer elements into their IoT platforms.

From a long-term perspective, insurance companies cannot afford to engage in price battles over commoditized products. As the IoT-driven data revolution progresses, the emphasis will shift from risk transfer to risk management. Insurers' stances will evolve from defensive to offensive as they aim to help policyholders prevent losses before they happen, resulting in decreased loss ratios and lower volumes of claims. Besides minimizing risk losses, IoT applications can help carriers resolve the traditional customer relationship dilemma by presenting their policyholders with additional points of contact and tangible benefit opportunities.

These prospects for vast improvement do not come without challenges. First, carriers may be challenged to entice skilled professionals to join their efforts in putting new technologically geared strategies into play. Beyond acquiring talent, insurance companies will need to foster a command of a host of analytic technologies as they enter the sphere, namely artificial intelligence (AI), drone machinery, big data, and application programming interfaces (APIs). Artificial intelligence platforms can perform advanced underwriting mechanics without the expenditure of human capital. Similarly, drones use embedded sensors and image analytics to analyze risk without requiring human supervision. Big data analytics play a key role in obtaining all-encompassing insights about a customer. The utilization of API can assist insurance companies in the collection of general information that can be applied to functions such as policy viewing, coverage analysis and payment, and claims processing. As these data capabilities expand, insurers' ability to discern truly predictive data from noise will become crucial and may require either partnering with external IoT experts or overhauling of legacy systems and corporate culture. Privacy concerns will be another hurdle for insurers to overcome to unlock the full potential of the IoT. Only 53 percent of people say they would be willing to divulge information on their driving, according to a Deloitte survey, and though discounts may prove sufficient to incentivize consumers to allow their behaviors to be monitored, a more sustainable long-term solution would likely be needed.[9]

The potential for the IoT to disrupt the traditional insurance industry is certainly possible. It is clear how the technology affords carriers the chance to buck the trend of product commoditization with personalized policies and bundled multiline offerings. With 38.5 billion IoT devices projected to be deployed globally by 2020 (according to Deloitte), the data monopoly is over for insurers, the result being a leveled playing field for smaller players and new entrants.[10]

InsurTech Disruptors Will Continually Challenge Traditional Providers

A significant competitive advantage of traditional insurers is that new potential competitors and carriers cannot meet the capital requirements necessary for effective risk pooling. As alternative risk-transfer mechanisms have emerged, this longstanding advantage of insurance carriers has been negated, eroding yet another barrier to entry. The influx of alternative capital has then resulted in a persistent surplus that has resulted in a prolonged soft market of lower premiums. The force driving this trend is actually twofold.

Primary insurers are ceding less of the risk, dampening demand, along with the continued growth of capital in the reinsurance market saturating supply. The most traditional of risk transfer mechanisms is the catastrophe (CAT) bond. These high-yield debt instruments have risen in popularity recently in the midst of a very low interest rate environment. Because they are not linked to the stock market or economic conditions, they are attractive for diversification purposes. However, many other forms of insurance-linked securities (ILSs) have arisen as means to transfer risk to investors in the capital markets. Industry-loss warranties are an alternative that offer payouts in a similar fashion as options. Collateralized reinsurance, perhaps the fastest growing segment of alternative reinsurance, is launched through a special-purpose contract that provides collateral equal to the maximum loss on the reinsurance contract. In comparison to CAT bonds, these vehicles are able to access a broader range of insurance risks. "Sidecars" are types of collateralized reinsurance structures where the investors themselves take on insurance risk for the benefit of the investment returns and underwriting profits. With these products having emerged as means of access to the insurance industry for investors who were once barred from entry, it is no surprise that fund managers are exploring insurance as an asset class. Hedge funds edging into the reinsurance market pose a particular risk as they continue to package risk-transfer capital in hopes to generate higher returns by employing more aggressive investment strategies than traditional insurance carriers can afford to undertake. If the expansion of ILSs continues, securitization may eventually fulfill the needs of the under-served, further weakening primary insurance demand and perpetuating the low-price environment.

The rise of crowdfunding through peer-to-peer (P2P) insurance networks presents a separate risk as their dynamics alter the risk-pooling dynamic of the conventional insurance model. A central appeal of the P2P business model is the potential to mitigate loss by eliminating fraud on the basis that small groups of likeminded insurers are less likely to file false claims, especially considering their eligibility to receive premium refunds if claims volume is low. Because such a large portion (10% according to Deloitte) of P&C losses are the result of fraudulent claims, the potential for the advent of P2P to lower the overall overhead costs of insurance is undeniable.[11] The lower the overhead costs required to operate in the insurance space, the more formidable of a threat alternative risk-transfer sources of capital become to standard carriers.

As with many of the other disruptive trends, alternative risk-transfer mechanisms can be viewed as enablers rather than true disruptors to incumbent insurers. Strategic steps can be taken on the part of carriers to either mitigate their impact or mimic their effect. Here, to disrupt their own operating models and reap the benefits of securitization, carriers can oversee capital market risk-transfer initiatives for their customers or even issue ILSs themselves to diversify their own risks.

CONCLUSION

Insurance has been viewed as an irreplaceable fixture of society for centuries. Over that time period, the industry and legacy players in it have adapted to survive and thrive. Nonetheless, the threat of disruption facing the insurance industry and its key players today poses a greater risk than ever before. It is important that this disruption is not viewed as a single hurdle. In fact, the quickening of technological innovation and adoption of change among consumers suggests that players in the industry will be tasked to constantly transform over the coming decades.

Speed is the name of the game here, presenting a problem to legacy insurance players who are encumbered by antiquated systems. As important as speed is in this battle, coherent and consistent long-term visions are even more crucial. Insurance companies and key players need to look far forward to not only stay paced with disruption, but proactively beat it to the punch. If today's key players fail to adapt, competition from capital markets and InsurTech firms offering innovative products and services may overtake once-dominant legacy insurers atop the insurance industry.

For banks, the increasing intersection of insurance and technology provides the potential for industry paradigms to shift and allow for new players to emerge as traditional insurance players evolve. While clearly impacting those banks already providing insurance products and services, this shift also provides an opening for those banks looking to add or expand their insurance offerings by leveraging InsurTech trends to expand services, increase profitability, and enhance their valuation. Beyond providing a potential source of non-interest income in a weak environment for spread banking revenues, InsurTech also offers an additional touchpoint to improve satisfaction among existing customers, attract new customers, and also gain additional insight into customer behaviors and patterns through the immense data created in InsurTech offerings. Over time, it will be interesting to see if most banks increasingly adopt InsurTech innovations and expand their insurance products and service offerings as these new trends continue to develop. For those forward-thinking banks that are able to leverage InsurTech appropriately, it may enhance profitability and valuation over the long term.

NOTES

1. This chapter was primarily authored by Lucas M. Parris, CFA, ASA/BV-IA and Michael Anthony. For more InsurTech information, visit Mercer Capital's website at mercercapital.com/industries/financial-institutions/insurance/.

 2. Lucas Parris, CFA, ASA-BV-IA, "Valuing Insurance Agencies," *Mercer Capital*, http://mercercapital.com/assets/Mercer-Capitals-Valuing-Insurance-Agencies-Lucas-Parris.pdf.
 3. Data in this paragraph based upon Mercer Capital research of data obtained from S&P Global Intelligence.
 4. "Insurance Tech Startup Funding Hits $2.65B in 2015 as Deal Activity Heats Up," *CB Insights*, January 29, 2016, https://www.cbinsights.com/blog/insurance-tech-startup-funding-2015/.
 5. Amit, "10 Reasons Why InsurTech Is Going to Be Important," *Let's Talk Payments*, April 4 2016, https://letstalkpayments.com/10-reasons-why-insurtech-is-going-to-be-important/.
 6. Ibid.
 7. SNL Financial.
 8. "Internet of Things Spending Forecast to Reach Nearly $1.3 Trillion in 2019 Led by Widespread Initiatives and Outlays Across Asia/Pacific," *International Data Corporation*, December 10, 2015, https://www.idc.com/getdoc.jsp?containerId=prUS40782915.
 9. Matt Clifford, Malika Gandhi, Charlotte Ryan, "Test Driving Telematics," *Deloitte*, Winter 2014, https://www2.deloitte.com/content/dam/Deloitte/us/Documents/strategy/us-strategy-test-driving-delematics-012815.pdf.
10. Michelle Canaan, John Lucker, Bram Spector, "Opting In: Using IoT Connectivity to Drive Differentiation," *Deloitte University Press*, June 2, 2016, https://dupress.deloitte.com/dup-us-en/focus/internet-of-things/innovation-in-insurance-iot.html#endnote-19.
11. Celia Ramos, Jim Kinzie, "A Call to Action: Identifying Strategies to Win the War Against Insurance Claims Fraud," *Deloitte*, https://www2.deloitte.com/content/dam/Deloitte/us/Documents/financial-services/us-fsi-a-call-to-action-080912.pdf.

Three

S ection Three covers a range of topics important to both executive/board members of traditional financial services companies like banks as well as FinTech companies and their partners and investors.

Chapter 9 delves deeply into FinTech partnerships and analyzes the key strategic questions facing both FinTech companies and banks when assessing potential partnerships. This chapter provides insights into how to look at these strategic questions with an eye toward how each strategy could potentially affect the valuation and profitability of banks and FinTech companies. For example, a key question that community banks face is "Should we focus on building our own FinTech platform/tools, selectively partner with Fintech companies, or acquire FinTech companies?" A key strategic question for FinTech companies is "Should we focus on developing partnerships with existing traditional financial services companies or should we focus more on disruption?"

Chapter 10 focuses on issues important to early-stage FinTech companies and investors/acquirers (including banks) and addresses the following questions: "How do you value an early-stage FinTech company?," "How do you value venture capital investments in early-stage FinTech companies?," and "When are valuations of early-stage FinTech companies needed?"

The next two chapters focus on key issues facing more mature FinTech companies and their bank partners/potential acquirers and look at two potential strategies. Chapter 11 focuses on the key issues related to steering a FinTech company through to a successful exit such as an acquisition or merger. Additionally, this chapter touches on key considerations for banks that may look to acquire FinTech companies. Key questions answered in this chapter include: "What are some recent historical trends in FinTech exit activity?," "How can acquirers analyze the potential valuation and financial impact of a FinTech acquisition?," "How can banks compare those growth opportunities to other more traditional growth opportunities like acquiring other banks or building branches?," "What are some challenges to structuring acquisitions of FinTech companies by traditional financial services companies like banks?," and "What are some ways that banks can structure a FinTech acquisition to minimize some of these issues?" **Chapter 12** focuses on key issues facing FinTech companies and their investors/partners when the company continues to operate independently and managing the business to maximize valuation and returns for shareholders. One key question addressed is: "What are ways to enhance liquidity if the FinTech company does not exit through an IPO or sale and continues to operate independently?"

Chapter 13 explores the question: "Is there a bubble in FinTech?" Up to this point, we have discussed the factors contributing to the excitement and interest in FinTech but this final chapter examines the potential over-exuberance in the sector. It also explores challenges for the sector as it continues to evolve and mature. Additionally, we present a case study of a FinTech company whose ending was not successful. Hopefully, this chapter will help banks and FinTech entrepreneurs realistically assess opportunities and market potential and ultimately enhance profitability and/or efficiency through proper utilization of FinTech.

CHAPTER 9

Partnering with a FinTech Company

INTRODUCTION

Banks are starting to realize that they must develop a strategy that considers how to evolve, survive, and thrive as technology and financial services increasingly intersect. A recent survey from *BankDirector* noted that bank boards are focusing more on technology with 75 percent of respondents wanting to understand how technology can make banks more efficient and 72 percent wanting to know how technology can improve the customer experience.[1]

For these reasons, a number of banks are seeking to engage in discussions with FinTech companies. The right combination of technology and financial services through a partnership has significant potential to create value for both FinTech companies and traditional financial institutions.

FinTech presents traditional financial institutions with a number of strategic options, but the most notable options include focusing on one or some combination of the following: building their own technology solution, acquiring a FinTech company, or partnering with a FinTech company. While we do not yet know which strategy will be most successful, we do know that discussions of whether to build, partner, or buy will increasingly be on the agenda of boards and executives of both financial institutions and FinTech companies for the next few years.

This chapter focuses on key considerations when contemplating a partnership between a traditional FinTech company and a traditional financial services institution—such as a community bank. Partnerships between banks and FinTech companies have been increasingly common in recent years. Venture capital data indicates that corporate partnerships with FinTech companies seem to be on the rise, with corporate participations in nearly one-third of all FinTech deals (32%), which is an increase over recent prior quarters.[2] Additionally, significant partnerships between traditional banks and FinTech companies have been announced recently. The news is also full of announcements related to co-creation opportunities where larger traditional financial institutions invest in innovation labs or accelerators to provide support for FinTech companies to grow and develop new concepts and technologies. For perspective, let's examine one FinTech niche where examples of partnerships are perhaps most evident—wealth management and the industry's response to robo-advisory. These include:

- Motif and JP Morgan (partnership announced in October 2015).
- UBS and SigFig (partnership announced in May 2016).
- FutureAdvisor, operating under the auspices of BlackRock, announced partnerships with RBC, BBVA Compass, and LPL in 2016.
- Personal Capital announced a partnership in July 2016 with AlliancePartners to offer its digital wealth management platform to approximately 200 community banks.
- Betterment and Fidelity (partnership announced in October 2014).

The interest in partnering appears to be coming from both upstart FinTech companies as well as traditional financial services companies. For banks, partnering with a startup is becoming an attractive option, as it allows the incumbent to give a FinTech solution, like robo-advisory, a test drive without wholly committing to the idea yet. For FinTech companies, the potential benefits include the expertise and customer feedback gained by rolling out their newest innovation to the established customer base of the bank while banks can more quickly and cheaply test a FinTech innovation with their customer base.

Any partnership should be studied carefully to ensure that the right metrics are used to examine value creation and returns on investment. Partnerships come with risk, such as execution and cultural issues, contingent liabilities, and potential regulatory/compliance issues. These risks must be balanced with the potential rewards, such as customer satisfaction/retention, shareholder value creation, and return on investment.

Conditions Driving Banks to FinTech Partnerships

There are a number of different reasons why a traditional bank might want to partner with a FinTech company, but one of the key drivers is the potential value creation for the bank's shareholders. As noted in Chapter 2, the valuation of a bank is typically reflective of three key elements: cash flow, risk, and growth. Partnerships that create value for the bank will likely serve to increase cash flow, reduce risk, or increase potential growth prospects. The trade-offs between increased cash flow and potential growth rates versus the additional risk are important to measure and analyze prior to entering into the partnership.

Certain FinTech partnerships offer the bank the ability to enhance revenue from expanding fee or net interest income while others offer the ability to lower costs through servicing deposits more cheaply. To the extent that the partnership has a direct positive impact on profitability through either increasing revenues (spread income or non-interest income) or lowering expenses, then the addition to shareholder value could be measured by applying a multiple to the after-tax earnings impact.

In addition to improving profitability, a partnership can also enhance the value of the bank by either reducing risk or enhancing growth prospects. These elements can be more difficult to measure but can be significant nonetheless. For example, a bank could partner with a cybersecurity FinTech company to reduce potential exposure in that area for the bank. A bank could also partner with a FinTech company that has a software solution that utilizes big data analytics to provide quicker alerts to financial difficulties of borrowers, thereby reducing charge-offs and enhancing underwriting. FinTech partnerships may also provide an additional touchpoint to improve the stickiness/retention of the client/customer.

To demonstrate the potential benefits of FinTech to community banks, let's consider the following example of two community banks: FinTech Community Bank and Traditional Community Bank. Both community banks have very similar financial characteristics, but one bank, FinTech Community Bank, elects to focus on developing a FinTech strategy and framework and focuses on developing and partnering with FinTech companies that provide mobile banking products that will increase convenience for customers and reduce costs as customers transition certain transactions from in-person branch visits to mobile. If the FinTech-oriented bank's mobile banking platform enables the bank to service customer accounts through digital channels rather than traditional in-person branches, an impact on the bank's profitability and in turn valuation will occur.

While reports vary as to the exact cost of servicing an account through a traditional in-person interaction versus a mobile device, most agree that serving customers through a mobile device can be a win-win for the bank, as it improves the convenience and accessibility of the bank to its customers. Mobile transactions are significantly cheaper than traditional in-branch visits and save the bank approximately $3.85 per branch transaction.[3] If we assume that FinTech Community Bank has 20,000 deposit accounts and each account shifts two transactions per month to mobile and away from in-person branch visits, this will result in approximately $150,000 in cost savings per month or an annual savings of approximately $1.8 million. (See Table 9.1.)

TABLE 9.1   Potential Cost Saving from Digital Focus

Costs to Service Deposits	$4.00
Costs to Service Digital Deposits	$0.15
Difference	$3.85
# of Deposit Accounts	20,000
Transactions Shifted to Mobile/Month	2
Pre-Tax Cost Savings per Month	$154,000
Pre-Tax Cost Savings to the Bank	$1,848,000

FinTech Community Bank's ability to lower costs relative to Traditional Community Bank helps it generate higher earnings, a lower efficiency ratio, and a higher return on assets (ROA) and equity (ROE). (See Table 9.2.)

This enhanced financial performance can have a significant impact on valuation. If we assume that both banks achieve the same P/E multiple range of 12.5× to 15× earnings, as an example, then the valuation range for the Traditional Community Bank is from $100 to $120 million compared to FinTech Bank's valuation range of $125 to $150 million. (See Table 9.3.)

While partnering with a FinTech company may appear to be a novel strategy for a bank, this strategy to assist the bank in expanding its digital offerings is not inconsistent with how the bank might have undertaken a traditional branch-building growth strategy. For example, a bank that builds a physical branch essentially partners with a number of companies to complete the project, like contractors, engineers, architects, and so forth. Similarly, a bank needs a variety of partners to build digital capabilities. One benefit to building digital capabilities over a traditional physical branch is that all of the bank's customers can benefit from digital capabilities, whereas only the customers who access and use the bank's new physical branch will benefit from it.

Conditions Driving More FinTech Companies to Bank Partners

Market conditions may also drive more FinTech companies to consider partnerships. Coming off recent years where both public and private FinTech markets were trending positively, the tail end of 2015 and the start of 2016 were unique as performance started to diverge. The performance of public FinTech companies was relatively flat through the first quarter of 2016 and signs of weakness were observed in certain niches (alternative/marketplace lending) and in some of the more high-profile FinTech IPOs. The median

TABLE 9.2 Community Bank Comparison

	Traditional Community Bank	FinTech Community Bank
Net Interest Income	36,000	36,000
Non-Interest Income	10,000	10,000
Non-Interest Operating Expenses	(31,050)	(28,750)
Pre-Tax, Pre-Provision Income	14,950	17,250
Provision Expenses	(2,160)	(2,160)
Pre-Tax Income	12,790	15,090
Taxes	(4,477)	(5,282)
Net Income	$8,314	$9,809
Return on Average Assets	0.83%	0.98%
Return on Tangible Equity	9.24%	10.90%
Average Equity	90,000	90,000
Average Loans	720,000	720,000
Average Earning Assets	900,000	900,000
Average Assets	1,000,000	1,000,000
Net Interest Margin	4.00%	4.00%
Non-Interest Income/Average Assets	1.00%	1.00%
Efficiency Ratio	67.50%	62.50%
Provision Expenses/Average Loans	0.30%	0.30%

TABLE 9.3 Price-to-Earnings and Valuation Ranges

	Implied Financial Performance			Price-to-Earnings Multiple			
	Net Income	ROAA	ROTE	10.0	12.5	15.0	17.5
	7,000	0.70%	7.78%	70,000	87,500	105,000	122,500
Traditional Bank	8,000	0.80%	8.89%	80,000	100,000	120,000	140,000
	9,000	0.90%	10.00%	90,000	112,500	135,000	157,500
FinTech Bank	10,000	1.00%	11.11%	100,000	125,000	150,000	175,000
	11,000	1.10%	12.22%	110,000	137,500	165,000	192,500

return of the FinTech companies that IPO'd in 2015 was a decline of 16 percent since IPO (through 3/31/16). For perspective, some recent prominent FinTech IPOs such as Square, OnDeck, and Lending Club are each down significantly in 2016 (down 28%, 53%, and 64%, respectively from 1/1/2016 to 5/18/2016). Also, the broader technology IPO slowdown in late 2015 continued into 2016 and FinTech IPOs were minimal in 2016.

However, optimism for FinTech still abounds and the private markets continue to reflect this optimism through robust investor interest and funding levels. In 2016, 334 FinTech companies raised a total of $6.7 billion in funding in the first quarter of 2016 (compared to 171 companies raising $3.2 billion in the first quarter of 2015) and Ant Financial (Alibaba's finance affiliate) completed an eye-popping $4.5 billion capital raise in April 2016.

While the factors driving this divergence in performance between public and private markets are debatable, the divergence is unlikely to continue indefinitely. A less favorable public market and less attractive IPO market creates a more challenging exit environment for those "unicorns" (startups valued at over $1 billion) and other private companies. Headwinds for the private markets could develop from more technology companies seeking IPOs and less cash flow from successful exits to fund the next round of private companies. Consequently, other strategic and exit options beyond an IPO are being considered by FinTech companies such as partnering with, acquiring, or selling to traditional incumbents (banks, insurers, and money managers).

The potential for partnerships is even more likely in FinTech, particularly here in the United States, due to the unique dynamics of the financial services industry, including the resiliency of traditional incumbents and the regulatory landscape. For example, consider a few of the inherent advantages that traditional banks have over non-bank FinTech lenders:

- **Better Access to Funding.** Prior to 2016, the interest rate/funding environment was very favorable and limited the funding advantage that financial institutions have historically had relative to less regulated nonfinancial companies. However, the winds appear to be shifting somewhat as rates rose in late 2015 and again in late 2016, and funding availability for certain FinTech companies has tightened. For example, alternative lenders are dependent, to some extent, on institutional investors to provide funding and/or purchase loans generated on their platform and a number have cited some decline in institutional investor interest.
- **Banks Still Have Strong Customer Relationships.** While certain niches of FinTech are enhanced by demand from consumers and businesses for innovative products and technology, traditional institutions still maintain the majority of customer relationships. As an example, the

2015 *Small Business Credit Survey* from the Federal Reserve noted that traditional banks are still the primary source for small business loans with only 20 percent of employer firms applying at an online lender. The satisfaction rate for online lenders was low (15% compared to 75% for small banks and 51% for large banks). The main reasons reported for dissatisfaction with online lenders was high interest rates and unfavorable repayment terms.

- **Regulatory Scrutiny and Uncertainty Related to FinTech.** Both the Federal Reserve and the OCC have made recent announcements and comments about ways to regulate financial technology. In the online lending area specifically, regulatory scrutiny appears to be on the rise with the Treasury releasing a whitepaper discussing the potential oversight of marketplace lending and the CFPB signaling the potential to increase scrutiny in the area. The lack of a banking charter has also been cited as a potential weakness and has exposed certain alternative lenders to lawsuits in different states.

For FinTech companies looking to overcome those inherent advantages of traditional banks, partnering with a traditional bank can be beneficial. As the result of the partnership, the FinTech company can scale more quickly, lower customer acquisition costs, and elevate their brand by partnering with a more established brand. In addition, accessing the knowledge and experience of the bank's management team, who often has more experience with the regulatory landscape, can prove invaluable.

Developing a FinTech Partnership Framework

While the potential benefits of FinTech partnerships are numerous, banks must put much consideration into prioritizing FinTech opportunities and determining which FinTech partners they will ultimately select. As discussed in Chapter 1, there is a vast array of FinTech companies focused on different FinTech niches and a significant number would benefit from having access to a bank's customer base. So, banks should be highly selective when picking and choosing FinTech companies that would best align with their strategy and help enhance profitability and valuation. In order to properly consider FinTech opportunities, banks need to develop a specific framework and criteria for potential FinTech partnerships so that they can focus on partnerships in areas that will be most beneficial to their bank and their customers and shareholders.

Basics of Corporate Finance and Investment Returns[4] To assist with developing an appropriate framework for FinTech partnerships, we first briefly review the basics of corporate finance and shareholder returns so that directors and managers of banks can make more informed financial decisions when considering FinTech partnerships. This brief review will help the board and management to determine strategy as it relates to interconnected financial decisions, such as capital budgeting, capital structure, and distribution policy. By understanding these three financial decisions better and their interaction with the company's strategic plan, managers and directors can make the optimal FinTech partnership decisions to generate shareholder returns and value.

There are two primary components of an investor's return: the return from reinvestment and the return from dividends. In order for value to be created, the returns from reinvestment decisions must meet or exceed the investor's required return. If that occurs, then the enhancement to either cash flow and/or future growth will offset the capital outlay. (See Table 9.4.)

Total return is often determined by the earnings retention policy and then the dividend policy would flow through. If your bank has favorable reinvestment opportunities, then the optimal strategy would likely be to attempt to grow through reinvestment and capital appreciation. Reinvestment lowers the potential for current returns in favor of future return growth. Creating value through the decision to reinvest versus distribute is a balancing act. Reinvestments are good for future growth and capital appreciation so long as the investments are made in productive assets. If the investments are made in unproductive assets, though, expected returns are lower and less capital appreciation occurs while current returns in the form of dividends are delayed.

FinTech companies and banks consist of a portfolio of projects. The range of the projects can vary and will likely expand as the company or bank grows. For example, a small community bank may have only a limited number of projects (FinTech or otherwise), whereas a large bank may have hundreds or even thousands of projects. Similarly, an early-stage FinTech

TABLE 9.4 Investment Returns for FinTech Company

	Current Income		Future Upside
Total Return =	Dividend Yield	+	Capital Appreciation
	Dividend		Value at End of Period
	Value		Value at Beginning of Period
Determined by Operating Performance	Board does have some discretion in determining these components.		
Total Return =	Dividend Yield	+	Capital Appreciation

company may be focused on only one or a handful of products/services, whereas a larger and more well-established FinTech company may have a number of products that have existed for several decades, as well as a vast pipeline of potential new products and initiatives. This helps to explain a key valuation difference between early-stage or smaller FinTech companies and larger companies. As investors examine the menu of potential investments, they are going to require a higher return for early-stage or smaller FinTech companies due to the greater risk of investing in a smaller, less diversified portfolio of projects.

Two basic elements of corporate finance are return and risk. A keen understanding of the two, and how they interact, is important for directors and managers to understand. We describe the best ways to analyze returns from FinTech acquisitions and partnerships in more detail at the end of this chapter (see also Chapter 10), but now let's briefly discuss risk.

One important factor to consider when assessing risk is that the riskiness of a project in isolation is less important than the riskiness of a project in conjunction with the rest of the portfolio of projects. We often hear from community bankers about their concerns regarding the risks inherent with FinTech investments or partnerships. While it is advisable that any potential FinTech partnership/investment be analyzed in terms of its potential riskiness, community bankers would be wise to consider the riskiness of potential FinTech opportunities relative to their existing portfolio of projects.

To better understand this point, let's consider the following example: two community banks are examining a relationship with an alternative lender that provides small business financing. Both banks determine that the relationship would enhance the bank's return on equity and provide an internal rate of return (IRR) (we discuss how to compute an IRR for a FinTech partnership in more detail in a later section of this chapter) that exceeds the bank's existing cost of equity. While the IRR from the FinTech partnership is the same for both banks, one bank elects to reject the relationship while the other elects to continue the partnership, yet both made the right strategic decision. Why?

Let's assume that the FinTech company that both banks looked at is Digital Lender, a hypothetical FinTech company that offers a digital lending solution that is specifically focused on providing loans to small- and medium-sized businesses. The first bank already had a higher-than-peer concentration of small business lending as it already had an SBA (Small Business Administration) lending platform and employed a number of small business-focused lenders. The first bank also already has a fairly diversified loan portfolio with above-peer margins. The second bank had a large concentration in agricultural and residential real estate loans, but did not have a very large small business lending portfolio. However, it believed there was an opportunity within its market area to offer small business loans due to a growing number of small businesses and a shortage of banks focused on this segment. However, the second bank had been unable to attract a lender with that expertise to the bank due to a talent shortage in their area and its minimal level of product offerings. Thus, the second bank foresaw the opportunity for the digital small business lending platform of Digital Lender to offer another touchpoint and product for it to go out and attract small business customers and start to add diversification to its loan portfolio. Furthermore, the second bank's net interest margin was below peer due to a higher-than-peer concentration of securities and need to reinvest those assets in higher yielding assets. Thus, the digital lending platform was a low-cost way for the second bank to enter into the small business segment, increase its net interest margin, and improve its diversification.

Consequently, different FinTech products and companies will appeal to different banks for different reasons. For a FinTech company looking to partner with a bank, it is important to recognize which bank provides the best fit for its products and services. For the bank seeking to partner with a FinTech company, it is similarly important to identify the potential opportunities within the broader FinTech industry that fit the bank's risk profile, return threshold, and long-term strategy. Similarly, it is important for the bank to assess which FinTech opportunities provide the added benefit of diversification and risk reduction relative to the bank's existing concentrations.

Basics of Valuation   To assist further with developing an appropriate framework for FinTech partnerships, we briefly review the basics of valuation so that directors and managers of banks and FinTech companies can better understand how FinTech partnerships can impact valuation.

The basic valuation equation is given here and the value of a FinTech company or bank can be broken down as follows:

$$\text{Value} = \text{Cash Flow} \times \text{Multiple}$$

$$\text{Value} = \text{Cash Flow} \times \left(\frac{1}{\text{Discount Rate} - \text{Expected Growth}} \right)$$

Value is a function of cash flow, risk, and growth and it is important to have a keen understanding of each valuation element in order to assess value creation.

- **Cash flow** is the portion of the expected net income of a business that remains for distribution after all necessary expenses, taxes, and reinvestments are made. A portion of net income is reinvested and the more that is reinvested in productive assets that generate a return in excess of the company's cost of equity, the more value is created over time.

- **Growth** is primarily influenced by two factors: inflation and reinvestment. Reinvestment only influences growth to the extent that funds can be allocated properly into projects whose returns exceed the company's cost of capital. The impact of the reinvestment decision will depend upon the owner's propensity to reinvest in the company and the prospects for generating growth for those reinvestments. If your bank or FinTech company has an abundance of projects that have expected returns in excess of your cost of capital (alternatively known as a number of growth opportunities), then it may be appropriate to retain a greater proportion of earnings to reinvest and fund future growth opportunities (like FinTech, new facilities, personnel, traditional bank acquisitions, etc.).

- **Risk** is an important consideration for any company, but it is particularly important for banks and FinTech companies. When thinking about risk, consider the following: *The absolute riskiness of the project/investment is often less important than the degree to which the addition of that investment/project changes the risk of the company's overall portfolio of projects.* For a bank considering a FinTech opportunity such as a potential partnership or acquisition of a FinTech company, it should consider the riskiness of the FinTech company's operations within the context of the bank's entire operations.

For example, consider that the community bank industry today has a greater concentration in real estate–related assets than it did approximately 30 years ago. This would seem counterintuitive coming off of the financial crisis, which was sparked from weak real estate conditions. Similarly, the operations of community banks are often concentrated to a limited geographic market area. This combination of having heavy real estate exposure in a limited geographic area can often have fatal consequences for community banks. Consequently, a community bank with a heavy concentration in real estate loans in a particular market may view an opportunity to partner with a FinTech company offering a new service (like consumer lending, payments, or insurance solutions) more attractively than a bank with a larger, more diversified portfolio. Even though the potential IRRs from the FinTech partnership are the same for both banks, the less diversified, real estate–oriented bank may desire the potential to expand and diversify revenue through enhancing FinTech offerings more than the larger, more diversified bank.

Basics of Capital Budgeting Now that we have discussed the basics of investor returns and valuation, let's discuss capital budgeting so that bankers can understand how they can consider FinTech partnerships in light of other capital budgeting decisions. Among the potential uses of cash, the decision regarding whether to make capital investments in a business either through reinvesting in the company (i.e., funding the development

TABLE 9.5 Capital Budgeting: Sources and Uses of Capital

Sources of Capital	=	Uses of Capital
Earnings		Capital Investment (including Acquisitions)
Borrowing		Debt Repayment
New Share Issuance		Shareholder Dividends
Monetize Assets/Sale Portion of Business		Share Repurchase

of another portfolio of projects) or through investing in other potential acquisitions or other FinTech partners is often dependent upon the potential returns of those projects and where those projects lie in the capital budgeting process. (See Table 9.5.)

The capital budgeting decision of whether to use cash generated to reinvest in the business or pay those available cash flows to shareholders or debt holders is driven by a number of factors. One key factor to consider is how many attractive capital projects are available to the company. For example, if the company has a plethora of capital projects available and a number that can be demonstrated to be value enhancing (i.e., the potential returns from the projects are in excess of the company's cost of equity), then the strategy to create value and utilize those funds optimally will likely be to invest those cash flows in the available capital projects. The difficult question then becomes prioritizing those capital projects and determining which ones offer the greatest potential to create value and maximize shareholder returns.

However, if it is deemed that there exists a dearth of capital projects that offer attractive returns (as measured by return on investment or internal rate of return relative to the company's cost of equity), then the optimal strategy will likely be to pass on reinvesting in the business and return some or a significant proportion of those earnings to shareholders in the form of dividends or share repurchases or to repay debt holders.

Thus, a key determinant of capital budgeting is determining how many capital projects are available and how attractive the potential returns on those capital investments are relative to the company's cost of capital. If attractive capital projects are available, then the company will likely want to focus on reinvesting earnings. If less attractive capital projects are available, then the company may want to focus on distributing earnings or repurchasing shares. (See Figure 9.1.)

Pulling It Together: FinTech Framework for Banks To help determine how attractive a FinTech partnership may be in order to compare it to an alternative capital project, an internal rate of return analysis can be utilized. IRR

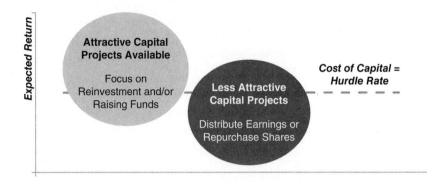

FIGURE 9.1 Attractive vs. Less Attractive Capital Projects

can be beneficial for managers of both FinTech companies and traditional financial services firms as an effective way to measure the relative merits of a variety of capital allocation decisions related to FinTech. Should your bank decide that it wants to develop a particular niche like wealth management, an IRR analysis can be prepared with a wide variety of potential strategies such as exploring the idea of acquiring a robo-advisor, partnering with a robo-advisor, building your own robo-advisory platform, or looking to partner with a traditional asset manager or RIA through either an acquisition or partnership.

While each of these options presents a unique set of considerations and execution issues, an IRR analysis can be prepared for each whereby you can determine the potential financial impact of each and determine which FinTech strategy provides the best potential return while also being consistent with the bank's long-term strategic plan and market potential. (See Figure 9.2.)

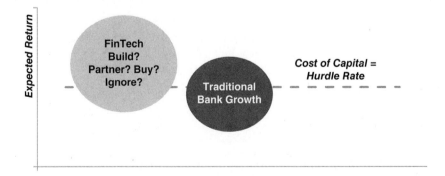

FIGURE 9.2 Considering Returns of FinTech Strategies

For a number of banks, their use of FinTech and other enhanced digital offerings represent one potential capital project that could demonstrate an attractive IRR and enhance value. This is one reason that FinTech has garnered so much attention from banks and the press in recent periods. However, one difficulty for most community bankers is the vast array of FinTech startups that have developed in the last few years and determining which FinTech niche or company offers the greatest potential returns and is the best strategic fit for the bank. Once the ideal FinTech niches are determined, the key strategic question becomes whether to build, buy, or partner in order to enter into that particular niche.

One way to develop a framework to determine which niches and FinTech companies are most attractive is to examine the IRRs from FinTech partnerships in different FinTech niches and compare that to the bank's cost of equity (or required return). Those partnerships and niches that offer IRRs in excess of the bank's cost of equity (or required return) would be attractive FinTech areas and companies to pursue as potential partners as they offer greater returns and would create value over time if the returns exceed the bank's cost of equity. One can also compare these returns to other more traditional growth options like acquiring other banks or building branches. Figure 9.3 provides an example of a FinTech framework for a community bank by comparing the IRRs for different FinTech partnership opportunities with the bank's cost of equity (i.e., the hurdle rate), which was assumed to be in the 10 percent range. For this particular bank, the bank technology and alternative lending niches appear to offer the most attractive potential returns relative to other niches and traditional bank deals.

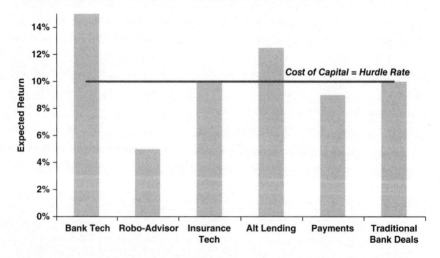

FIGURE 9.3 Hurdle Rates for Transactions

One reason that FinTech partnerships can appear to be so attractive in the current environment is that bank returns on equity are being pressured by the low interest rate environment. For example, the median community bank ROE is in the 6–10 percent range in mid-2016 compared to 10–15 percent pre–financial crisis. As banks consider different FinTech niches and strategies, it will be important to consider the IRR for different FinTech partnerships and compare those to traditional acquisition strategies, as well as their cost of equity, to determine whether to enter into them.

How to Assess Potential Financial Returns from Partnerships

We now provide an example of an internal rate of return analysis and discuss how to analyze the potential returns and value creation from a FinTech partnership. As previously discussed, by analyzing the key metrics used to measure the potential returns from a FinTech partnership, banks can assess which FinTech companies and structures will be most beneficial to the bank. An internal rate of return analysis can be used to assess FinTech partnerships and determine which partnership may be right for your bank.

Internal Rate of Return Analysis   An internal rate of return analysis derives the discount rate that equates the cash outlays to initiate the partnership (cost to utilize the technology/software, roll out the product, etc.) to the earnings generated from the partnership. The IRR can also be compared to the company's cost of equity to determine whether the potential partnership creates value for the acquirer's shareholders. To the extent that the IRR is greater than the cost of equity, value is created as the investment in the partnership is generating a return in excess of the company's cost of equity.

To illustrate how to use IRR to analyze a FinTech partnership, let's consider the following. A FinTech company approaches a bank or vice versa about new software products that will provide the bank with additional revenue opportunities from new deposit product offerings that increase non-interest income. The costs of the products are an initial installation fee of $100,000 and $275,000 for the next few years to pay for the software license. The software is expected to increase revenue by approximately $300,000 in Year 1 and then grow incrementally thereafter. The IRR analysis allows the bank to model the potential rate of return from the investment (22%) and also analyze the potential pickup in ROE (12 to 20 bps) and compound annual growth rate in equity (~5%) over the next five-year period (see Table 9.6).

Since the IRR is above the typical cost of equity and ROE of most community banks, the FinTech partnership would appear to enhance the

TABLE 9.6 FinTech Partnership Example

	Initial	Year 1	Year 2	Year 3	Year 4	Year 5
Cost Outlay	(100,000)	(275,000)	(275,000)	(275,000)	(275,000)	(275,000)
Revenue Enhancement*		300,000	306,000	312,120	318,362	324,730
Total Cash Flows	(100,000)	25,000	31,000	37,120	43,362	49,730
Internal Rate of Return	22%					

*The enhancement to revenue could come from either the increase of spread or non-interest income or the reduction of expenses.

	Pre-Partnership					
Bank Equity	20,000,000	19,900,000	20,895,000	21,939,750	23,036,738	24,188,574	25,398,003
Incremental Pickup to ROE		0.12%	0.14%	0.16%	0.18%	0.20%
Compound Annual Growth Rate in Equity	4.89%					

TABLE 9.7 FinTech Partnership: IRR and ROE Spread

FinTech Partnership

	IRR	Bank ROE	IRR – Bank ROE
Adding Product	22%	10%	11.9%

bank's ROE and create enough value to support the potential expenditure. (See Table 9.7.)

The nice thing about both the IRR and the IRR less COE metric (return on investment minus cost of equity) is that you can compare these metrics across different FinTech partnerships or other more traditional strategic alternatives to assess which option makes sense. However, both metrics are very sensitive to different assumptions. IRR, for example, can be very sensitive to the pro forma earnings stream as well as the terminal value multiple utilized. IRR can also be very sensitive to assumptions such as the revenue synergies and the bank's cost of equity.

Investing in a FinTech Partner

Another item to consider when analyzing FinTech partnerships is whether the bank would also like to invest in the FinTech company. One could make a compelling case that banks should seriously consider such investments. Recall in Chapter 3 the significant value created for both the FinTech companies and the traditional community banks that invested in FinTech companies like Visa and MasterCard. A combination investment/partnership has a number of advantages for both the bank and the FinTech company.

- The bank can benefit the FinTech company by advocating for its product to their fellow bankers and by providing useful insights into real-world issues experienced within their customer base as they interact with the offering—along with insights into how the regulatory agencies view the product.
- The bank can enhance returns should the FinTech company be successful.
- By making a minority investment, the accounting treatment is more favorable for the bank (i.e., no goodwill creation). We address the accounting considerations related to FinTech acquisitions more fully in Chapter 11.

For these reasons, the bank may have more to consider beyond just whether to engage in a partnership with the FinTech company and the bank may consider whether to invest in the FinTech company's next funding round, or even acquire the FinTech company outright. There are a number of factors to consider; however, determining the IRR of each scenario can help the bank identify which option may be most favorable.

Let's look at the same FinTech partnership and consider a strategy whereby the bank also makes a minority investment in the FinTech company (see Table 9.8). This strategy generates a higher internal rate of return assuming both an investment and exit within the next five years; however, it also requires more capital to be allocated to the project (i.e., it will be more expensive).

The bank may then also want to examine the potential IRR for a full acquisition of the FinTech company (see Table 9.9). In this case, the bank can again run an IRR analysis and compare the results to the other two strategies—being a minority investor and/or just utilizing the FinTech company's products.

Once all three options (partnership only, partnership plus minority investment, and partnership through full acquisition) are modeled, the bank can compare the potential internal rates of return of each option and determine which generates the highest potential return. As shown in Figure 9.4, each structure enhances the bank's returns; thus a partnership on some level ought to be pursued. What's more, the bank could elect to test the FinTech company's product initially (i.e., partner only) and then retain the option to invest or acquire the company later.

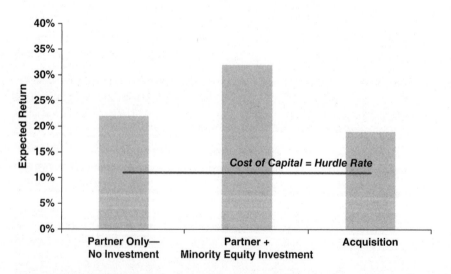

FIGURE 9.4   FinTech Partner/Invest in/Acquire Analysis

TABLE 9.8 Equity FinTech Partner (Minority Shareholder)

	Initial	Year 1	Year 2	Year 3	Year 4	Year 5
Cost Outlay	(100,000)	(250,000)	(250,000)	(250,000)	(250,000)	(250,000)
Equity Investment	(1,000,000)					
IPO/Sale Proceeds						4,000,000
Revenue Enhancement*		300,000	300,000	300,000	300,000	300,000
Total Cash Flows	(1,100,000)	50,000	50,000	50,000	50,000	4,050,000
Internal Rate of Return	32%					

*The enhancement to revenue could come from either the increase of spread or non-interest income or the reduction of expenses.

	Pre-Partnership					
Bank Equity	20,000,000	19,900,000	20,895,000	21,939,750	23,036,738	24,188,574	30,398,003
Incremental Pickup to ROE		0.24%	0.23%	0.22%	0.21%	13.32%
Compound Annual Growth Rate in Equity	8.73%					

TABLE 9.9 FinTech (Full Acquisition)

Internal Rate of Return (Full Acquisition)	Closing	Year 1	Year 2	Year 3	Year 4	Year 5
Deal Consideration	(25,000)					
Closing Costs	(2,000)					
Opportunity Cost of Cash		(1,000)	(1,000)	(1,000)	(1,000)	(1,000)
Cash Flows Generated from Target		0	1,000	2,000	3,000	4,000
Terminal Value						60,000
Total Cash Flows	(27,000)	(1,000)	0	1,000	2,000	63,000
Internal Rate of Return	**19%**					

In this example, the partnership plus the minority equity investment produces the highest internal rate of return and thus the largest spread over the bank's return on equity. Therefore, this strategy would be most conducive to creating strategic value for the bank. However, other considerations may be important enough to tilt the bank to another structure. For example, investing in the FinTech company requires additional capital be deployed to the investment, which means greater risk accrues. Therefore, the expected potential return should be higher for an equity partnership than a non-equity partnership in order to be worth the additional risk of the investment (see Table 9.10).

Other Key Questions When Thinking About FinTech Partnerships

Beyond the financial decisions and return analyses discussed previously in this chapter, there are additional items for a community bank to consider when partnering with a FinTech company.

TABLE 9.10 FinTech Partnership and ROE Spread Comparison

FinTech Partnership	IRR	Bank ROE	IRR - Bank ROE
Adding Product	22%	10%	11.9%
Product + Equity Investment	32%	10%	22.4%
Complete Acquisition	19%	10%	9.1%

- **Is the bank comfortable with the FinTech company's risk profile?** Managing risk is a key responsibility of managers and directors of financial services companies. Risk is inextricably linked with performance in highly leveraged entities like banks. Growth absent an appropriate consideration of risk can lead to poor outcomes. For example, a bank that aggressively expands into a new lending area may see a few years or quarters of higher interest income wiped out quickly by credit losses on poorly underwritten loans. Thus, it is critical for banks to understand and manage the potential risk from their FinTech partnership and ensure that the risk is appropriate for their institution. Banks are also more highly regulated than non-bank FinTech companies. Therefore, it is important for the bank to assess the suitability of the partnership given their risk appetite and regulatory/compliance burdens. For FinTech companies seeking banking partners, it is important to understand the regulations and compliance burdens of banks and be prepared to address those concerns. However, these regulations may also offer opportunities for FinTech companies to provide "RegTech" solutions and expand their revenue and product mix.

- **What will the regulatory reaction be?** It is not uncommon for most banks to relay to their regulators their intent to enter into a significant partnership with a FinTech company. This may be the preferred method, as opposed to asking for approval after the fact. When presenting the FinTech partnership, banks may need to be able to demonstrate the potential of the partnership to enhance the bank's product offerings and expand its services to a larger customer base within the bank's market area. The bank may also need to demonstrate that the additional risk of entering into the partnership is offset by the potential to enhance the bank's returns and/or profitability. The regulatory vetting process often is a significant hurdle for bank/FinTech company partnerships. However, overcoming that hurdle can provide an advantage for the FinTech company and the bank once complete because many competitors may not attempt it.

- **Who will maintain the primary relationship with the customer?** There are certain FinTech solutions that allow the bank to improve its ability to serve and enhance its relationship with customers. For example, a bank that offers a white-labeled technology solution may enhance its product offering while still remaining the primary contact for the customer. However, certain FinTech solutions and partnerships may create a dilemma for banks and their partners as they work together. If a bank partners with a FinTech company for a new lending product or payment offering, several key questions arise, including: Who will ultimately service the customer's account? Will the bank remain the primary contact for the customer during this process or will it transfer to the FinTech company? Who will own the customer relationship or will it be shared?

■ **Is the partnership consistent with the bank's long-term plan?** The Office of the Comptroller of the Currency (OCC) issued a whitepaper on March 31, 2016, titled "Supporting Responsible Innovation in the Federal Banking System: An OCC Perspective."[5] The OCC defines responsible innovation in this whitepaper as: "The use of new or improved financial products, services, and processes to meet the evolving needs of consumers, businesses, and communities in a manner that is consistent with sound risk management and is aligned with the bank's overall business strategy."

The OCC whitepaper then discusses eight principles related to responsible innovation. One of the eight principles is: "Encourage banks of all sizes to integrate responsible innovation into their strategic planning." The whitepaper notes that a decision to offer innovative products should be aligned "with the bank's long-term business plan rather than following the latest fad or trend." The OCC goes on to note that partnerships should help the bank achieve its strategic objectives and consider traditional strategic planning criteria (such as consistency with the bank's risk profile, business/capital plan), and the decision should consider both realistic financial projections and exit strategies. Thus, banks should ensure that the FinTech partnerships are consistent with their long-term strategic plan and be prepared to demonstrate that to both their boards and regulators.

CONCLUSION

FinTech partnerships can be attractive to banks for many of the reasons cited in this chapter and they are increasingly becoming more common. Partnerships with banks can also prove to be beneficial for FinTech companies. For those bankers interested in exploring FinTech partnerships, the task can be daunting, given the number of FinTech niches and companies that are focused on unbundling traditional financial services offerings. By relying on the appropriate strategies, frameworks, and return analyses for analyzing and structuring potential FinTech partnerships, forward-thinking bankers can leverage FinTech to enhance profitability and create value for their banks. The vast array of FinTech companies and their desire to partner with banks can be turned into a positive for those banks utilizing the framework and analysis discussed in this chapter as they can afford to be selective and prioritize which FinTech partnerships are most attractive to the bank.

NOTES

1. Emily McCormick, "2015 Growth Strategy Survey," *Bank Director*, August 2015, http://www.bankdirector.com/download_file/view_inline/4268.
2. "The Pulse of Fintech," Q2 2016 by *KPMG and CBInsights*, August 17, 2016.
3. Daniel Huang, "Mobile's Rise Poses a Riddle for Banks," *Wall Street Journal*, December 18, 2014, http://www.wsj.com/articles/mobiles-rise-poses-a-riddle-for-banks-1418945162. While data is limited in regard to the cost comparison of a mobile versus a traditional transaction, this article cites a survey that showed an average cost of $0.17 for digital transactions versus $4.00 for an interaction with a bank teller.
4. The material in this section was adapted with permission from "Corporate Finance in 30 Minutes," by Travis W. Harms, CFA, CPA/ABV, *Mercer Capital*, August 2016, http://mercercapital.com/financialreportingblog/corporate-finance-in-30-minutes/.
5. "Supporting Responsible Innovation in the Federal Banking System: An OCC Perspective," Office of the Comptroller of the Currency, March 2016, https://www.occ.gov/publications/publications-by-type/other-publications-reports/pub-responsible-innovation-banking-system-occ-perspective.pdf.

CHAPTER 10

Early Stage FinTech Valuation Issues

INTRODUCTION

The excitement around FinTech is evident in several areas, including the outperformance of the publicly traded FinTech companies relative to the broader market, the increase in the number of both FinTech unicorns and venture capital and corporate/bank investments in FinTech companies, and increasing M&A activity in the sector. Up to this point, we have discussed FinTech as an area that has been the beneficiary of additional funding and investor interest and highlighted potential benefits for community banks. Factors driving optimism toward FinTech include technology advancement, evolving consumer behavior and expectations for digital delivery of financial services, and regulatory response to the financial crisis, which has served to create opportunities for emerging, less regulated FinTech companies.

This chapter seeks to help investors, entrepreneurs, and potential partners—such as community banks—better understand valuation mechanics for early-stage FinTech companies. It covers:

- When an early-stage FinTech company will need a valuation performed —such as for equity compensation
- Unique considerations when assessing and valuing FinTech companies
- How investor preferences can impact valuation
- Unique valuation issues related to valuing venture capital interests in FinTech companies (given that the level of venture capital investments in FinTech has grown in recent periods and venture capital firms face increasing pressure from investors, auditors, and regulators to enhance disclosure and processes related to valuations of portfolio interests)

For those FinTech entrepreneurs reading this, we encourage you to extend your corporate and strategic planning dialogue to include valuation. Sooner or later circumstances requiring an external valuation will arise. Early awareness of the valuation process and key valuation drivers will minimize the likelihood of unpleasant surprises and increase the likelihood of creating significant value.

WHY YOU SHOULD HAVE A VALUATION PERFORMED

"Nowadays people know the price of everything and the value of nothing."

—Oscar Wilde, *The Picture of Dorian Gray*

The above quote seems especially apt in the FinTech industry. The implied values of high-profile, private FinTech companies, based on the stock price paid by investors in a recently completed funding round, are often misreported in the headlines of news articles. The problem with these headlines is that the shares purchased often include investor preferences, which obscures the prices paid by investors for those particular shares and overstates the value of the company when that price is applied to other shares.

Consider the following example: investors in a late-stage funding round get a number of economic rights, control rights, and preferences associated with their preferred shares that earlier investors and common shareholders did not have. Those later-stage investors invest $100 million into the company and then pay $1,000 per preferred share. Since the implied value is approximately $1 billion—based upon the $1,000 price in the recent financing round and 1 million common and preferred shares outstanding after the round—headlines will note that a new FinTech unicorn has arrived. This overstates the company's value, however, since the majority of the shares outstanding do not have the same rights and preferences as those purchased in the most recent financing round.

For these reasons, valuing venture-backed FinTech companies can be complicated, particularly those with several different share classes and preferences across the capital structure. These valuations can have very real consequences for stakeholders (specifically employees and other investors) and they can also provide a number of benefits to the company over the long-run. Some benefits of having a valuation performed are summarized ahead.

To Measure Value Creation Over Time

One of the best performance scorecards for managers, investors, and directors of companies is to measure value creation over extended time periods.

For public companies, returns can be measured easily by comparing the company's total return (percentage change in share price plus dividend yield) to other benchmark measures, such as the broader market, industry, and/or peers. For example, a publicly traded payments company whose shareholders have achieved a total return of 10.0 percent can note on their scorecard that their performance has outpaced the returns from the S&P 500 and Mercer Capital's FinTech Payments Index, which were up 4.0 and 4.6 percent, respectively, in the 12 months ended June 30, 2016.

For private companies, putting together a scorecard measuring value creation can be difficult. Since annual valuations are not typically performed, there is no accurate measure to assess value creation. Some privately held financial services companies, like banks, can often proxy value creation without annual valuations by tracking growth in book value or returns on equity (net income divided by equity). However, it is more difficult for private FinTech companies to track their progress and value creation over time by comparing an earnings measure to a balance sheet measure since near-term earnings are often sacrificed for the sake of top-line growth. Balance sheet measures can also have little connection to earnings capabilities as a number of assets created in technology companies (like customer databases, intellectual property, patents, and the like) are intangible and nonphysical in nature and are not recorded on the balance sheet. Additionally, dividends (the other element of shareholder return) are often delayed or minimal as available cash flow is reinvested to fund future growth.

It is possible to measure value creation for private FinTech companies by having annual valuations performed by an outside third-party. Consider Table 10.1 for a private FinTech company that details the total returns to shareholders over a trailing three-year period based upon dividends paid as well as the change in value per share from the valuation performed.

Using this valuation and dividend information, this private FinTech company can then compare its returns to other benchmark measures such as peers or publicly traded FinTech companies, the broader market as a whole, and the FinTech industry. These comparisons allow managers, the board, and stakeholders to see how their performance has compared and develop their own scorecard (see Figure 10.1).

For Planning Purposes

Valuations of early-stage FinTech companies tend to increase as milestones are achieved and revenue and profitability improve. Valuations of an early-stage FinTech company will inherently require the development of a set of financial projections that can be overlaid with significant milestones over the projection period. Additionally, the capital investment needed

TABLE 10.1 Change in Value per Share

Valuation Date	Value per Share	Dividend per Share	Total Return (Change in Share Price + Dividend Yield)	Cumulative Dividends
6/30/2016	$12.90	$0.30	45%	$1.60
12/31/2015	$12.90	$0.30	42%	$1.30
6/30/2015	$12.20	$0.25	32%	$1.00
12/31/2014	$11.55	$0.25	23%	$0.75
6/30/2014	$10.30	$0.25	8%	$0.50
12/31/2013	$9.00	$0.25	–8%	$0.25
6/28/2013	$10.00	na	0%	

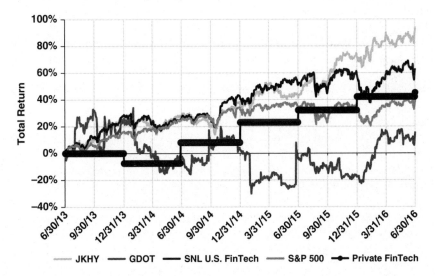

FIGURE 10.1 Comparison of Returns to Benchmark Measures
Source: S&P Global Market Intelligence

to achieve those milestones may also be considered as well as potential dilution from future funding rounds. This forecast can serve to provide a roadmap against which to compare future performance and value creation, as well as to contemplate future strategic decisions. For example, consider a FinTech company that is determining whether to pivot to a model focused on partnering with community banks rather than their current plan, which is to disrupt community banks. The partnership model might result in more rapid growth in terms of customers and top-line revenue but at a lower margin, whereas the disruption strategy might result in slower top-line growth and similar margins initially. By comparing the partnership model to the preexisting disruption forecast in the valuation analysis, management will be able to more accurately compare the two strategies and determine which model may result in higher cash flows, shareholder returns, and valuations.

For Other Stakeholders, Including Employees and Early-Stage Investors

FinTech companies often attract top talent by offering stock ownership and the ability for employees to share in the potential upside should the company's valuation improve over time. Additionally, FinTech companies can often have complex capital structures with venture, corporate (including banks), and/or private equity investors having preferences related to their particular shares that rank-and-file employees do not. While this can certainly be a recipe for success for some technology companies that are able to successfully exit at higher valuations through a sale or IPO, it can make the valuation process challenging and these valuations can have very real consequences for stakeholders, particularly employees and venture capital investors. There have been examples where employees have suffered, and even lost money, based upon paying taxes at valuations higher than the company executed in an exit through a sale. While the exposure to a decline in performance and/or pricing based on market conditions or company performance is unavoidable, it is important to have a valuation process with formalized procedures to demonstrate compliance with tax and financial reporting regulations. As the number of FinTech venture capital investments is growing, valuation practices are coming under greater scrutiny, and these investments generally need to conform to accounting standards (U.S. GAAP or IFRS) in order to provide useful information to investors and withstand auditor scrutiny.

Certainly, the prospects for scrutiny from auditors, SEC, and/or the IRS are possible but very real tax issues can also result around equity compensation for employees.

VALUATION CONSIDERATIONS FOR FINTECH COMPANIES

A valuation looks at the key financial, operational, and regulatory considerations of the subject company. Valuing an early-stage company can be tricky as they often have valuation needs distinct from more mature companies. Early-stage FinTech companies are even trickier to value given FinTech's unique industry dynamics and complex regulatory environment, which either facilitates or thwarts future growth and profitability. When valuing a FinTech startup, it is important to consider a number of different issues. While not all-inclusive, the following provides several key considerations when valuing FinTech companies.

Market Characteristics and Potential Impact

FinTech companies tend to operate within a given market niche. How successful the company operates within that particular market can be the most significant factor in the exit valuation of a startup. Understanding market dynamics of different segments and the potential competitive contours within those segments is a critical element of the valuation process. For a FinTech startup, significant market factors can include the market's absolute size and growth prospects.

Measures for evaluating a particular FinTech market can include determining the size of the total market that the product is targeting and then how much market share might be available to be captured or disrupted by the new technology or innovative product. For example, the potential for a new consumer loan product may first consider the size of the consumer lending market, the existing composition of traditional lenders, and the potential market share that the new product could take. Once the total amounts of loan originations are estimated, then the potential income related to those originations should be estimated. The potential income related to the loans will be impacted by strategic decisions and the business model of the startups. For example, the profitability and forecast will need to take into account whether the lender retains the loans on their balance sheet (in which case spread income would be a more important factor) or sells the loans (in which case the income may be related to gains on sales, origination fees, and servicing fees).

Determining the startup's potential market can be challenging, specifically for companies focusing on innovative markets or presenting a revolutionary offering that may create a new market. In those situations, it is difficult to grasp the level of possible customer adoption or disruption that the startup may be able to achieve. As an example, estimating the potential market share for a bitcoin exchange can be difficult given the ability or inability to forecast customer adoption due to the newness of the market. However, even in these situations an analyst can triangulate the market potential by examining the total possible market size under different consumer adoption scenarios, analyzing certain trends of consumer adoption in other markets where bitcoin is more widely accepted, and examining whether the conditions within this particular market are ripe for greater levels of consumer adoption and market disruption.

Other FinTech companies may offer improvements upon existing procedures. For example, a FinTech company may focus on RegTech and develop a technology offering that assists traditional incumbents (e.g., banks) with their compliance burden. In this case, the market potential may be easier to estimate as one has some proxy for it such as the number of banks dealing with compliance issues and the possible revenue from selling the product.

Management Team

Given the limited financial and operating history and the uncertainty around the startup's ability to achieve projected financial results inherent in any early-stage company, qualitative factors such as the quality and experience of the management team are important. This is particularly true in FinTech companies where knowledge of the regulatory and competitive landscape is especially crucial. A management team that has significant financial services experience in a particular niche (payments, lending, banking, insurance, wealth management, etc.) can enhance its value compared to a team that only consists of highly technical founders/entrepreneurs with minimal or no experience in financial services.

Intellectual Property and Intangible Assets

Ownership and legal protection related to intellectual property and other intangible assets—such as an assembled workforce, key customer relationships, or strategic partnerships—can provide a significant competitive advantage over future or existing competitors and also provide greater revenue streams. Thus, a qualitative consideration of intellectual property and other intangible assets is important to the value of a startup enterprise and tends to be value-enhancing when in place, adequately documented, and demonstrated to potential investors. Valuing these items may help in a potential acquisition should the potential acquirer be a traditional financial incumbent who is subject to capital requirements. In Chapter 11, we discuss the considerations related to valuing intangible assets acquired in FinTech deals in greater detail.

Stages of Development

Startups often set certain milestones and track their progress in achieving those milestones. The meeting of milestones (or the lack thereof) can affect the valuation of a startup. The potential impact on valuation from achieving a milestone varies depending on the significance of the milestone. Significant milestones for FinTech companies can include completion of an initial round of financing, proof of concept, regulatory approval, attracting a significant partner, delivery of product/solution to customers, and/or profitability.

As each milestone is achieved, the level of risk/uncertainty around the startup decreases and value is created. Later-stage milestones often generate larger increases in value than earlier-stage milestones. Additionally, later-stage companies have greater certainty around the likelihood of potential exit events (such as M&A/IPO), which tends to provide tighter ranges for valuation.

When the valuation considers future funding rounds and the potential dilution from additional capital raises, a staged financing model is often prepared. An example of the output of this model is provided in Table 10.2. The potential timeline, milestones, and valuation insights can provide a planning

TABLE 10.2 Value Stages

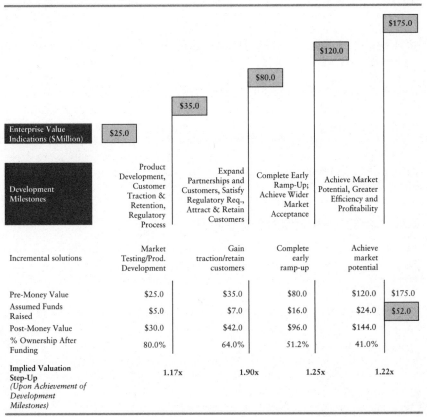

	Market Testing/Prod. Development	Gain traction/retain customers	Complete early ramp-up	Achieve market potential	
Incremental solutions					
Pre-Money Value	$25.0	$35.0	$80.0	$120.0	$175.0
Assumed Funds Raised	$5.0	$7.0	$16.0	$24.0	$52.0
Post-Money Value	$30.0	$42.0	$96.0	$144.0	
% Ownership After Funding	80.0%	64.0%	51.2%	41.0%	
Implied Valuation Step-Up *(Upon Achievement of Development Milestones)*	1.17x	1.90x	1.25x	1.22x	

roadmap for a FinTech company to follow and set expectations for future funding rounds.

Regulatory Overlay

An important consideration for valuing a FinTech company is its regulatory environment. Financial services companies (banks, insurance, asset managers, brokers, etc.) are heavily regulated relative to companies operating in other segments of the economy. The regulated nature of financial services is a double-edged sword. Regulations can make growth difficult for FinTech companies, impede the implementation of breakthrough technologies, and make the process of selling the company long and arduous. Alternatively, regulations can be an extremely valuable moat around a FinTech company that has successfully navigated its regulatory maze, protecting it and helping it thrive. Opportunities exist for the FinTech sector, but it takes careful consideration of the regulatory environment for FinTech investors and entrepreneurs.

For a FinTech company, assessing its regulatory environment and requirements can be challenging. FinTech companies are often at the forefront of innovation, which means rules are still taking shape. However, regulatory expectations and requirements can have a significant impact on value. If regulatory requirements are stringent and limit the ability of a company to offer its products or services, the cash flow forecast can be impacted and, thus, value as well. Furthermore, the instability of regulatory actions or requirements can significantly impact the firm's risk profile. For example, an alternative lender relying on emerging digital platforms and algorithms to develop a unique way to underwrite and originate loans faces a complex regulatory environment that is just beginning to examine this new technology.

Trade-Offs between Risk and Growth

Against this backdrop, we discuss the basics of valuing a FinTech company while acknowledging that each company is unique. The process tends to revolve around three primary valuation elements: earnings/cash flow, risk, and growth. The three primary valuation elements are more forward-looking; however, the past will often serve as a proxy for the company's future performance and market potential.

Significant trade-offs can exist among the three primary valuation elements (cash flow, risk, and growth), particularly for financial services companies whose financial performance is often more closely linked to the balance sheet and credit risk taken than other companies. As an example, an alternative lender's earnings, dividend-paying capacity, and growth can be enhanced in the short- to intermediate-term by taking more risk and making more loans while the impact of the decision (usually credit losses) may not be evident for several years. A well-reasoned, defensible valuation should consider the potential trade-offs and the implications of higher earnings and growth today versus potential issues in the future.

Regulatory requirements can also significantly impact the inherent risk of the company. Consequently, the cash flow forecast for a startup company must be assessed in light of the regulatory requirements that are in place or expected to be in place. This may require multiple forecasts based upon different regulatory scenarios.

Additionally, the ability of a FinTech company to scale may be limited by distinct regulatory requirements in different states or countries. In some places, for example, banks are limited in how much balance sheet growth they can achieve by capital requirements. Thus, regulatory requirements can have a significant impact on future cash flows that can be generated and earnings retention/dividend decisions.

Valuation Approaches

There are three general approaches to determining business value: asset, income, and market. Under each approach there are specific ways to determine value that are commonly referred to as valuation methods. Each of these approaches is typically considered and then weighted to provide an indicated value or range of value for the company and, ultimately, the specific interest or share class of the company.

The Asset Approach The asset approach determines the value of the subject business by examining the cost that would be incurred by the relevant party to reassemble the company's assets and liabilities. For startup technology companies, the asset approach is generally inappropriate as they are not typically (internally) capital-intensive businesses, although the asset approach can sometimes be relevant after recently completed funding rounds. What's more, the balance sheet can be remarkable if there are excess or non-operating assets or contingent liabilities that need to be considered apart from the value of the firm's ongoing operation.

The Market Approach The market approach determines the value of the subject company by utilizing valuation metrics from transactions in comparable companies or historical transactions in the subject company. For startups that have completed funding rounds, consideration of those valuation metrics can be important and provide meaningful valuation indications. Due to different rights and preferences associated with different share classes, though, indications of value from a recent funding round for a particular equity class—like preferred stock in a startup—may not be entirely comparable to another class, such as common stock. FinTech startups are often funded by a number of financing rounds and different classes of equity and this complicates the determination of enterprise value based solely on a given share value for one particular class. However, the share prices in these prior funding rounds can provide helpful valuation anchors from which to test the reasonableness of the updated valuation range.

Market data derived from publicly traded FinTech companies and FinTech acquisitions for which deal pricing and multiples are available can also serve as key valuation inputs. For example, pricing multiples and margins of more mature FinTech companies that have exited, or are publicly traded, can provide insights for potential exit values.

For early-stage companies, market metrics can provide valuable insight for potential valuations and financial performance of a FinTech company once it matures. For mature companies, recent financial performance can be directly compiled to serve as a valuable benchmarking tool. Potential investors can also discern how the market might value the private company based on pricing information from comparable public FinTech companies.

Table 10.3 provides detail related to valuation multiples and margin information for publicly traded FinTech companies at June 30, 2016.

An overview of pricing multiples for FinTech acquisitions through the first half of 2016 for which deal values and pricing information is available is presented in Table 10.4.

TABLE 10.3 Public Market Information: Multiples & Margins (as of June 30, 2016)

Segment	Price/ LTM EPS	Price/ 2016 (E) EPS	Price/ 2017 (E) EPS	Enterprise Value/ LTM EBITDA	Enterprise Value/ FY16 (E) EBITDA	Enterprise Value/ FY17 (E) EBITDA	Enterprise Value/ LTM Revenue	EBITDA Margin
FinTech— Payments	28.4	18.0	16.2	14.7	10.9	9.9	2.8	21.7%
FinTech— Solutions	36.5	24.6	21.8	16.6	12.4	11.3	3.4	21.1%
FinTech— Technology	39.6	27.4	23.3	16.9	13.2	12.1	3.9	13.8%

TABLE 10.4 Overview of FinTech M&A Activity (Comparisons)

	1H16	FY 15	FY 14
Deal Activity			
# of Deals	102	195	169
Total Reported Deal Value ($M)	$13,228.4	$49,057.9	$16,675.2
Median Reported Deal Value ($M)	$87.5	$73.5	$39.0
Median Pricing Metrics			
Deal Value/Revenue	2.11	3.56	2.72
Median Deal Value ($USD Million)			
Payments	229.0	67.5	40.8
Technology	71.2	35.0	48.1
Solutions	42.0	162.5	32.5

Source: S&P Global Market Intelligence

The Income Approach The income approach can also provide a meaningful indication of value for a FinTech company. It relies upon specific considerations for the business's expected cash flows, risk, and growth prospects relative to the market. The most common valuation method under the income approach for valuing early-stage FinTech companies is the discounted cash flow (DCF) method. The DCF method determines value based upon the present value of the expected cash flows for the enterprise.

Under the DCF method, the analyst develops a discrete projection of future revenues, expenses, and cash flow and discounts those back to the present at an appropriate discount rate. Key elements of the DCF method include:

- **Forecast of Expected Future Cash Flows.** The cash flow forecast should be for a discrete period, typically ranging from three to ten years, until the company can achieve a stable cash flow stream. The financial performance indication from assessing the market approach and analyzing the performance of publicly traded FinTech companies can provide valuable perspective as to potential growth rates and margins in the forecast.
- **Terminal Value.** The terminal value is the value of the company once mature and profitable and equals the value of all the cash flows beyond the immediate, discrete forecast period. The terminal value is typically determined by capitalizing cash flow (or some other performance metric) at the end of the forecast period. Capitalization methods for the terminal value vary from single-period capitalizations utilizing variations of the

Gordon Growth model (the Gordon Growth model is "used to determine the intrinsic value of a stock based on a future series of dividends that grow at a constant rate"[1]) to the application of current or projected market multiples derived from financial measures at the end of the forecast period.

■ **Discount Rate.** The discount rate is used to discount the forecasted cash flows to the present. Investors typically require or expect a return on the money that they invest in a particular company. Early-stage FinTech investors require higher returns than late-stage investors for myriad reasons, but most notably due to the higher risk associated with an early-stage company. Discount rates tend to decline over time for the FinTech company as it reaches certain milestones and the company matures. For example, an early-stage FinTech company that has developed a new FinTech product but is in stealth mode and has not started to generate revenue and service customers will likely receive a higher discount rate than a mature FinTech company that has been operating profitably for the last 20–30 years.

The sum of the present values of all the forecasted cash flows (both the discretely forecasted periods and the terminal value) provides the indication of value for a specific set of forecast assumptions. For startup FinTech companies, the cash flow forecasts are often characterized by a period of operating losses and capital needs early in the enterprise and then an expected payoff for distributions/repurchase as profitability improves or some exit event, such as an IPO or sale, occurs.

Synthesizing Valuation Indications and Reaching a Conclusion

Once determined, multiple valuation approaches are then considered to provide lenses through which to assess value and generate tests of reasonableness against which the different indications of value can be evaluated. It would be unusual for the indicated values from the various methodologies and approaches employed to align perfectly. Furthermore, value indications from the market approach can be volatile and investors in private companies think longer-term in our experience. Because valuation is more of a descriptive exercise than a prescriptive one, this is a perspective we often consider. The more enduring indications of value can often come from income approaches, such as DCF models, which are often more representative of the actual behavior of real-world buyers and sellers of interests in FinTech companies, particularly early-stage companies.

A Hypothetical Example of a Valuation of an Early-Stage FinTech Company

Let's look at a hypothetical example of valuing an early-stage FinTech company to provide additional perspective on the valuation process. Digital Advisory, a robo-advisory firm that began operations in 2014, offers digital wealth management services whereby the company leverages the use of technology to service client accounts and investments are largely selected by software and complex algorithms. Digital Advisory operated in stealth mode for its first six months while the company built its software/digital platform. Once unveiled to the public, Digital Advisory began gathering assets through digital advertising and content marketing. The company gathered approximately $100 million in assets in the first full year of operations before growing to $1 billion by mid-2016. Digital Advisory expects to continue growing and taking market share from traditional wealth managers and RIAs. Their five-year forecast shows them growing to over $10 billion in AUM within five years. Consistent with Digital Advisory's AUM growth, revenues and profitability were also forecasted to grow over the five-year period as demonstrated in Figure 10.2.

In order to test the reasonableness of this forecast, the market potential for the robo-advisory segment was examined. Estimates for the size of the robo-advisory segment vary but there are relevant data points for comparison. For example, Schwab estimated the automated investment advisory

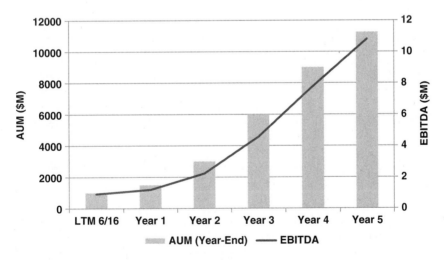

FIGURE 10.2 Digital Advisory's 5-Year Forecast

segment at $400 billion but Goldman noted that this might be conservative given the size of retail AUM in the United States of over $10 trillion.[2] Goldman also noted that PWC projected North America AUM to grow at a 5.1 percent compound annual growth rate from $34 trillion in 2012 to $49 trillion by 2020, which would serve as a tailwind for automated investment advisory.[3] Meanwhile, A.T. Kearney estimated the robo-advisory segment to be managing $2 trillion by 2020.[4]

While the amount of retail AUM that would switch to automated investment advisory is debatable, the potential market share for the segment is clearly quite large and there is evidence that some proportion of consumers are starting to prefer the existing robo-advisor platforms. For example, if one assumes that robo-advisory takes a 10 percent share of forecast retail AUM in the PWC study and reached that by 2020, then the robo-advisor segment would hold approximately $1.6 trillion of AUM ($12 trillion growing at 5.1% annually for 5 years times 10%), which is also relatively consistent with the A.T. Kearney forecast. Digital Advisory's projected AUM of $10 billion appears reasonable and potentially achievable in light of its historical growth and the market potential for the robo-advisory segment as it represents less than 1 percent of the $1.6 trillion projected market for robo-advisory in 2020.

Margins for publicly traded asset managers were also examined to assess the reasonableness of Digital Advisory's forecast. Digital Advisory's forecast EBITDA margin in Year 5 was 35 percent and appeared reasonable when compared to the publicly traded traditional asset managers whose median EBITDA margin was 38 percent in the trailing 12 months ended June 30, 2016.

After analyzing Digital Advisory's financial forecast and testing its reasonableness, the projections were utilized to develop an indication of value for Digital Advisory. Digital Advisory's value was determined as a function of the company's interim cash flows generated over the forecast period, as well as a terminal value (based upon Digital Advisory's forecasted cash flow times a capitalization factor).

Interim Cash Flows. The interim cash flows were estimated as a function of Digital Advisory's estimated profitability over the forecast period.

Terminal Value. The terminal value was estimated based upon Digital Advisory's free cash flow based upon a financial forecast at the end of the forecast period times a capitalization factor (i.e., multiple). The capitalization factor shown in Table 10.5. is based upon two factors: the required return estimated for Digital Advisory (the Weighted Average Cost of Capital shown below) minus their estimated growth.

TABLE 10.5 Terminal Value Calculation
($Millions)

2020 Free Cash Flow		6.1
Terminal Growth Rate		6.0%
Terminal Year Free Cash Flow		6.4
WACC	17.5%	
– Terminal Growth Rate	–6.0%	
Terminal Capitalization Rate	11.5%	
Terminal Capitalization Factor		8.70
Terminal Value		56.0
Discounting Periods		4.5
Discount Factor	18%	0.484
Present Value of Terminal Value		**$ 27.12**

TABLE 10.6 Test of Reasonableness for Terminal Value

2020 EBITDA	10.81
Implied Terminal Value/Terminal EBITDA	5.19
2020 AUM	11,250
Implied Terminal Value/2020 AUM	0.50%

Since data on privately held FinTech companies is often limited, terminal value multiples can often be compared to multiples of publicly traded FinTech companies in similar niches to test their reasonableness. The median valuation multiples for publicly traded traditional asset managers was 1.6 percent of AUM and 11.8× EBITDA at June 30, 2016, which were both above the implied terminal value multiples for Digital Advisory but appear reasonable given Digital's lower fee schedule relative to traditional advisors. (See Table 10.6.)

The valuation of Digital Advisory equals the sum of the interim cash flows and the terminal value discounted to the present at an appropriate discount rate. Digital Advisory's estimated enterprise value was $35 million. Digital Advisory's valuation as a percentage of current AUM was 3.5 percent, which appeared reasonable given Digital Advisory's expected growth rate and the terminal value as a percentage of terminal AUM at 1.50 percent, which also reflects the lower realized fees as a percentage of AUM for Digital Advisory compared to the realized fees for the broader asset management industry. (See Table 10.7.)

TABLE 10.7   Valuation Conclusion for Digital Advisory ($Millions)

			Projected			
		Year 1	Year 2	Year 3	Year 4	Year 5
Free Cash Flow to Firm		0.1	0.8	2.2	4.2	6.1
Discounting Periods		0.5	1.5	2.5	3.5	4.5
Discount Factor	17.5%	0.9225	0.7851	0.6682	0.5687	0.4840
Present Value of Cash Flow		0.11	0.60	1.47	2.39	2.94
Present Value of Discrete Cash Flows		7.51				
+ Present Value of Terminal Value		27.12				
Total Capital Value		34.64				
– Total Interest Bearing Debt		0				
Indicated Equity Value		34.64				
Indicated Value: DCF Method		$35.00				

WHAT ABOUT PREFERENCES AND FINTECH VALUATIONS?

We noted previously in this book and in other venues that the headline valuation number in a private fundraising round is often not the real value for the company.[5] Rather, the price per share in the most recent private round reflects all of the rights and economic attributes of the share class. These rights and economic attributes are commonly not the same for all shareholders, particularly investors in earlier fundraising rounds. As Travis Harms, a colleague at Mercer Capital, notes: "It's like applying the pound price for filet mignon to the entire cow—you can't do that because the cow includes a lot of other stuff that is not in the filet."[6]

While a full discussion of investor preferences and ratchets is beyond the scope of this chapter, they are fairly common in venture-backed companies and thus the valuation dilemma is fairly common. Recent studies by Fenwick & West on unicorn fundraisings noted that the vast majority offered investors some kind of liquidation preference.[7]

Beyond presenting implications for valuation of the various share classes, the combination of investor preferences and a decline in pricing relative to prior funding rounds can often result in pricing declines being felt asymmetrically across the capital structure and result in a misalignment of incentives. John McFarlane, Sonos CEO, noted this misalignment when he stated: "If you're all aligned, then no matter what happens, you're in the same boat.... The really high valuation companies right now are giving out preferences—that's not alignment."

A real-world example of this misalignment and the potential valuation implications was reported in a *New York Times* story in late 2015 regarding Good Technology, a unicorn that ended up selling to BlackBerry for approximately $425 million in September 2015. While a $425 million exit might be considered a success for a number of founders/investors, the transaction price was less than half of Good's purported $1.1 billion valuation in a private round.[8] The article noted that while a number of investors had preferences associated with their shares that softened the extent of the pricing decline, many employees did not. "For some employees, it meant that their shares were practically worthless. Even worse, they had paid taxes on the stock based on the higher value."[9]

As the Good story illustrates, the valuation process can be challenging for venture-backed companies, particularly those with several different share classes and preferences across the capital structure and these valuations can have very real consequences for stakeholders, particularly employees. Thus, it is important to have valuation processes and procedures in place in order to demonstrate compliance with tax and financial reporting regulations when having valuations performed. Certainly, the prospects for scrutiny from auditors, SEC, and/or the IRS are possible but very real tax issues can also result around equity compensation for employees.

Given the complexities in valuing venture-backed companies and the ability for market/investor sentiment to shift quickly, it is important to have a valuation professional who can adequately assess the value of the company, and understand the attributes of each share class as well as the market trends prevalent in the industry. The valuation professional should attempt to gain a thorough understanding of the economics of the most recent funding round to provide a market-based anchor for valuation at a subsequent date. Once the model is calibrated, the valuation professional can then assess what changes have occurred (both in the market and at the subject company) since the last funding round to determine what impact if any that may have on valuation.

SPECIAL ISSUES: VALUATIONS FOR OTHER STAKEHOLDERS

As noted earlier in this chapter, two other common reasons why an early-stage FinTech company will need to have an external valuation performed are for equity compensation related to employee ownerships and for financial statement reporting purposes for early-stage investors such as venture capital funds, banks, and/or private equity. We discuss both of these topics in greater detail in this section. First, we discuss issues specific to valuations for employee ownership and then we discuss valuation issues for early-stage investors. While potentially relevant for a number of different players in FinTech, these discussions should be particularly useful for both bankers, who potentially invest in or form subsidiary companies focused on FinTech, and entrepreneurs, who have stakeholders such as employees with equity compensation and investors that have unique valuation issues.

Equity Incentives

Many technology companies provide equity compensation to their employees so they can share in the benefits of rising stock prices. There are several types of equity incentive instruments to consider. We discuss a few in greater detail, although we note that the list is not all-inclusive. The equity incentive instrument that can be the most beneficial for a particular FinTech company and its employees will vary depending upon the specific situation.

The following discussion relates to potential incentive, tax, and dilution implications for both the issuer and the holder for three types of equity incentive instruments. Given their complexity, we strongly urge you to obtain competent legal and tax advice before implementing any of the following plans.

Stock Options   The holder of a stock option has the ability to purchase a specific number of shares at some point in the future at the strike price (a predetermined price). Typically, options have a vesting period that allows the holder to purchase shares in a particular time period and an expiration date. For example, an option holder may have the option to purchase 1,000 shares at $10.00 per share over a four-year period and the options are subject to a vesting schedule whereby up to 250 shares vest each year. If the option holder doesn't exercise the option, then the options expire.

Options can be granted in two forms:

1. **Nonqualified Options.** This is the simpler option type as it allows the holder to pay income tax on the difference between the value of the stock and the strike price at the date they are exercised. The company receives a corresponding tax deduction upon exercise.
2. **Incentive Stock Options (ISOs).** ISOs allow the holder to defer taxation.

Restricted Stock   Restricted stock is an outright grant of shares that are typically restricted for a period of time (perhaps on sale or transfer). The stock typically vests in stages and is treated as compensation upon vesting. Advantages related to restricted stock include eligibility for dividends, no cash payment requirement for the shares by employees, the ability for the holder to vote, the ability to provide some value even if the FinTech company's stock price drops, and the ability to offer less dilution as it typically requires fewer shares to be granted for the same level of compensation.

Stock Appreciation Rights Stock appreciation rights (SARs) provide the holder with the appreciation in value of the underlying stock from when they were granted until they are exercised. SARs can provide certain benefits, including the holder is not required to pay a strike price to acquire the security, employee benefits are provided to companies with shareholder restrictions, such as S corporations, and limited ownership dilution as the appreciation is typically settled in cash rather than shares. Benefits to SARs holders are taxed upon exercise as ordinary income.

Tax Issues Related to Equity Compensation

It can be very important for private companies—especially those that are sponsored by private equity, banks, and/or venture capital funds—to have a strong valuation process. As the size of the company as well as the size of the grants to employees increase, one can expect the level of potential scrutiny related to equity compensation grants to increase. Additionally, as the capital structure of the company becomes more complex, this can increase the valuation challenges and level of difficulty in demonstrating compliance with tax and financial reporting regulations. However, management can minimize total compliance costs by having the valuation procedures appropriate to the situation correct the first time.

409A Compliance The potential for scrutiny related to 409A compliance can come from many sources, including auditors, the SEC, and the IRS. Additionally, Section 409A compliance is also important when considering mergers and acquisitions. For example, buyers need to ensure that the target company is in compliance with 409A so that they do not encounter hidden costs that might transfer to them upon the closing of the transaction. Examples of potential costs and issues that might arise for the buyer include liability for the target's failure to pay the appropriate tax obligations, breach of contract claims, and gross-up payments due to executives from excise taxes. For the seller, it is important to demonstrate to the buyer that your company has been in compliance with Section 409A such that the buyer does not adjust the potential purchase price downward and/or does not consider the acquisition due to concerns about potential costs and exposure related to 409A compliance.

For all of these reasons, it is important for companies to develop a quality valuation process related to equity compensation grants so that compliance with Section 409A is achieved. The rules are very complex, but they can be navigated such that the outcomes of the compensation program are achieved and shareholder and employee interests are appropriately aligned through a well-designed plan.

Given the importance of Section 409A compliance, and valuation procedures within that context, let's cover a few basics that you will want to know about Section 409A.[10]

- **When does Section 409A apply to my company?** Section 409A applies to those companies offering nonqualified deferred compensation, an arrangement whereby an employee receives compensation in a later tax year than that in which the compensation was earned. Two common forms of incentive compensation in private companies, a stock option or stock appreciation right, can potentially be within the scope of Section 409A. For example, a stock option or SAR that is issued "in the money" could be subject to Section 409A since the value of the shares granted exceeds the strike price of the option. Therefore, in order to avoid being subject to Section 409A, the employer needs to demonstrate that the stock options and SARs are issued "at the money" (the strike price is equal to the fair market value of the shares) or "out of the money" (the strike price is greater than the fair market value of the shares granted).
- **What are the consequences of Section 409A?** Should the stock options or SARs granted to employees be subject to Section 409A, then employers are responsible for normal withholding and reporting obligations with respect to the amount that should be included in the employee's gross income under Section 409A. Amounts includible within the employee's gross income are also subject to income tax equal to 20 percent of the compensation that should be included in gross income and also interest on prior underpayments. The tax levied related to Section 409A can be difficult for the employees that received the options since no cash has typically been received that could be used to pay the tax absent an exercise of the option and sale of the underlying stock. For these reasons, most companies attempt to structure their equity compensation plans such that the stock options and SARs qualify for exemption under Section 409A by setting the strike price of the stock option or SAR at grant date below the stock's fair market value. In order to structure their equity compensation grants appropriately, companies need to determine the fair market value of their stock to assist with determining the appropriate strike price for options and SARs.
- **How does one determine the fair market value of the stock?** Against this backdrop, we typically encourage clients to have an independent appraisal performed by an individual or firm that has an educational

background in finance and valuation, significant experience both in the company's industry as well as in preparing independent valuations/ appraisals, and relevant professional credentials (ASA, ABV, CBA, CVA, or CFA). For FinTech companies, we also note the importance of hiring a valuation professional or firm that has significant experience in the financial services and technology industry so that the valuation appropriately reflects and considers the unique nature of FinTech companies and the industry and regulatory environment in which they operate.

The IRS regulations note that "fair market value may be determined through the reasonable application of a reasonable valuation method" and goes on to state that if a method is applied reasonably and consistently, such valuations will be presumed to represent fair market value, unless shown to be grossly unreasonable. While fair market value is not defined specifically in Section 409A, it is defined in IRS Revenue Ruling 59-60 as "the price at which the property would change hands between a willing buyer and a willing seller when the former is not under any compulsion to buy and the latter is not under any compulsion to sell, both parties having reasonable knowledge of the relevant facts."[11]

Based on these instructions, one can presume that a reasonable valuation considers many of the factors noted previously in this chapter as well as the asset, market, and income approaches to derive a value for the enterprise and then also considers the specific control and liquidity characteristics of the subject interest in that enterprise.

Early-Stage Investors

As the number of FinTech venture capital (VC) investments is growing, VC fund valuation practices are coming under greater scrutiny from VC investors (limited partners). VC investments also generally need to conform to accounting standards (U.S. GAAP or IFRS) in order to provide useful information to investors and withstand auditor scrutiny. Lastly, valuing VC investments can be difficult due to their illiquid nature and FinTech VC investments can be particularly challenging due to the wide variety of FinTech niches (payments, technology solution providers, crowdfunding, P2P lenders, etc.).

Against this backdrop, it is useful to examine how to value venture capital portfolio investments. While key fundamental valuation drivers such as profitability, growth prospects, and risks vary among FinTech niches, the process undertaken by an independent valuation firm should be robust and provide comfort to all interested parties (investors, fund managers, and auditors).

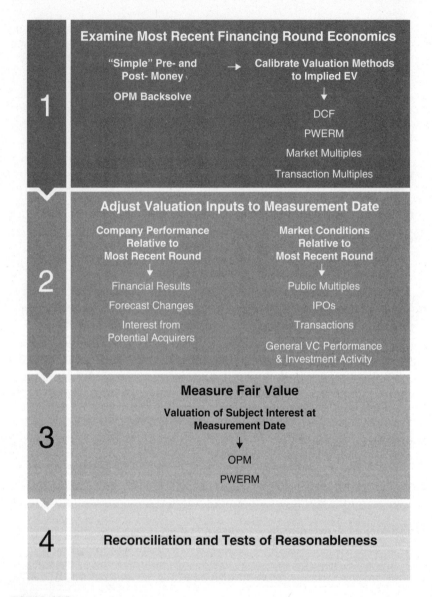

FIGURE 10.3   Process to Value FinTech VC Investments
Source: Mercer Capital

Figure 10.3 outlines our process when providing periodic fair value marks for venture capital fund investments in pre-public companies.[12]

1. **Examine the most recent financing round economics.** The transaction underlying the initiation of an investment position can provide three critical pieces of information from a valuation perspective:

- Size of the aggregate investment and per share price
- Rights and protections accorded to the newest round of securities
- Usually, but not always, an indication of the underlying enterprise value from the investor's perspective

Deal terms commonly reported in the press focus on the size of the aggregate investment and per-share price. The term *valuation* is usually a headline-shorthand for implied pre- or post-money value that assumes all equity securities in the company's capital structure have identical rights and protections. While elegant, this approach glosses over the fact that for pre-public companies, securities with differing rights and protections should and do command different prices.

The option pricing method (OPM) is an alternative that explicitly models the rights of each equity class and makes generalized assumptions about the future trajectory of the company to deduce values for the various securities. Valuation specialists can also use the probability-weighted expected return method (PWERM) to evaluate potential proceeds from, and the likelihood of, several exit scenarios for a company. Total proceeds from each scenario would then be allocated to the various classes of equity based on their relative rights. The use of PWERM is particularly viable if there is sufficient visibility into the future exit prospects for the company.

The economics of the most recent financing round helps calibrate inputs used in both the OPM and PWERM.

- Under the OPM, a backsolve procedure provides indications of total equity and enterprise value based on the pricing and terms of the most recent financing round. The indicated enterprise value and a set of future cash flow projections, taken together, imply a rate of return (discount rate) that may be reasonable for the company. Multiples implied by the indicated enterprise value, juxtaposed with information from publicly traded companies or related transactions, can yield valuation-useful inferences.
- Under the PWERM, in addition to informing discount rates and providing comparisons with market multiples, the most recent financing round can inform the relative likelihood of the various exit scenarios.

In addition to the quantitative inputs enumerated above, discussions and documentation around the recent financing round can provide critical qualitative information, as well.

2. **Adjust valuation inputs at measurement date.** Between a funding round and subsequent measurement dates, the performance of the company and changes in market conditions can provide context for any adjustments that may be warranted for the valuation inputs. Deterioration in actual financial performance may warrant revisiting projected cash flows while improvements in market multiples for similar companies

may suggest better pricing could be available at exit. Interest from potential acquirers (or withdrawal of prior interest) and general IPO trends can inform inputs related to the relative likelihood of the various exit scenarios.

3. **Measure fair value.** Measuring fair value of the subject security entails using the OPM and PWERM, as appropriate and viable, in conjunction with valuation inputs that are relevant at the measurement date. ASC 820 defines fair value as, "The price that would be received to sell an asset or paid to transfer a liability in an orderly transaction between market participants at the measurement date."[13]

4. **Reconciliation and tests of reasonableness.** A sanity check to scrutinize fair value outputs is an important element of the measurement process. Specifically, as it relates to venture capital investments in pre-public companies, such a check would reconcile a fair value indication at the current measurement date with a mark from the prior period in light of both changes in the subject company and changes in market conditions.

The probability-weighted expected return method determines the value of a company by evaluating potential proceeds from, and the likelihood of, several exit scenarios for a company. Total proceeds from each scenario would then be allocated to the various classes of equity based on their relative rights. The use of PWERM is particularly viable if there is sufficient visibility into the future exit prospects for the company.

In using the PWERM to value a company, the first step is to consider the possible outcomes for the company. For most venture capital and/or private equity–backed companies, there are four main potential outcomes for the business: IPO, strategic sale, liquidation value, and a downside scenario where the company underperforms the initial business plan and achieves an outcome that is below the first two scenarios (IPO and/or strategic sale).

Once the scenarios are identified, the company is valued under each scenario. When determining the assumptions for a PWERM analysis, it is important to consider the valuation assumptions relative to the company's lifecycle, market trends, industry outlook, economic cycle, and other factors as well. Then, the key variables to consider are:

- The probability of achieving each scenario.
- The time period necessary to achieve each scenario. The timing of the events will vary, with a downside scenario or liquidation often likely to occur more quickly than a strategic sale or IPO.
- Expectations of future capital needs in order to consider future dilution to existing shareholders from future capital raises.

A Hypothetical Example of the Valuation of a FinTech Venture Capital Investment

Let's assume we are valuing a venture capital investment made by Cypress Capital (a FinTech venture capital firm) in Digital Advisory (a robo-advisory firm we discussed earlier in this chapter). Cypress Capital hires FinTech Valuation Company to perform the valuation and they use a PWERM analysis in the following manner. First, they develop the following scenarios and estimated exit values for Digital Advisory in each scenario as shown in Table 10.8 (Scenario 1—IPO; Scenario 2—Strategic Sale; Scenario 3—Downside Case; and Scenario 4—Liquidation).

TABLE 10.8 Scenarios for PWERM Analysis ($000)

Scenario #1: IPO			
Expected Time Until Event (Years)	5		
	Revenue	**EBITDA**	**AUM**
Forward Perf. Measures	$31,000	$11,000	$10,000,000
times: Selected Multiples	3.0	10.0	1.15%
Estimated Values—IPO	$93,000	$110,000	$115,000
Weights Applied	33.33%	33.33%	33.33%
Estimated Exit Value (IPO)	$106,000		
Scenario #2: Strategic Sale			
Expected Time Until Event (Years)	5		
	Revenue	**EBITDA**	**AUM**
Forward Perf. Measures	$31,000	$11,000	$10,000,000
times: Selected Multiples	3.8	12.5	1.44%
Estimated Values—Sale	$116,250	$137,500	$143,750
Weights Applied	33.33%	33.33%	33.33%
Estimated Exit Value (Sale)	$133,000		
Scenario #3: Downside Case			
Expected Time Until Event (Years)	5		
Est. Strategic Sale Value	$133,000		
times: Selected Multiple	0.5		
Estimated Value—Downside Case	$66,500		
Weight Applied	100.00%		
Estimated Value (Downside)	$67,000		
Scenario #4: Liquidation/Dissolution			
Expected Time Until Event (Years)	3		
Cumulative Invested Capital	$20,000		
times: Est. Recovery Multiple	50.00%		
Estimated Value (Liquidation/ Dissolution)	$10,000		

TABLE 10.9 Synthesizing the PWERM Analysis ($000)

Scenario Description	Scenario 1 IPO	Scenario 2 Strategic Sale	Scenario 3 Downside Case	Scenario 4 Liquidation/Dissolution
Exit Enterprise Value	$106,000	$133,000	$67,000	$10,000
Scenario Weight	25.0%	25.0%	25.0%	25.0%
Implied Enterprise Value Analysis				
Expected Dilution	0.00%	0.00%	0.00%	0.00%
Ent. Value Attributable to Existing Capital Prov.	$106,000	$133,000	$67,000	$10,000
Discount Periods	5	5	5	3
Indicated Enterprise Value	$26,000	*Rounded*		

Synthesizing the Analysis and Reaching a Conclusion The concluded value of Digital Advisory is $26 million (see Table 10.9) based on the discounted present value of the estimated enterprise value at the end (i.e., exit) of each scenario multiplied by the probability of achieving each scenario.

CONCLUSION

Valuation issues are increasingly important for FinTech companies, particularly early-stage companies. While the simplicity of a rule-of-thumb valuation is appealing, valuation can be a complex exercise that has real-world implications for investors and employee shareholders. Furthermore, the potential scrutiny of the IRS, the SEC, auditors, and investors—combined with the potential liability associated with poorly constructed valuations—make it critical that value be determined and articulated in a reasonable manner.

The process of having a valuation performed can also be valuable for both management and directors. The knowledge gleaned from the valuation process provides insights and identifies key risk and growth opportunities that can improve the company's strategic planning process. That strategic planning process might build to a successful liquidity event in the form of a sale or IPO or the development of a stable company that can operate independently for a long time. Thus, both FinTech entrepreneurs and their potential venture and bank investors need to have a keen understanding of valuation issues so that they can comply with and respond to potential scrutiny of their valuations, build value in their FinTech companies by improving one of the three key valuation elements (improving cash flow, lowering risk, and/or enhancing growth), prepare for a potential exit through a sale or IPO, and measure value creation over time to ensure that they are achieving adequate returns on their efforts.

NOTES

1. Gordon Growth Model, *Investopedia: Terms,* http://www.investopedia.com/terms/g/gordongrowthmodel.asp.
2. "The Future of Finance Part 3," *Goldman Sachs Report,* March 13, 2015.
3. PWC Press Release, February 10, 2014.
4. Insights from the A.T. Kearney 2015 Robo-Advisory Services Study: "Hype vs. Reality: The Coming Waves of Robo Adoption," June 2015.
5. Travis W. Harms, "Unicorn Valuations: What's Obvious Isn't Real, and What's Real Isn't Obvious," *Mercer Capital's Financial Reporting Blog,* September 11, 2015, http://mercercapital.com/financialreportingblog/unicorn-valuations-whats-obvious-isnt-real-and-whats-real-isnt-obvious/.

6. Sujan Rajbhandary, "A Few Thoughts on Valuing Investments in Startups: An Interview with Travis Harms," *Mercer Capital's Financial Reporting Blog*, November 6, 2015, http://mercercapital.com/financialreportingblog/a-few-thoughts-on-valuing-investments-in-startups-an-interview-with-travis-harms/.

7. Barry J. Kramer, Khang Tran, and Nicole Harper, "The Terms Behind Unicorn Valuations: As of December 31, 2015," *Fenwick & West*, February 10, 2016, https://www.fenwick.com/publications/pages/the-terms-behind-the-unicorn-valuations-as-of-december-31-2015.aspx.

8. Katie Benner, "When a Unicorn Start-Up Stumbles, Its Employees Get Hurt," *New York Times*, December 23, 2015, http://www.nytimes.com/2015/12/27/technology/when-a-unicorn-startup-stumbles-its-employees-get-hurt.html?_r=0.

9. Ibid.

10. The material in this section was adapted with permission from "8 Things You Should Know About Section 409A," by Travis W. Harms, CFA, CPA/ABV, *Mercer Capital's Financial Reporting Blog*, July 10, 2015.

11. American Society of Appraisers, *ASA Business Valuation Standards©* (revision published November 2009), "Definitions," p. 25.

12. The material in this section was adapted with permission from "How to Value Venture Capital Portfolio Investments," by Sujan Rajbhandary, CFA, *Mercer Capital's Financial Reporting Blog*, May 8, 2015.

13. ASC 820-10-20 (formerly SFAS 157, paragraph 5).

CHAPTER 11

Acquiring a FinTech Company

INTRODUCTION

An acquisition of a FinTech company by a bank may be more beneficial than a partnership between the two. Acquisition allows the acquirer to fully integrate the FinTech innovation into its business model and also to fully control the relationship with the customer. The acquirer also has control over the strategic direction of the technology and whether the technology will be offered to competitors.

There are, however, downsides for community banks to an acquisition strategy compared to a partnership strategy. First, acquisitions can be very expensive, particularly when compared to a partnership. There is also the potential for significant valuation differentials between banks and FinTech companies. Thus, bank acquirers have to be significantly capitalized and funded to execute the transaction. This is a key reason why most FinTech acquisitions to date have been undertaken by larger financial services providers who have more capital and resources.

Additionally, there are other acquisition challenges for banks, including the following:

- **Goodwill Creation.** Acquisitions of FinTech companies tend to create more goodwill than acquisitions of other banking entities. For example, over 90 percent of the purchase price is often accounted for as goodwill in acquisitions of FinTech companies. This is significantly higher than traditional bank acquisitions. This is important to bankers because it creates greater dilution of book value and reduces capital ratios, which are important to regulators, managers, and stakeholders. Book value dilution and earn-back periods are often proxies that bankers and investors look at when measuring value creation and examining the potential success of a bank acquirer's acquisition. Lastly, capital levels are important to banks as they serve as a cushion for the bank in the event of weak performance. In addition, the regulatory emphasis on capital ratios tends to serve as a governor on the amount of balance sheet growth that the bank can achieve. The potential for greater book value dilution for FinTech deals can be a difficult pill to swallow.

■ **Cultural Differences.** Cultural differences are always a consideration in any acquisition; however, they can be especially acute when attempting to combine the culture of an early-stage, high-growth FinTech company with a mature, traditional bank. Cultural differences can be most profound around risk and compliance. A traditional financial institution is a regulated entity. FinTech companies are often managed and controlled by their founders, who possess an entrepreneurial mindset. This entrepreneurial mindset can be a great benefit to the traditional financial institution eventually. In the interim, differences can arise because FinTech companies are often hyper-focused on growth and customer acquisition, whereas banks are often focused on compliance and mitigating risk. For example, banks know extremely well the trade-off between risk and growth. Most banks could increase the number of loans made in the next few quarters by loosening their underwriting standards, but this could negatively influence the bank's returns in later years when credit issues surface. Many of the banks that failed during and after the financial crises were the community banks that had the highest growth and performance metrics in the years prior to the crisis.

■ **Value Gaps.** An issue that often arises when a bank is considering the acquisition of a FinTech company is how to manage the valuation differential between the two entities. As noted in prior chapters, valuation is primarily related to three variables: cash flow, risk, and growth. While these key valuation variables are the same for both FinTech companies and traditional banks, the resulting multiples can be remarkably different and often result in FinTech companies priced at a significant premium to traditional banks.

For example, a mature traditional incumbent bank may have a history of generating cash flow at a 10 percent return on equity, risk comparable to the majority of other similarly sized public banks, and growth potential consistent with a mature company. A high-growth FinTech company may have minimal profitability today as profit margins on core products are offset by expenses to grow staff and scale in order to capture more market share. Risk is still perceived high as the FinTech company has only been in operation for 5 years and the product has not been tested at scale during a full credit/economic cycle. The FinTech company also has high growth potential because only 1 percent of a potential trillion-dollar market is captured thus far.

The FinTech company's stock is priced at a valuation multiple of around 100× historical earnings, 50× next year's earnings, and 20× two-years' forward earnings while the traditional community bank is priced at 15× trailing 12 months' earnings, 14× next year's earnings, and 13× two-years' forward earnings. This differential in valuation multiples can be a difficult obstacle in structuring a transaction, particularly if the acquirer is offering stock as part of the consideration to be paid to the seller.

- **Traditional Deal Metrics for Bank Deals Do Not Fit.** Certain traditional metrics utilized to analyze deals between traditional financial service providers do not fit as well in FinTech acquisitions. FinTech companies have less asset- and capital-intensive balance sheets. Thus acquisitions are priced at significant premiums to book value and often result in significant tangible book value dilution initially. While expense savings and potential efficiencies drive traditional financial services acquisitions, FinTech acquisitions are often driven by growth and revenue enhancements.

For those bankers considering an acquisition, this chapter explores the unique considerations of acquiring a FinTech company in light of the challenges discussed.

RECENT TRENDS IN FINTECH M&A ACTIVITY

Since mid-1993, there have been approximately 2,300 FinTech transactions with an average of approximately 100 transactions annually. The pace of FinTech deal activity has increased recently with approximately 200 transactions in 2015 and 180 transactions in 2014. Similar to the uptick in deal activity, deal values and pricing appear to be rising with the median deal value for transactions announced since 2010 being approximately $40 million compared to a median of approximately $30 million on all FinTech deals since the early 1990s. While these represent averages across a wide variety of deals and only a fraction of the deals have reported pricing information available, these median deal values can be informative to potential investors, partners, and entrepreneurs as they consider frames of reference for potential exit values for their companies and investments.

As detailed in Figure 11.1, 2015 represented a near-term high for FinTech M&A volume and pricing with 195 announced deals and a median deal value of $74 million. Transaction pricing multiples are often limited for transactions within the sector and thus meaningful pricing multiples and deal terms are difficult to find.

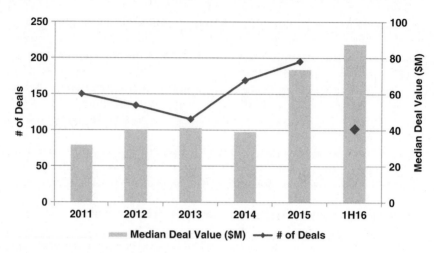

FIGURE 11.1 FinTech M&A Overview 2011–2016
Source: S&P Global Market Intelligence

The Largest FinTech Exits of All Time

Table 11.1 provides the top-10 largest acquisitions of FinTech companies located in the United States.

There are several interesting takeaways from this list of some of the largest FinTech transactions. First, the transactions involve target FinTech companies that are widely dispersed across different FinTech niches. Second, 5 of the 10 transactions occurred after the onset of the financial crisis, which is unusual within the financial services industry where we have seen a pullback in larger deals since the crisis. Third, the composition of the acquirers is notable in that none of the acquirers are traditional banks, which lends credence to the notion that it is difficult for banks to structure a transaction with some of the largest, most highly valued FinTech companies. Additionally, only three deals involved traditional financial institutions as acquirers—an insurance broker (Willis Group/Towers MOE), an asset manager (KKR/First Data), and a broker-dealer (ICE/Interactive Data). This might imply that the largest FinTech companies may face difficulty being acquired by traditional financial services companies. It is interesting that several involved nonfinancial acquirers like Hewlett Packard, Xerox, and so on. One notable FinTech acquisition that did not quite make our top-10 list, but that also provides an example of a nonfinancial acquirer, is EBay's acquisition of PayPal in the late 1990s. One might expect the trend of minimal bank acquisitions to change over time as more traditional financial institutions take notice and more creative deal structures are considered.

TABLE 11.1 Top-Ten FinTech M&A Exits

Buyer Name/ Target Name	Announce Date	Deal Value $M (Reported)	Deal Value, Incl. Debt Assump. $M (Reported)	Target Niche	Target Description
Kohlberg Kravis Roberts & Co./First Data Corporation	4/1/2007	26,264	28,781	Payment Processors	First Data Corp. provides electronic commerce and payment solutions including merchant transaction processing services for businesses
Hewlett-Packard Company/Electronic Data Systems Corporation	5/13/2008	12,578	13,272	Outsourcing	Information technology equipment and services company
Solar Capital Corp./SunGard Data Systems Inc.	3/27/2005	11,043	11,597	Investments Technology	Provider software and services to education, financial services, and public sector organizations
Quintiles Transnational Holdings Inc./IMS Health Holdings Inc.	5/3/2016	9,002	13,539	Insurance/ Healthcare Solutions	Merger of equals; Quintiles is a provider of support services for pharmaceutical, biotech, and medical companies and individuals while IMS Health Holdings is a leading provider of information and technology services to clients in the healthcare industry
Willis Group Holdings Public Limited Company/ Towers Watson & Co.	6/30/2015	8,647	8,829	Outsourcing	Merger of equals; Towers Watson is a global professional services company that helps organizations improve performance through effective people, risk and financial management.

(continued)

189

TABLE 11.1 (*Continued*)

Buyer Name/ Target Name	Announce Date	Deal Value $M (Reported)	Deal Value, Incl. Debt Assump. $M (Reported)	Target Niche	Target Description
First Data Corporation/ Concord EFS Inc.	4/1/2003	7,533	NA	Payment Processors	An electronics transaction processor and parent to Memphis, TN–based Concord EFS National Bank
Xerox Corporation/ Affiliated Computer Services Inc.	9/28/2009	6,714	9,044	Outsourcing	Provides process outsourcing support in areas that include finance, human resources, information technology, transaction processing, and customer care
SAP AG/Sybase Inc.	5/12/2010	5,923	NA	Banking Technology	Provides enterprise and mobile software solutions for information management, development, and integration worldwide
Investor group/Ceridian Corporation	5/30/2007	5,318	NA	Payroll & Administrative Solutions	Provides human resource and payroll processing solutions, including payroll, benefits administration, tax compliance and payment processing; the company also provides payment processing and issues credit cards, debit cards and stored value cards
Intercontinental Exchange Inc./ Interactive Data Holdings Corporation	10/26/2015	5,265	5,265	Financial Media & Content	Provider of financial market data, analytics, and related trading solutions

TABLE 11.2 Acquisitions of FinTech Companies (1/1/2005–6/30/2016)

	Traditional Financial Institutions Buying FinTechs			Others Buying FinTechs	
	Banks	Insurers	Money Managers	Online Brokers	FinTech Cos.
Number of Deals	153	205	179	2	1,222
Median Deal Value ($M)	$41	$25	$39	$349	$25
Trans Value/ Revenue	1.5	1.9	2.8	NA	2.2
Trans Value/EBITDA	8.0	8.6	9.3	NA	13.4
Goodwill as % of Deal Value	99.5%	96.8%	100.0%	95.3%	98.2%

Source: S&P Global Market Intelligence

Who Acquires FinTech Companies?

As detailed in Table 11.2, there have been approximately 540 acquisitions of FinTech companies by traditional financial institutions in the United States. Acquisitions by traditional financial institutions represented approximately one-third of total FinTech acquisitions in the last 10 years. Traditional financial institutions (banks, insurers, and money managers) are acquiring FinTechs at a lower rate than other companies. Approximately two-thirds of FinTech companies were acquired by nonfinancial companies (including other FinTech companies). Traditional financial institutions also tend to pay a lower multiple than traditional FinTech companies.

Within the traditional financial institution segments, insurers were the entity most likely to acquire a FinTech company while banks had the lowest number of acquisitions. Those FinTech companies acquired by banks to date have typically been the largest financial institutions acquiring smaller FinTech companies.

Of those transactions where traditional financial institutions acquired FinTech companies, only 15 had reported deal values greater than $1 billion. There were five FinTech companies acquired by banks where the purchase price was greater than $1 billion; three of those deals were in the payments niche and two in the investments technology niche. The median deal value to revenue multiple was 2.3× for those five largest FinTech deals where a bank was an acquirer. The acquirers in the majority of those larger FinTech deals were some of the largest publicly traded banks in the nation (Bank of America, Citigroup, Bank of New York Mellon, and U.S. Bancorp).

TABLE 11.3   Acquisitions of Traditional Banks by FinTech Companies (1/1/2005–6/30/2016)

	FinTechs Buying Traditional Financial Institutions			
	Banks	Insurers	Money Managers	Specialty Finance
Number of Deals	3	47	47	11
Median Deal Value ($M)	$11	$11	$12	$56
Goodwill as % of Deal Value	46.9%	92.7%	95.3%	0.0%

Source: S&P Global Market Intelligence

How Often Have FinTech Companies Acquired Traditional Financial Institutions?

FinTech companies acquiring traditional financial institutions (like banks, insurance, wealth managers) were much rarer and generally smaller transactions. Of the transactions where FinTech companies acquired traditional financial institutions, there were no acquisitions where the deal value was greater than $1 billion and only five where the deal value exceeded $100 million:

- Of those five transactions where the deal value was greater than $100 million, three involved acquisitions of wealth managers while two involved acquisitions of specialty finance companies. Three involved larger FinTechs that are publicly traded. Intuit, FIS, and FiServ each had one larger acquisition of a traditional financial institution during the period analyzed.
- No FinTech companies acquired banks in the last 5 years and only three were reported in the last 10 years. The most recent bank acquisition by a FinTech company was Green Dot Corporation's purchase of a small bank for approximately $15 million in the first quarter of 2010. There were several online brokers that acquired banks from the late 1990s to the mid-2000s.
- For those FinTech companies that have acquired traditional financial institutions, the majority of acquisitions have been acquisitions of wealth managers and insurers. (See Table 11.3.)

METRICS TO ANALYZE FINTECH TRANSACTIONS

Previously, we noted that bankers often struggle with analyzing acquisitions of non-banks like FinTech companies due to the difficulty in developing the appropriate metrics to compare non-bank deals to traditional bank deals. To help address these issues, we discuss metrics in the following and provide examples that can be useful when assessing potential returns and value creation for a potential FinTech acquisition.

Internal Rate of Return

An internal rate of return (IRR) analysis derives the discount rate that equates the cash outlays to complete the transaction (deal consideration plus any transaction closing costs) to the earnings generated from the transaction. The IRR can also be compared to the company's cost of equity (COE) to determine if the potential transaction creates value for the acquirer's shareholders. To the extent that the IRR is greater than the cost of equity, value is created as the capital invested in the acquisition target is generating a return in excess of the company's cost of equity. A Morgan Stanley study examined the IRR less the cost of equity for bank transactions and determined that those deals with a higher IRR less COE created greater returns for the shareholders of the buyer over the two-year period following the deal announcement.[1] One downside to IRR is that it is often subject to a number of assumptions and is quite sensitive to those assumptions.

To provide an example of an IRR analysis for a FinTech acquisition, let's consider the following scenario. A community bank (Hometown Community Bank) is presented with two acquisition opportunities:

1. A FinTech company (FinTech Target)—an online, non-bank lender that successfully originates and services auto loans through a digital platform. FinTech Target generates revenue from loan fees, servicing revenues related to the loans, as well as sales of the loans to the secondary market. FinTech Target reported a net income of $4 million and equity of $12 million for the most recent trailing 12-month period.
2. A traditional bank (Traditional Bank Target)—a community bank in a nearby market. Traditional Bank Target appears attractive due to its focus on commercial and business lending as well as being in a more attractive geographic area than Hometown Community Bank. Traditional Bank Target reported net income of $4 million and equity of $50 million for the most recent trailing 12-month period.

The CFO of Hometown Community Bank is tasked by the board with analyzing the two acquisitions. She hired an outside firm to help assess the two opportunities. The value determined for FinTech Target was $100 million, based upon their net income of $4 million and a P/E multiple of 25×. The Traditional Bank Target was valued at approximately $80 million, based upon their net income of approximately $4 million and

P/E multiple of 20×. In order to analyze and compare the potential returns from both acquisitions, Hometown Community Bank's CFO put together a Value Creation ScoreCard for both deals and then analyzed them using the different measures.

As detailed in Table 11.4, the IRR for FinTech Target was 24 percent, which was higher than the 7 percent IRR for Traditional Bank Target. Although the purchase price and multiple for the FinTech acquisition was higher than the bank acquisition, the combination of the anticipated revenue growth from the FinTech lending platform as well as the revenue growth and potential expense savings from rolling the platform out to the bank's existing customers would contribute to higher incremental cash flows, terminal value, and IRR for the FinTech acquisition.

Return on Investment

Return on investment (ROI) is typically measured by comparing the target's earnings contribution inclusive of fully implemented synergies to the purchase price for the acquisition. By comparing this measure of return to the company's cost of equity, managers and directors can determine whether they can generate a return from the acquisition in excess of what they could get from the company (i.e., the company's cost of equity). One benefit of this measure is that it is relatively straightforward and allows for comparison across deals, including traditional and nontraditional deals such as a FinTech acquisition.

So let's examine our potential acquisition of FinTech Target and Traditional Bank Target to assess which return on investment is higher and how they compare to the acquiring bank's return on equity (see Table 11.5).

Synergies to Premium

This is typically only applied to publicly traded companies whereby one can analyze the transaction price and then compare that price to the trading price prior to announcement. It is difficult to apply for privately held deals since we do not have a trading price prior to the acquisition. However, this method can be applied should the privately held company have a typical valuation performed, and thus you have an indication of value for the company excluding any control premium.

Let's assume that the control premium for both acquisitions was approximately 35 percent of the purchase price and compare the synergies to premium measures for both. A control premium represents the amount that an acquirer would pay above the target's price for a minority interest (in most cases, for public companies this represents the trading price prior to deal

TABLE 11.4 Hometown Community Bank: Acquisition Analysis

FinTech Acquisition (000s)

	At Announcement	Year 1	Year 2	Year 3	Year 4	Year 5
Purchase Price	(100,000)					
After-Tax Cash One-Times	(4,000)					
After-Tax Opportunity Cost of Cash		(2,000)	(2,000)	(2,000)	(2,000)	(2,000)
Target's Estimated Net Income		4,000	6,000	8,400	10,920	13,104
Terminal Value					Source	262,080
Incremental Cash Flow	(104,000)	2,000	4,000	6,400	8,920	273,184
Internal Rate of Return	24%					

Bank Acquisition (000s)

	At Announcement	Year 1	Year 2	Year 3	Year 4	Year 5
Purchase Price	(80,000)					
After-Tax Cash One-Times	(3,200)					
After-Tax Opportunity Cost of Cash		(1,600)	(1,600)	(1,600)	(1,600)	(1,600)
Target's Estimated Net Income		5,000	5,300	5,618	5,955	6,312
Terminal Value						94,680
Incremental Cash Flow	(83,200)	3,400	3,700	4,01	4,355	99,392
Internal Rate of Return	7%					

1) Assumes cash one-time items at 4% of purchase price

2) Cost of cash related to funding acquisition (onetime outlays times 2% cost of cash

3) Terminal value based on Year 5 net income and a price/earnings multiple of 15× (bank) and 20× (FinTech)

TABLE 11.5 Hometown Community Bank: ROI and COE Comparisons

FinTech Acquisition

Purchase Price	100,000,000
Net Income (Fully Phased In)	13,104,000
ROI (FinTech)	13.1%
Cost of Equity (Trad'l Bank)	11.0%
ROI – Cost of Equity	2.1%

Bank Acquisition

Purchase Price	80,000,000
Net Income (Fully Phased In)	5,300,000
ROI (Trad'l Bank Deal)	6.6%
Cost of Equity (Trad'l Bank)	11.0%
ROI – Cost of Equity	−4.4%

announcement) to be able to control the company. In periodic reviews of bank transactions for which the target was publicly traded, we often see control premiums in the range of 20 to 40 percent on average, so our 35 percent assumption here seems reasonable.

Per Table 11.6, the FinTech acquisition compares favorably because the present value of the synergies (i.e., revenue enhancements) that are forecast to be picked up in the FinTech acquisition exceeded the premium paid.

TABLE 11.6 Hometown Community Bank: Synergies to Premium ($000)

	FinTech Acq.	Bank Acq.
Synergies (After-Tax)	4, 500	1,000
Div. by COE	11%	11%
Present Value of Synergies	40,909	9,091
− Acquisition Costs	(4,000)	(3,200)
Present Value of Net Cost Saves	36,909	5,891
Premium Paid	26,000	20,000
PV of Synergies/Premium Paid	*142%*	*29%*

The metrics are less favorable on the transaction for the bank acquisition whose synergies largely relied upon expense savings as the present value of these synergies was below the premium paid.

Historically financial services mergers have focused on expense savings as drivers of transactions. In fact, expense savings are typically a key driver (if not the primary driver) in a number of financial services mergers. Revenue enhancements, such as taking core products or expertise offered at the target, are often secondary considerations for banks. Banks considering FinTech acquisitions, however, will need to shift that thinking a bit as the key driver of synergies for these FinTech transactions may be revenue enhancements. Ally Financial Inc.'s (ticker on NYSE is "ALLY") acquisition of TradeKing announced in early 2016 was an example of a bank thinking creatively and focusing more on revenue enhancements as opposed to cost savings (see Chapter 7 for more information on the acquisition). ALLY is an over $150 billion asset bank headquartered in Michigan and TradeKing is a discount online brokerage firm that was known for its low-cost equity trades at approximately $5 per trade.

Executives of both Ally and TradeKing talk about the creative thinking behind the acquisition.

> *Banking and brokerage should be together so you can save and invest—and easily move money between the two.*
> —**Don Montanaro, TradeKing, CEO**[2]

> *We have a good composition of customers across all demographic segments, from affluent boomers to millennials. Our customers have been happy with our deposit products, but are asking for more from the online bank.*
> —**Diane Morais, Ally Bank, CEO**[3]

While the Ally Financial transaction offers an example of unorthodox thinking from a traditional financial services provider, this is not the norm for bank transactions.

Whereas the focus of a FinTech transaction is typically revenue enhancement, a FinTech transaction may result in expense savings for the acquiring bank. The expense savings will likely come from reducing the bank's existing staff or costs via the FinTech's technology offering.

TBV Accretion/Dilution and Earn-back Period

Book value per share immediately prior to and immediately after the acquisition (i.e., pro-forma inclusive of the impact of acquiring the target) can also be important metrics to analyze for a potential acquisition by a bank. Typically, an acquisition will result in tangible book value dilution initially after the transaction closes. Transactions (even banks acquiring other banks) often result in goodwill creation once the fair value of the assets and liabilities acquired is determined and the purchase price is allocated. The buyer then focuses on how long it will take to earn back the initial dilution by examining how many years it will take for the buyer's tangible book value per share to return to where it was prior to closing the acquisition. A typical range of earn-back periods can be three to five years.

An example of tangible book value dilution and earn-back period for the FinTech acquisition by Hometown Community Bank is presented in Table 11.7.

TABLE 11.7 Hometown Community Bank: TBV Accretion/Dilution and Earn-back Period for FinTech Acquisition

FinTech Acquisition

Impact on Tangible BVPS	Prior Year	Post-Acquisition				
		Year 1	Year 2	Year 3	Year 4	Year 5
Pro-Forma TBVPS per Share	$35.00	$41.20	$48.61	$57.43	$67.74	$79.38
– Standalone TBVPS	$75.00	$79.20	$83.61	$88.23	$93.08	$98.16
= Accretion/(Dilution)		−48.0%	−41.9%	−34.9%	−27.2%	−19.1%

Pro-Forma TBV Estimate ($M)	Pre-Acq.	Pro-Forma
Acquirer Common Equity	150	150
Less: Goodwill & Intangibles	0	(80)
Acquirer Tangible Common Equity	150	70
TBV Accretion/ (Dilution)—%	−53.3%	
TBV Accretion/ (Dilution)—$	$40.00	
TBV Earn-back Period	~5 Yrs	

TABLE 11.8 Hometown Community Bank: TBV Accretion/Dilution and Earn-back Period for Traditional Bank Acquisition

Traditional Bank Acquisition

Impact on Tangible BVPS	Prior Year	Post-Acquisition				
		Year 1	Year 2	Year 3	Year 4	Year 5
Pro-Forma TBVPS per Share	$54.50	$61.20	$68.26	$75.69	$83.52	$91.76
– Standalone TBVPS	$75.00	$79.20	$83.61	$88.23	$93.08	$98.16
= Accretion/(Dilution)		–22.7%	–18.4%	–14.2%	–10.3%	–6.5%

Pro-Forma TBV Estimate ($M)	Pre-Acq.	Pro-Forma
Acquirer Common Equity	150	150
Less: Goodwill & Intangibles	0	(41)
Acquirer Tangible Common Equity	150	109
TBV Accretion/ (Dilution)—%	–27.3%	
TBV Accretion/ (Dilution)—$	$20.50	
TBV Earn-back Period	~3 Yrs	

Table 11.8 presents an example of the tangible book value dilution and earn-back period for the traditional bank acquisition.

As shown, the FinTech acquisition results in a higher amount of tangible book value dilution initially and the earn-back period is longer than a traditional bank deal. This reflects several factors, including the valuation differential (i.e., the FinTech acquisition has a higher multiple of earnings), the FinTech company's balance sheet being less asset intensive (and thus, by implication, has less book value), and accounting differences between the purchase price allocations for bank and FinTech deals (we dive deeper into this issue later in this chapter).

While TBV accretion, dilution analysis, and earn-back period can provide useful benchmarking information when considering a transaction, these metrics provide limited insight into how much value may be created.

For example, book value dilution can be greatly affected by the stock/cash mix of consideration paid for the transaction, as well as the relative P/TBV multiples between the buyer and seller. What's more, the key determinant of the financial success of a merger or acquisition tends to be the pro-forma earnings stream that the combined entity can generate once the acquisition is fully integrated. Tangible book value dilution and accretion does not consider this as directly as some other value creation measures.

EPS Accretion/Dilution

Earnings per share accretion and dilution analysis compares the acquirer's earnings per share immediately prior to and immediately after the acquisition (i.e., pro-forma inclusive of the impact of acquiring the target). Typically, an acquisition that is set to enhance the value of the target will include an improvement in the buyer's earnings per share either immediately or within a year or two after the onetime costs of the acquisition are realized.

Per Table 11.9, the FinTech acquisition results in greater earnings per share accretion than the bank transaction after Year 1, as the FinTech deal costs more to execute and provides less accretion in Year 1. However, the FinTech acquisition ultimately provides greater earning power and potential once fully integrated.

Similar to TBV accretion/dilution analysis, this metric can also be of limited usefulness as it suffers from some of the same shortcomings. For example, the mix of consideration as well as the relative P/E multiples between the buyer and seller can skew the metrics.

TABLE 11.9 Hometown Community Bank: EPS Accretion/Dilution Comparison

FinTech Acquisition

	Prior Year	Post-Acquisition				
		Year 1	Year 2	Year 3	Year 4	Year 5
Pro-Forma EPS		$7.20	$8.41	$9.82	$11.31	$12.64
Trad'l Bank Standalone EPS	$5.00	$5.20	$5.41	$5.62	$5.85	$6.08
= Accretion/(Dilution)		38.5%	55.5%	74.7%	93.3%	107.7%

Traditional Bank Acquisition

	Prior Year	Post-Acquisition				
		Year 1	Year 2	Year 3	Year 4	Year 5
Pro-Forma EPS		$7.70	$8.06	$8.43	$8.83	$9.24
Trad'l Bank Standalone EPS	$5.00	$5.20	$5.41	$5.62	$5.85	$6.08
= Accretion/(Dilution)		48.1%	49.0%	49.9%	50.9%	51.9%

Putting It All Together

Now that both potential acquisitions have been analyzed, it comes down to making a decision as to which acquisition will be most favorable for the bank. A summary of the results of each value creation measure is provided in the Value Creation Scorecard in Table 11.10.

In our view, the FinTech acquisition is the most beneficial from a financial perspective as it has more favorable value creation measures in the categories that tend to be stronger measures for analyzing long-term success. It provides greater earnings and higher returns despite having a higher acquisition price. For example, the FinTech deal clearly outpaces the bank acquisition when comparing the potential return on investment to the acquirer's existing cost of equity. What's more, the negative spread in that measure for the bank transaction is a red flag. As previously noted, in a study of bank acquisitions by Morgan Stanley, bank stocks with transactions having a higher spread between IRR and the cost of equity have outperformed over the two years following the acquisition while EPS accretion and dilution had little predictive power.[4] Additionally, the ROI or IRR less COE metric is the only metric that considers the bank's cost of equity directly, and the bank's existing profitability can influence the attractiveness of acquisitions or partnerships. Thus, a key measure to assess value creation is comparing the IRR to the bank's cost of equity. A lower cost of equity for a bank, all else equal, will lower the threshold for potential FinTech deals and enhance the potential for value creation.

TABLE 11.10   Value Creation Scorecard

	FinTech Acquisition	Traditional Bank Acquisition	More Favorable Deal	Strength of Value Creation Measure
Internal Rate of Return	24%	7%	FinTech	Very Strong
ROI Less COE	2.1%	−4.4%	FinTech	Very Strong
Synergies to Premium	142%	29%	FinTech	Very Strong
TBVPS Accretion/ Dilution and Earn-back Period	~50% initially; 5 YR Earn-back	~30% initially; 3 YR Earn-back	Bank	Neutral
EPS Accretion/ Dilution	~50% Fully Phased In	~75–100% Fully Phased In	FinTech	Neutral

The Value Creation Scorecard also reveals that the FinTech transaction could result in greater tangible book value dilution and is also more dependent upon synergies achieved from successfully growing and integrating the FinTech company post-acquisition. As such, it may be advisable to consider structuring the transaction to minimize the potential tangible book value dilution and also withhold a portion of the consideration to provide ample reward for the existing owners and managers of FinTech Target post-closing. The traditional bank acquisition would not be as conducive to withholding forms of consideration as the synergies to be achieved in that transaction are largely from expense savings by removing duplicative and redundant costs—a significant portion of which could include letting go of higher level executives of Traditional Community Bank Target. Since those synergies to be achieved through expense savings are smaller, can be achieved quickly, and don't require assistance from the senior managers of Traditional Community Bank Target, withholding consideration does not seem necessary for the traditional bank acquisition.

ACCOUNTING CONSIDERATIONS AND GOODWILL CREATION IN FINTECH DEALS

Accounting considerations are important for traditional financial services companies since they often face regulatory requirements on capital levels. Regulatory capital ratios also often require certain intangible assets resulting from acquisitions be excluded from the regulatory capital calculation. As such, pro-forma capital ratios resulting at the end of an acquisition and a consideration of the amount of time that it can take to earn back any dilution are important considerations for bankers as they assess FinTech acquisitions. FinTech acquisitions often include a greater proportion of the purchase price being allocated to goodwill and intangibles than traditional bank deals. This can serve as an impediment to structuring and executing FinTech acquisitions for traditional banks. Additionally, bankers often track book value per share growth as a proxy for value creation over time, so this measure often receives significant management and board-level attention when assessing acquisition opportunities.

To better understand accounting considerations for FinTech deals and how they can differ from traditional bank deals, the following discussion examines the basics of goodwill and intangible assets and highlights some key accounting considerations for FinTech deals. In his 1937 book,

The Interpretation of Financial Statements, Ben Graham defined goodwill as follows:

> *Intangible Asset purporting to reflect the capitalization of excess future profits expected to accrue as a result of some special intangible advantage held, such as good name, reputation, strategic location, or special connections. In practice, the amount at which goodwill is carried on the balance sheet is rarely an accurate measure of its true value.*[5]

While progress has been made to improve goodwill measurement since 1937, the accuracy of intangible assets like goodwill is still debatable and many investors continue to question their reliability.

Debates persist within the accounting profession over the pros and cons of two primary accounting models to measure goodwill—historical cost and fair value. The key points of the debate tend to center around the trade-offs between the reliability of historical cost and the relevance of fair value (Figure 11.2).

Historical cost tends to imply that an asset is recorded on the balance sheet at its original cost, which is often reliable in that the cost can be easily identified. However, the original cost of the asset may lack relevance as time passes from the original purchase date. Fair value implies that the asset's value is determined based upon an estimated fair value using different assumptions and methodologies. The fair value model is more relevant in that it may reflect the asset's present value, but can be less reliable due to the assumptions and difficulty in verifying the value. Another critique of fair value accounting is that it can be costly and time consuming as companies often have to engage valuation firms to determine the fair value of balance sheet items. In addition, the reviews from both managers and auditors can also be time-consuming.

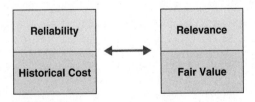

FIGURE 11.2 Accounting Models
Source: Mercer Capital

While these debates have persisted for years, there has been movement within the accounting profession toward the fair value model. The assets of FinTech companies are typically nonphysical. While the Financial Accounting Standards Board (FASB) is considering adding this topic to its rule-making agenda, these intangible assets are largely invisible to investors (unless they are acquired) because internally generated intangible assets are not reported on the balance sheet. Acquired assets are often recorded at fair value because it more adequately captures the value of certain nonphysical assets generated by FinTech companies.

Following the acquisition of either a FinTech company or a traditional bank, ASC 805 *Business Combinations* requires firms to recognize and measure the fair value of acquired identifiable assets, including any customer-related intangible asset. Fair value, for the purposes of both acquisition accounting and impairment testing, is defined in ASC 820 *Fair Value Measurement* as:[6]

> *The price that would be received to sell an asset or paid to transfer a liability in an orderly transaction between market participants at the measurement date.*

In particular, fair value is defined from the perspective of market participants rather than a specific party. Accordingly, valuation of customer-related intangible assets should be based on market participant assumptions.

In order to demonstrate the differences in goodwill typically resulting following the fair value determinations in both a traditional bank and FinTech deal, let's consider the following examples. Both examples assume that the target (a traditional bank in the first example and a FinTech company in the second example) is acquired for a cash purchase price of $80 million.

Accounting for a Traditional Bank Deal

Table 11.11 details the assets, liabilities, and common identifiable intangible assets acquired in a typical bank acquisition.

Table 11.12 provides an example of the changes to the target bank's balance sheet at closing as the acquired assets, such as the loans and intangible assets (like depositor customer relationships), are fair valued. The traditional bank acquisition results in approximately 50 percent of the purchase price being allocated to goodwill.

The traditional bank acquisition results in a decline in the acquirer's tangible equity as the goodwill created in the acquisition impacts the acquirer's balance sheet (Table 11.13). The goodwill created, as well as the additional assets acquired, reduced the bank's tangible-equity-to-asset ratio from 14.3 percent prior to the acquisition to 7.2 percent after the acquisition.

TABLE 11.11 Assets, Liabilities, and Common Identifiable Intangible Assets in a Typical Bank Acquisition

Fair Value—Bank Acquisition

Assets	Liabilities
Securities	Certificates of Deposit
Loans	FHLB Advances
Premises & Equipment	Trust Preferred Securities
Identifiable Intangible Assets	
Depositor Customer Relationships (Core Deposit)	
Borrower Relationships	
Customer Relationships	
Insurance	
Trust/Asset Management	
Merchant Processing	
Employment Agreements	

TABLE 11.12 Changes to Target Bank's Balance Sheet at Closing ($Millions)

Fair Value—Bank Acquires Another Bank

Target's Balance Sheet at Closing	Book Value	Fair Value
Securities	100	100
Loans (Net of Reserve)	375	370
Other Assets	25	25
Depositor Customer Relationships	0	5
Goodwill	0	36
Total Assets	**500**	**536**
Demand Deposits	300	300
Time Deposits	125	130
FHLB Advances	25	26
Total Liabilities	*450*	*456*
Total Equity	*50*	*80*
Total Liabilities & Equity	**500**	**536**
Goodwill & Intangibles as % of Purchase Price		*51%*

TABLE 11.13 Pro-Forma Balance Sheet for Traditional Bank Acquisition ($Millions)

Fair Value—Bank Acquires Another Bank

Pro-Forma Combined	Bank Acquirer	Target Bank	Consolidation Adjustment	Pro-Forma
Securities	200	100	(80)	220
Loans (Net of Reserve)	800	375	(5)	1,170
Other Assets	50	25	0	75
Depositor Customer Relationships	—	—	5	5
Goodwill	—	—	36	36
Total Assets	1,050	500		1,506
Demand Deposits	600	300	0	900
Time Deposits	250	125	5	380
FHLB Advances	50	25	1	76
Total Liabilities	900	450	6	1,356
Total Equity	150	50	0	150
Total Liabilities & Equity	1,050	500		1,506
Equity/Assets	14.3%	10.0%		10.0%
Tangible Equity	150	50		109
Tang. Equity/Assets	14.3%	10.0%		7.2%

Accounting for a FinTech Deal

Table 11.14 details the assets, liabilities, and common identifiable intangible assets acquired in a FinTech company acquisition. A FinTech company's balance sheet may consist largely of nonphysical assets and may also have little or no relevance to the potential operating performance of the company. Per Table 11.14, the acquired FinTech company has a significantly smaller balance sheet than the bank (Table 11.11), which results in the FinTech company's balance sheet increasing when fair valued. Additionally, the goodwill created is much greater than the amount created in the typical bank acquisition.

Note that a significantly higher proportion of the purchase price is allocated to goodwill in the FinTech acquisition (Table 11.15) than the bank acquisition (Table 11.12). This results in lower tangible equity at the acquiring bank post-closing and a lower tangible-equity-to-asset ratio.

TABLE 11.14 Assets, Liabilities, and Common Identifiable Intangible Assets in a FinTech Acquisition

Fair Value—FinTech Acquisition

Assets	Liabilities
Securities	Funding Lines
Loans (if held on balance sheet)	Debt
Premises & Equipment	
Identifiable Intangible Assets	
Customer Relationships	
Trademarks	
Employment Agreements	
Non-Competes	
Earn-outs	
Developed Technology	
Patents	

The FinTech acquisition also results in a decline in the bank acquirer's tangible equity as the goodwill created in the acquisition impacts the acquirer's balance sheet (Table 11.16). The goodwill created, as well as the additional assets acquired, reduced the acquiring bank's tangible-equity-to-asset ratio further than the traditional bank deal from 14.3 percent prior to the acquisition to 6.6% after the acquisition (compared to 7.2 percent for the traditional bank deal).

This analysis of goodwill creation provides greater detail to the example from earlier in this chapter (see Tables 11.7 and 11.8) where we detailed how different tangible book value dilution and earn-back period analyses can look for FinTech and traditional bank acquisitions. FinTech acquisitions often have a much higher proportion of the purchase price accounted for as goodwill, which results in greater dilution and a longer earn-back period when compared to traditional bank transactions. This book value dilution can often be an impediment to banks acquiring FinTech transactions.

Tangible book value dilution and an estimate of how long it will take to earn back that dilution has historically been an important consideration for banks considering acquisitions. While this focus, and perhaps obsession, with tangible book value dilution can seem odd to a FinTech board or founder, it can make sense in light of the broader banking landscape. A bank's growth is typically limited by the level of tangible book value and

TABLE 11.15   Changes to Target FinTech's Balance Sheet at Closing ($Millions)

Fair Value—Bank Acquires FinTech Company

Target's Balance Sheet at Close	Book Value	Fair Value
Cash	4	4
A/R	4	4
Prop, Equip, Software	3	3
Other Assets	3	3
Identifiable Intangibles	0	18
Goodwill	12	62
Total Assets	**26**	**94**
Accounts Payable	1	1
Short-Term Debt	1	1
Long-Term Debt	12	12
Total Liabilities	*14*	*14*
Total Equity	*12*	*80*
Total Liabilities & Equity	**26**	**94**
Goodwill & Intangibles as % of Purchase Price		*100%*
Identifiable Intangibles Include:		
Customer Relationships		12
Non-Compete Agreements		2
Developed Technology		2
Tradename		2
Total Acquired Identifiable Intangible Assets		**18**

leverage as measured by regulatory capital ratios. While regulatory capital ratios and how they are calculated tend to vary from country to country, acquisitions by banks in the United States typically require a regulatory application to be filed and approved. A key aspect of this process is demonstrating that the bank's pro-forma capital ratios remain strong and in excess of regulatory minimums after the closing of the acquisition. Regulatory capital ratios often require certain intangible assets to be excluded from the regulatory capital calculation. Therefore, FinTech deals can be more dilutive to book value and thus viewed as less attractive than traditional bank acquisitions. Furthermore, bankers often track book value per share growth as a

TABLE 11.16 Pro Forma Balance Sheet for FinTech Acquisition ($Millions)

Fair Value—Bank Acquires FinTech Company

Pro Forma Combined	Bank Acquirer	Target FinTech	Consolidation Adjustment	Pro Forma
Securities	200	4	(80)	124
Loans (Net of Reserve)	800	—	—	800
Prop, Equip, Software	10	3	—	13
Other Assets	40	7	—	47
Identifiable Intangibles	—	—	18	18
Goodwill	—	12	50	62
Total Assets	1,050	26		1,064
Demand Deposits	600	—	—	600
Time Deposits	250	—	—	250
FHLB Advances	50	—	—	50
Other Liabilities	—	14	—	14
Total Liabilities	900	14	—	914
Total Equity	150	12	—	150
Total Liabilities & Equity	1,050	26		1,064
Equity/Assets	14.3%	46.2%		14.1%
Tangible Equity	150	—		70
Tang. Equity/Assets	14.3%	0.0%		**6.6%**

proxy for value creation over time and this measure often receives significant management and board-level attention.

While tangible book value dilution is an important deal metric, it tends to be impacted significantly by the nature of the consideration paid, as well as the relative comparison of P/TBV multiples for the target and the acquirer. Deals that have the largest amount of tangible book value dilution tend to include those where a company with a low P/TBV multiple acquires one with a higher P/TBV multiple. Tangible book value dilution also tends to be greatest for those acquisitions where the target has high or potentially high profitable and a less capital-intensive balance sheet. This tends to fit the profile of many potential deals between banks and FinTech companies.

Despite the intense focus on book value dilution and earn-back analyses, it may not be the best metric for FinTech deal analysis. Banking represents the classic mature industry where greater economies of scale are often achieved through acquisitions and tend to drive higher profitability. While expense savings are often a primary driver of traditional bank mergers, though, revenue enhancements often drive FinTech deals. A FinTech partnership or acquisition can be viewed differently in that there is typically no overlap in the services/staff with the existing bank, so the transaction must be viewed through a different lens. That lens is one that considers the additional revenue that may be gained by expanding the technological offering/product to the bank's existing customer base.

To better assist with the understanding of goodwill creation in FinTech deals, let's also discuss customer relationships and tradenames whose fair value is often determined in a FinTech acquisition. On July 1, 2013, Total System Services (TSYS), a prepaid payment processor, acquired all the outstanding voting stock of NetSpend, a leading provider of GPR prepaid debit and payroll cards and related financial services to underbanked consumers in the United States. Under terms of the merger agreement, TSYS paid approximately $1.4 billion (primarily cash consideration) with $1.0 billion, or nearly 74 percent of the purchase price, allocated to goodwill and $480 million allocated to intangible assets. TSYS noted that the goodwill arising from the acquisition consisted largely of the expansion of the customer base, differentiation in market opportunity, and economies of scale expected from combining the operations. The largest intangible assets were customer relationships ($318 million) and tradenames ($44 million). So, how are valuations of tradenames and customer relationships determined and what are the primary drivers? The following section will examine this issue more closely.

Customer Relationships

A key intangible asset for firms operating in many industries is customer relationships. Firms devote significant human and financial resources to develop, maintain, and upgrade customer relationships. In some instances, customer contracts give rise to identifiable intangible assets. More broadly, however, customer-related intangible assets consist of the information gleaned from repeat transactions, with or without underlying contracts. Firms can and do lease, sell, buy, or otherwise trade such information, which is generally organized as customer lists.

Customer relationships can be a key intangible asset that is booked concurrent with the closing of a FinTech acquisition. For example, an aspect important to understand when evaluating customer relationships in the payments industry is where the FinTech Payments Company is in the payment loop. This will drive who the customer is and the unit economics. Merchant acquirers typically have contracts with the merchants themselves and the valuable relationship lies with the merchant and the dollar volume of transactions processed over time, whereas the valuable relationship with other payments companies—such as a prepaid or gift card company—may lie with the end-user and their spending/card usage habits over time.

How to Value Customer-Related Assets[7]   Customer relationships are typically valued based upon an income approach (i.e., a discounted cash flow method) where the expected future cash flows from customer relationships are forecasted and then discounted to the present at a market rate of return.[8] The *multiperiod excess earnings method* (MPEEM) is typically used to value these intangible assets.

MPEEM involves estimation of the cash flow stream attributable to a particular asset. The cash flow stream is discounted to the present to obtain an indication of fair value. The most common starting point in estimating future cash flows is the prospective financial information prepared by (or in close consultation with) the management of the subject business.

In applying the MPEEM to customer-related assets, valuation professionals first identify the portion of prospective revenues that are expected to be generated through repeat business from customers existing at the valuation date. It is often useful to examine estimated future revenue as the product of revenue per customer and the number of retained customers. Fair value measurement requires that valuation professionals consider prospective revenue from a market participant perspective and exclude any firm-specific synergies that may be embedded in the prospective financial information prepared by management.

The expectation of repeat patronage creates value for customer-related intangible assets. Contractual customer relationships formally codify the expectation of future transactions. Even in the absence of contracts, firms look to build on past interactions with customers to sell products and services in the future. Two aspects of repeat patronage are important in evaluating customer relationships:

1. Not all customer contact leads to an expectation of repeat patronage. The quality of interaction with walkup retail customers, for instance, is generally considered inadequate to reliably lead to expectations of recurring business.
2. Even in the presence of adequate information, not all expected repeat business may be attributable to customer-related intangible assets. Some firms operate in monopolistic or near-monopolistic industries where repeat patronage is directly attributable to a dearth of acceptable alternatives available to customers. In other cases, it may be more appropriate to attribute recurring business to the strength of the tradenames or brands.

As discussed earlier, customer-related assets derive value within a finite period as the numbers of customers that provide repeat business can be expected to decline over time. Good estimates of expected attrition can be obtained by conducting statistical analyses of historical customer turnover and revenue growth rates. When historical customer data of sufficient quality is not available, it may be necessary to rely on management estimates or an examination of industry characteristics in developing customer attrition rates.

After the identification of prospective revenues attributable to the base of customers existing at the valuation date, valuation professionals estimate earnings based on expected profitability of the business. It is important to consider only the operating costs relevant to the base of existing customers from a market participant perspective. Marketing costs that are expected to be necessary in finding new customers and firm-specific cost synergies, for instance, are not relevant in projecting earnings on expected revenue from existing customers.

Customer-related intangible assets depend on the existence of other assets to provide value to the firm. Most assets, including fixed assets and intellectual property, are essential in creating products or providing services. The act of selling these products and services enables firms to develop relationships and collect information from customers. In turn, the value of these relationships depends on the firms' ability to sell additional products and services in the future. Consequently, for firms to extract value from customer-related assets, a number of other assets need to be in place.

Cash flow attributable to the customer-related asset is isolated from the estimated earnings by assessing contributory charges for other assets of the subject business. As discussed earlier, a number of other assets need to be in place for firms to extract value from customer-related assets. The contributory charges represent economic rent equivalent to returns on and returns of assets necessary to produce goods or services marketed to the customers.

Tradenames

Whether it is the name of an entire business or a single product, tradenames can represent substantial value in business transactions and are recognized as a marketing-related intangible asset under ASC 805, which states:

> *Trademarks are words, names, symbols, or other devices used in trade to indicate the source of a product and to distinguish it from the products of others.*

How to Value a Tradename[9]   The relief from royalty method is used to determine the fair value of a trademark or tradename. The method seeks to measure the incremental net profitability generated by the owner of the subject intangible asset through the avoidance of royalty payments that would otherwise be required to enjoy the benefits of ownership of this asset.

Applying the relief from royalty method requires several steps:

1. **Determine the future use of the trademark.** How will the acquired asset be used? Will it be phased out over time or is it a crucial part of the business? Do management's expectations for the trademark differ from those of a market participant?
2. **Determine the expected stream of revenue related to the trademark.** If there are multiple products or service lines, what are the projected revenues for each product line and its associated trademarks or product names? How long are the associated products or services expected to generate revenue? For some businesses this may be into perpetuity (e.g., Coca Cola), but for a trademark associated with certain technology or products, it may only be a few years.
3. **Determine an appropriate royalty rate to apply to the expected revenue stream.** What would a market participant pay to license a similar trademark? What do the structure and terms of the transaction indicate about the value of the trademark? The presence of earn-out payments that are based on a percentage of revenue can serve as an indicator for base royalty rate. Additionally, higher margin products generally demand higher royalty rates. Market data concerning various royalty rates can be found in SEC filings, legal agreements, or by providers such as RoyaltySource Intellectual Property Database. Royalty rates that are comparable to the subject transaction should be reflective of transactions in the relevant industry.
4. **Determine an appropriate discount rate to measure the present value of avoided royalty payments.** The risks associated with a trademark may differ from the risk of the business as a whole. Identifying additional risks or benefits ensures a more accurate measurement of the fair value of the trademark.

Ways to Overcome Some of the Accounting Challenges

Now that we have more closely examined some of the accounting challenges with FinTech deals, particularly for bank acquirers, let's discuss one way to overcome some of the accounting challenges: contingent consideration. Contingent consideration (like earn-outs, retention bonus, and non-compete agreements) can be favorable to banks that acquire FinTech companies for a number of reasons, including:

- **More Favorable Accounting Treatment.** The fair value of these items is determined at the acquisition closing date and recorded on the buyer's pro-forma balance sheet at those fair values. Since they tend to be structured with payments to be made in the future and are dependent upon certain things being achieved, the fair value of those payments tends to be discounted relative to the total value of the payments. For example, the fair value of an earn-out structure whereby the buyer owes the seller $15 million over a three-year period based upon the achievement of certain performance metrics (such as revenue targets) would only be recorded at a portion of the $15 million to reflect that the present value of a probability-weighted stream of those payments would be below that total amount. In Table 11.17, we assume that $15 million of consideration was withheld into an earn-out. The amount of goodwill recorded is below the amount absent this structure ($45 million of goodwill compared to $62 million with no contingent consideration) and pro-forma tangible-equity-to-asset ratios are higher for the acquirer (7.0% in Table 11.17 versus 6.6% in our prior example in Table 11.16).

- **Better Aligns Incentives for Post-Close Success.** One important way that FinTech acquisitions are different than traditional bank deals is that the acquirer is often interested in retaining the top talent and management of the FinTech company. In a traditional bank deal, the primary drivers are often cost savings that will result from eliminating overlapping or redundant expenses and personnel. However, FinTech companies typically bring technical expertise and products that the bank does not currently offer and thus the bank needs to insure that the existing personnel and team remains in place to run the FinTech service line. By withholding certain of the consideration, the acquirer is able to incentivize and hopefully retain key FinTech personnel and management so that they can continue to grow and enhance pro-forma earnings.

- **Can Address the Valuation Gap between Buyer and Seller.** As noted previously, FinTech companies are often younger and have higher growth prospects than more mature traditional financial services companies like banks. Thus, they tend to often be valued based on forecasts of future earnings performance in excess of where their earnings are today as milestones are met and revenue and customers grow. However, there can often be a difference between the expectations of future performance between buyers and sellers and this can result in differences regarding valuation today and being able to execute deals. Thus, contingent consideration can be used to bridge these valuation gaps and provide some protection to the buyer in the event that the seller underperforms their performance metrics while also providing some upside to the seller should they achieve the performance thresholds outlined in the earn-out and achieve the maximum potential payments.

TABLE 11.17 Fair Value Accounting Example of Traditional Bank Acquiring FinTech Company

Fair Value—Bank Acquires FinTech

Target's Balance Sheet at Close	Book Value	Fair Value	Pro-Forma Combined	Bank Acquirer	Target FinTech	Consolidation Adjustment	Pro-Forma
Cash	4	4	Securities	200	4	(65)	139
A/R	4	4	Loans (Net of Reserve)	800	—	—	800
Prop, Equip, Software	3	3	Prop, Equip, Software	10	3	—	13
Other Assets	3	3	Other Assets	40	7	—	47
Identifiable Intangibles	0	18	Identifiable Intangibles	—	—	18	18
Goodwill	12	57	Goodwill	—	12	45	57
Total Assets	26	89	Total Assets	1,050	26		1,074
Accounts Payable	1	1	Demand Deposits	600	—	—	600
Short-Term Debt	1	1	Time Deposits	250	—	—	250
Long-Term Debt	12	12	FHLB Advances	50	—	—	50
Contingent Liabilities	0	10	Contingent Liabilities	—	—	10	10
Total Liabilities	14	24	Other Liabilities	—	14	—	14
Total Equity	12	65	Total Liabilities	900	14	—	924
Total Liabilities & Equity	26	89	Total Equity	150	12	—	150
			Total Liabilities & Equity	1,050	26		1,074
Goodwill & Intang. as % of Purchase Price		115%	Equity/Assets	14.3%	46.2%		14.0%
			Tangible Equity	150	—		75
Identifiable Intangibles Include:			Tang. Equity/ Assets	14.3%	0.0%		7.0%
Customer Relationships		12					
Non-Compete Agreements		2					
Developed Technology		2					
Tradename		2					
Total Acquired Identifiable Intangible Assets		18					

Given the high proportion of goodwill potentially involved in a Fin-Tech acquisition and the potential impact on a traditional financial institution acquirer's regulatory capital ratios, we discuss ways that deals can be structured to minimize the creation of goodwill. *Earn-outs*, or contingent consideration, can be used to both reduce goodwill creation and also address potential valuation gaps, particularly when the acquirer has difficulty determining future earnings or growth potential of a FinTech company. To the extent that the owners of the FinTech company are also employees and there is a strong desire to keep them in place post-closing, the acquirer may be able to provide those employees with employment agreements (including non-compete agreements and/or retention bonuses) that allow for lower deal values as a portion of consideration is effectively provided to the owners as part of their compensation.

Contingent Consideration or Earn-outs Contingent consideration (earn-outs) are typically payments based on the future performance—financial or nonfinancial—of the target. Earn-outs represent one way that a transaction can be structured to minimize the amount of goodwill created and are often used when the acquirer has difficulty in determining the present value or future growth rate of a selling company. A contingency provision can provide:

- Protection for the buyer against overvaluation of the seller.
- Can close the gap in performance expectations between buyer and sellers.
- Allow the buyer to share post-acquisition risk with seller by making some consideration contingent on future performance.
- An incentive for the owner to remain and continue to successfully run the business.
- The ability for the seller to participate in the upside post-transaction.

While it is difficult to know with certainty, as they are more common in acquisitions of private companies that may not be reported, a few studies have noted that earn-outs and contingent consideration are relatively common, particularly in technology acquisitions. For example:

- Earn-outs were included in 25 percent of deals in 2012 (versus 19% in the 2006 version of the study, 29% in 2008, and 38% in 2010).[10]
- Approximately 19 percent of transactions had contingent consideration in the purchase price with contingent consideration representing 14 percent of median total purchase consideration.[11]

There are a variety of reasons why earn-outs are more prevalent in technology, including those noted previously as well as uncertainty inherent in markets with rapidly evolving competitive environments.[12]

Another study within the technology sector noted that:

- 16 percent of the deals had contingent consideration, representing a median of 18 percent of total purchase consideration.
- Range of purchase consideration as a percentage of deal value was 1 percent to 54 percent.[13]

Retention Bonuses   Another option to consider is a retention bonus, which is a temporary reward intended to prevent someone from leaving post-close. Retention bonuses are typically driven by concerns about the long-term success of the deal and a desire to provide incentives to critical employees. They can be critical in transactions where a key driver is the staff and management of the target.

How prevalent are they?

- 62 percent of deals in one survey include retention programs primarily for senior executives and those critical to long- or short-term success.

How are they structured?[14]

- Median retention bonus as a percentage of base salary is 45 percent for executives critical for long-term success as well as senior management.
- Indicated that those critical in the longer-term are often paid in installments over a 24-month period.
- In the United States, 26 percent of retention bonuses are paid in four or more payments.

Non-Compete Agreements   Non-compete covenants are a staple in most purchase agreements. These agreements are usually designed to protect the buyer in the event that one of the selling shareholders/managers decides to pocket their deal proceeds and start a competing venture. They have become more widely used in recent years and increasingly appear in the news, though not always in the most favorable of contexts. Proponents argue that such agreements protect firms' intellectual property and prevent the loss of key employees, customers, suppliers, and trade secrets. Others would suggest that non-competes stifle innovation by limiting competition and employee mobility.

Though different states follow different rules regarding non-competes—with some even outlawing the practice all together—several common criteria are generally followed:

- The agreement must be supported by consideration at the time it is signed.

■ It must protect a legitimate business interest of the employer.

■ The agreement has to be reasonable in scope, geography, and time.

From an accounting perspective, non-compete agreements are identifiable intangible assets (per ASC 805) and may require a fair value measurement along with other intangible assets like tradenames, patents, technology, and customer relationships. The value of a non-compete agreement can vary considerably by industry, business size, and factors specific to the individuals covered under the agreement. However, the valuation methodologies are similar whether the agreement is being valued for GAAP or tax compliance.

The value of an individual's non-compete to a corporation can become important in the context of acquiring a business, particularly in acquisitions of FinTech companies by traditional financial institutions whose pro-forma regulatory capital ratios are important to consider when assessing the deal. NCAs derive value from their ability to reduce the risk in business acquisitions by minimizing the loss of employees, customers, and suppliers. In a purchase price allocation, the value of a non-compete agreement is typically calculated as the difference between entity value on an as-is basis with present employees intact and a hypothetical firm value, assuming that the acquirer is unable to obtain assurances that key employees would remain active and, further, would not seek to compete with the acquired company for a specified period of time.

SPECIAL ISSUES TO CONSIDER WITH FINTECH M&A

In a FinTech transaction, there are also certain other non-accounting special issues to consider. We discuss two of these issues, fairness opinions and dissenter's rights—knowledge of both is beneficial for the buyer as well as the seller.

Fairness Opinions[15]

A fairness opinion is an opinion, usually prepared in a brief letter, in which an independent financial advisor (typically an investment banking firm, valuation firm, or a specialized firm with appropriate credentials) renders an opinion that a proposed transaction is fair, from a financial point of view, to the shareholders (or a special group of shareholders) of a company. It typically involves a review of the transaction from a financial point of view, including price, consideration to be received, and other financial terms of the transaction.

Fairness opinions are typically issued to the company's full board of directors or to special, independent committees of the board on or around the date proximate to when the buyer or seller are planning to vote on the proposed merger. Fairness opinions are viewed by many as recognition that the board of directors acted in good faith and in the interest of all shareholders (or the relevant class of stakeholders). It is designed to assist directors in making reasonable business decisions and to provide protection under the *business judgment rule.*

Transactions, particularly those involving public companies, often result in some form of legal challenge (i.e., litigation), and a board that relies upon a fairness opinion in their decision process regarding a significant transaction has taken steps to create a safe harbor.

The business judgment rule is a concept developed in U.S. case law that presumes that the directors' decisions are informed and reflect good faith, care, and loyalty to shareholders. The business judgment rule generally requires the following: a business decision is made; the board exercised due care in the process of making that decision; the board in this case acted independently and objectively (as a disinterested party might have acted); the board's decision was made in good faith; and there was no abuse of discretion in making the decision.

Fairness opinions initially became significantly more common following the expansion of the business judgment rule to encompass a requirement for informed decisions in the landmark case, *Smith v. Van Gorkom* [488 A.2d 858 (Supreme Court of Delaware, 1985)]. Some important business lessons from the Court's decision in *Smith v. Van Gorkom* include:

- The presence of a merger premium alone, as compared to the market price of the selling company, was not a sufficient reason to approve the merger, and directors were obligated to seek other sound valuation advice.
- The board made efforts believed to have a curative effect on any shortcomings, including hiring an investment banker to seek competitive bids and attaining the overwhelming support of the majority of shareholders.
- The Delaware court ruled that negligence occurred because the procedures for reaching the decisions were inadequate.
- The directors were held personally liable for a multimillion-dollar judgment (beyond insurance coverage) for breach of their fiduciary duty.

In summary, the lessons of *Smith v. Van Gorkom* should cause directors to insist that significant transactions are presented to competent experts who can speak to the legal, valuation, and disclosure issues. The application of the Court's findings is a matter of legal judgment and expert legal counsel should be sought to assure that a board involved in a merger is complying fully with state and federal statutes and related court decisions.

Fairness opinions can also be utilized to obtain an independent analysis of the transaction when conflicts of interest are present with the firm's other advisors on the transaction. For example, many investment banking firms that are hired to represent a buyer or seller in a transaction are frequently also retained to provide a fairness opinion on the same transaction. This can create a potential conflict of interest if the investment banking firm has a financial interest in the transaction or an existing relationship with the company or other parties involved in the transaction. Boards often would be well-advised to retain a truly independent firm to issue a second fairness opinion in such case (particularly in light of FINRA's Rule 2290). FINRA's Rule 2290 requires firms issuing fairness opinions to disclose conflicts and work processes, which has resulted in an increased need for fairness opinions and even second fairness opinions not issued by the investment banker.

Using a tennis analogy again, a fairness opinion can be the equivalent of a player asking the umpire for their opinion on a line call and using the instant replay system to challenge the call. It provides an independent and third-party review of the transaction that can serve to provide some security that the transaction (or in the case of tennis, the "line call") is fair.

While the fairness opinion itself is typically a short document, the supporting work behind the fairness opinion letter is considerable. The completion of analytical work is critical to the development of the fairness opinion. A fairness opinion should be based upon a number of considerations, including a review of at least the following five factors.

1. Financial performance and factors affecting earnings for the buyer, target, and the combined company
2. Dividend-paying history and capacity of the target and the combined company
3. Pricing of transactions involving comparable companies
4. The investment characteristics of the acquirer if stock is received (including growth prospects and future profitability before and after the transaction)
5. The merger agreement and its terms

Factor #3 will typically require the financial advisor to perform a valuation of the seller (i.e., the FinTech company being acquired). We discussed how to value a FinTech company in Chapter 10 and those basic valuation concepts and methods would again be applicable here. The valuation range would likely consider a valuation based upon a projection of future earnings (i.e., a discounted cash flow analysis) and consideration of the pricing of comparable transactions and publicly traded companies (i.e., a market approach).

In addition to these five factors, the consideration of a number of other elements of the transaction may be necessary. The financial advisor may also perform a "sell-now versus sell-later" analysis for the seller, or evaluate the buyer's shares when stock is a form of consideration. Typically, the valuation of the buyer's shares considers the company's historical performance, growth prospects, and an assessment of risk. Additionally, a comparison of the buyer's performance relative to a peer group as well as the valuation history of the company over market cycles can be important.

Both process and value are important considerations when evaluating fairness. Important questions to consider in the review of the process include: Did the board make an intentional decision to engage in a transaction, or is the company's involvement the result of a reaction to initiative(s) from outside? Who initiated the transaction? Was there any preliminary analysis of pricing or shareholder options prior to the initiation of the transaction process? What type of process was undertaken (i.e., negotiated sale, limited auction, or full auction)?

When reviewing alternative transactions, directors, managers, and their financial advisors should note that not all offers are directly comparable. Other factors to consider when evaluating pricing include the type of consideration paid (i.e., all stock, a consideration of both stock and cash, or all cash) and the terms of the transaction (including contingent consideration). For example, a consideration of how the exchange ratio is structured can also be important. Exchange ratios can be fixed (either at announcement or closing), variable (i.e., floats to provide a dollar amount of consideration based upon the acquirer's stock price), or some hybrid where the ratio floats within a specified band. Additionally, an examination of the value of the subject transaction to the seller's shareholders should be performed in certain situations. For example, items like contingent consideration (such as earn-outs) and escrow arrangements need to be evaluated and their contribution to the overall deal value estimated.

Fairness opinions do not predict where the target or acquirer's stock price will trade in the future, nor does it guarantee that the selling company received the best possible price for the company. Fairness, similar to valuation, is also a range concept, and the fairness of a transaction can range from very fair, to marginally fair, to unfair. The advisor reviews the process, the valuation, and the facts and circumstances of the transaction and provides the board with confidence about its decision and the merits of the opinion.

Dissenters' Rights

Contrary to the silence that usually occurs after the phrase "Speak now or forever hold your peace" is uttered in marriage ceremonies, the voice of dissent is being heard more frequently from shareholders dissenting to corporate unions. Appraisal, or dissenters' rights, actions occur when shareholders dissent to a transaction and petition the court to determine the "fair value" of their shares. Dissenting actions are on the rise and have begun to receive considerable attention from attorneys, investors, and other dealmakers. For perspective, 40 appraisal action cases were brought in 2014 and 38 have been filed through August 2015 with claims totaling $2.1 billion, compared to just $129 million three years ago.[16] The press also has noted the rising use of appraisal arbitrage whereby hedge funds and activists purchase shares after a deal is announced and then dissent to trigger an appraisal action. Whether this is positive or negative for capital markets is subject to debate, although one could argue additional price discovery is not all bad.

As long as M&A activity remains robust, we would not expect the volume of appraisal actions to decline much given two recent high-profile awards to dissenters. In mid-2015, dissenters in connection with Albertson's acquisition of Safeway Inc. received a 26 percent premium to the acquisition price, resulting in payments totaling more than $127 million.[17] In August 2015, the Delaware Chancery Court granted a 20 percent premium to dissenters in Dell's going-private transaction, resulting in an estimated $148 million award for dissenters (before statutory interest is applied).[18] The Dell and Albertson decisions are consistent with some studies concluding that Delaware courts tend to award a fair value greater than the merger price.[19] Further, the interest rate credited to the dissenter (discount rate plus 5.0%) between closing and the court's decision may be an incremental inducement to dissent given the current rate environment.

While high-profile awards may be an inducement for more dissenting actions, it should be noted that dissenters do not always receive a higher price. A Delaware ruling in June 2015 awarded dissenters in Cypress Semiconductor's 2012 acquisition of Ramtron International Corporation lower consideration (the merger price less synergies) while another Delaware ruling in October 2015 determined that the merger price in BMC Software Inc.'s going-private transaction in September 2013 represented fair value.[20]

Bank acquirers (and FinTech sellers) should consider the possibility of dissenters. Neither industry is immune to appraisal actions.

A key question when considering dissenters and appraisal actions is: "What is fair value?" Fair value in a dissenting shareholder action is not the same concept as fair value used in certain accounting contexts, nor is the fair market value standard used in many regulated transactions. Statutory fair value is defined in the corporate statutes of each state while case law provides the courts' interpretation of the statutes. Delaware case law is the most extensive.

Fair value usually is defined as the value of the dissenter's shares immediately before the action giving rise to the right to dissent without considering the impact of the transaction. Courts in some states view fair value as a control value, but without attributes that a strategic acquirer might consider relevant (e.g., merger synergies). Not surprisingly, disparate valuations can result from the application of premiums related to control and/or discounts related to minority status or illiquidity/marketability. Disagreements also can stem from the approaches used to value the shares. For example, consider the following quote from the *Weinberger v. UOP* case that the valuation "must include proof of value by any techniques or methods which are generally considered acceptable in the financial community and otherwise admissible in court."[21]

While acknowledging that each FinTech company, transaction, and appraisal action is unique, valuing a FinTech company is, by its nature, forward-looking with history serving as a guide. The process tends to revolve around three primary elements: earnings/cash flow, risk, and growth. Significant trade-offs can exist among these three elements. For example, a FinTech company's earnings, dividend-paying capacity, and growth can be enhanced in the short- to intermediate-term by taking more risk while the impact of the decision (usually credit losses) may not be evident for several years. A well-reasoned, defensible valuation will need to consider the potential trade-offs and the implications of higher earnings and growth today versus potential issues in the future.

Two common approaches to valuing a FinTech company in an appraisal action include the following:

- **Income Approach.** The discounted cash flow (DCF) method is an income approach whereby the FinTech company's value is determined by summing the present value of cash flows generated from excess capital generated over the forecast period and the terminal value at end of forecast period. Key variables in a DCF method include distributable cash flow (i.e., existing and internally generated capital that is in excess of a reasonable threshold level), the terminal value multiple to apply to earnings in the terminal period, and the discount rate.
- **Market Approach.** Using the market approach, a FinTech company's value is determined based upon comparisons to transactions in publicly traded FinTech companies, acquisitions of both privates and public FinTech companies, and/or transactions in the company's own stock. The guideline public company or guideline transactions method involves utilizing pricing multiples derived from publicly traded FinTech companies bearing similarities to the subject company such as business model, FinTech niche, and profitability. Common FinTech company

valuation multiples include price/revenue, price/EBITDA, and price/ earnings. Applying the guideline group multiples, inclusive of adjustments for fundamental differences between the subject company and the guideline groups if necessary, can provide meaningful indications of value.

As in the BMC Software decision referenced previously, courts have found that the acquisition (or transaction) price can be representative of fair value. We previously discussed the topic of fairness from a financial point of view and the importance of process in M&A transactions. These same points often become key elements in appraisal actions and determining whether the merger price is a reasonable indication of the FinTech company's fair value. While the process is tricky to assess in any transaction, a process that is limited and favors insiders or particular bidders in the transaction may be viewed as flawed and provide less convincing evidence that the merger price is consistent with fair value.

FinTech is unique in that regulations are important as well as a firm understanding of the unique dynamics of the industry. It is important that the valuation of the FinTech company in an appraisal action be prepared by an appraiser who is well versed in both valuation techniques and the FinTech industry. The appraiser should understand key valuation concepts as well as have a sound understanding of key factors/trends driving the FinTech industry, identify the impact of industry and regulatory trends on the subject FinTech company, and deliver a reasoned and supported analysis in light of these trends.

CONCLUSION

When presented with strategic options related to FinTech, banks may increasingly seek to acquire a FinTech company to enhance their returns, diversify product offerings, and ultimately increase their valuation. However, there are a number of challenges with properly analyzing and structuring FinTech deals. Additionally, banks must develop an appropriate framework and return metrics to appropriately consider and compare FinTech deals to other FinTech deals as well as traditional bank deals.

NOTES

1. "Midcap Banks: Bank Buyers Beware—Let's Use the Right Metrics for Assessing Value Creation in Bank M&A," *Morgan Stanley*, March 9, 2016.
2. Theresa W. Carey, "Ally, Fidelity to Launch Robo-Advisory Services," *Barron's*, April 23, 2016, http://www.barrons.com/articles/ally-fidelity-to-launch-robo-advisory-services-1461385575.

3. Ibid.

4. Ibid.

5. Andrew Everett, "Book Review: The Interpretation of Financial Statements," *The Key Point*, April 8, 2016, https://thekeypoint.org/2016/04/08/the-interpre tation-of-financial-statements/.

6. ASC 820-10-20 (formerly SFAS 157, paragraph 5).

7. The material in this section was adapted with permission from "Valuation of Customer-Related Assets," by Lucas M. Parris, CFA, ASA-BV/IA, *Mercer Capital's Financial Reporting Blog*, January 11, 2016.

8. The specific name of the technique varies and could include the *multiperiod excess earnings method (MPEEM), the distributor method, the with-and-without method, and the differential cash flows method.*

9. The material in this section was adapted with permission from "What's in a Name: Valuing Trademarks and Trade Names," by Travis W. Harms, CFA, CPA/ABV, *Mercer Capital's Financial Reporting Blog*, August 7, 2016.

10. "Review of 136 Private Target Transactions Closing in 2012," *American Bar Association (ABA), Private Target Merger & Acquisitions Deal Points Study: Financial Deal Points*, http://www.americanbar.org/content/dam/aba/ administrative/business_law/deal_points/2015_private_study.authcheckdam .pdf.

11. "2012 Purchase Price Allocation Study," *Houlihan Lokey*, hl.com/us/press/ insightsandideas/3938.aspx.

12. "2012 Contingent Consideration Study—Earn-out Structuring and Valuation," *Duff & Phelps*, August 2012, http://www.duffandphelps.com/assets/pdfs/ publications/articles/2012%20contingent%20consideration%20study.pdf.

13. "2012 Purchase Price Allocation Study," *Houlihan Lokey*, September 4, 2013, hl.com/us/press/insightsandideas/3938.aspx.

14. *Source:* Survey of M&A Retention and Transaction Programs by Mercer, subsidiary of Marsh & McLennan Companies, http://www.mercer.com/ content/dam/mercer/attachments/global/MandA/Mercer-Survey-of-Retention- and-Transaction-Programs.pdf.

15. Andrew K. Gibbs, CFA, CPA/ABV and Jay D. Wilson, Jr., *The Bank Director's Valuation Handbook* (Peabody Publishing, LP, 2009), pp. 77–84.

16. Liz Hoffman, "Dole Executives Ordered to Pay $148 Million in Buyout Lawsuit," *Wall Street Journal*, August 27, 2015, http://www.wsj.com/articles/dole- executives-ordered-to-pay-148-million-in-buyout-lawsuit-1440686542.

17. Steven M. Hecht, "Settling Safeway Shareholders Achieve Substantial Premium within Six Months of Closing," *Appraisal Rights Litigation Blog*, June 4, 2015, http://www.appraisalrightslitigation.com/2015/06/04/settling-safeway-share holders-achieve-substantial-premium-within-sixmonths- of-closing/.

18. Steven M. Hecht, "Dole Appraisal Case Yields 20% Premium," *Appraisal Rights Litigation Blog*, August 27, 2015, http://www.appraisalrightslitigation .com/2015/08/27/dole-appraisal-case-yields-20-premium/.

19. Jeremy Anderson, Jose P. Sierra, "Unlocking Intrinsic Value through Appraisal Rights," *Law360*, September 10, 2013, www.law360.com.

20. Steven M. Hecht, "Delaware Chancery Looks to Merger Price in BMC Software Ruling," *Appraisal Rights Litigation Blog*, October 23, 2015, http://www

.appraisalrightslitigation.com/2015/10/23/delaware-chancery-looks-to-merger-price-in-bmc-software-ruling/; Steven M. Hecht, Brandon M. Fierro, "With Unreliable Management Projections and No Market-Based Models, Delaware Chancery Pegs Fair Value to Merger Price," *Appraisal Rights Litigation Blog*, July 6, 2015, http://www.appraisalrightslitigation.com/2015/07/06/with-unreliable-management-projections-and-no-market-basedmodels-delaware-chancery-pegs-fair-value-to-merger-price/.

21. *Weinberger v. UOP, Inc.* (Del. 1983), CaseBriefs, http://www.casebriefs.com/blog/law/corporations/corporations-keyed-to-klein/mergers-acquisitions-and-takeovers/weinberger-v-uop-inc/.

CHAPTER 12

Liquidity Options Beyond a Sale

INTRODUCTION[1]

In Chapter 11, we noted that mature, successful FinTech companies, particularly the largest, most highly valued ones, are difficult to acquire given their size and valuation, which limits the pool of potential buyers.

Recent market trends are favorable for FinTech; however, these trends may not last indefinitely and any slowdown could temper M&A activity and liquidity options for FinTech companies. Should market conditions cool and exit options through a traditional sale be limited, FinTech companies and their stakeholders, which will likely increasingly include banks, may need a strategy adjustment to include liquidity options other than a traditional sale to a third-party. Consequently, this chapter discusses liquidity alternatives other than a third-party sale and may be particularly relevant for FinTech entrepreneurs, bankers, and their stakeholders.

Some of the best tennis players have the ability to alter their game depending upon the conditions and add a wrinkle in important moments that their opponent has previously not seen before. Similar to a great baseline tennis player who adapts his or her game and commits to moving forward in the court more on grass (a court surface that rewards that strategy more), FinTech founders and investors may need to consider a strategy adjustment depending upon market and industry conditions present. These strategic options can be extremely important to entrepreneurs and shareholders of FinTech companies, as they ultimately determine the potential returns that they will receive for their investments.

While institutional investors often have a portfolio of investments and the performance of one can offset the lack of performance of the other, the net worth of individual owners of private FinTech companies can be concentrated in the company itself and this can be dangerous. For example, let's consider the portfolio of Mr. Smith, a successful FinTech entrepreneur who

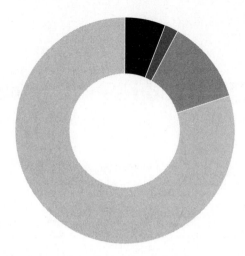

■ **Fixed Income** ■ **Cash** ■ **Public Equity Portolio*** ■ **Private FinTech Co.**

* Diverse mix of domestic (large, small, and midcap) stocks as well as international stocks

FIGURE 12.1   Mr. Smith's Portfolio Including His FinTech Portfolio

helped found a FinTech company, grow it into a successful and profitable operation, and now has a significant ownership position in the company. Mr. Smith's net worth is highly concentrated in the stock of his private FinTech company. Therefore, creating value and measuring and managing returns from this private company investment are extremely important to him. Liquidity is also a primary concern to investors and owners like Mr. Smith as investments in private companies are often illiquid, which creates a difficult situation for those investors seeking some diversification of their interest given their concentrated positions (See Figure 12.1).

This combination of concentrated positions in private companies and a desire for liquidity among the investors is often one reason that companies look to a traditional exit like a third-party sale. However, sometimes a third-party sale is not possible given market, industry, or other conditions. For owners such as Mr. Smith, we discuss other liquidity options.

LIQUIDITY OPTIONS

Other avenues for liquidity aside from a third-party sale are detailed in Table 12.1 and we discuss options under each strategy ("Holding On," "Selling In," or "Selling Out") in the sections that follow.

TABLE 12.1 Liquidity Options

Holding On	Selling In (Family, Management)	Selling Out (Financial Buyer, Strategic Buyer)
Dividends (Regular, Special, Leveraged Recap)	Management Buy-In	Private Equity
Share Redemptions	ESOP	Third-Party Sale (Financial Buyer)
	Generational Transfers	Third-Party Sale (Strategic Buyer)
	Trust Ownership	IPO

Holding On

This section discusses considerations for those FinTech companies that elect to "hold on" and make the financial decision to pass on reinvesting in the business and return a flexible, indeterminate amount of those earnings to shareholders in the form of shareholder dividends or share repurchases.

Dividends Dividends correspond to the portion of earnings available for distribution after paying all taxes and accounting for all net reinvestment in the business. Mature FinTech companies and banks that are generating earnings consistently will want to consider their dividend policies. Below we list a few common dividend policies for companies and the types of companies that most benefit from having those policies.

1. **No Dividend Paid at All.** Companies paying no dividends include those that pay no dividends ($0 in dividend payments) and S corporations whose shareholders/members/partners receive no economic dividend as they only receive distributions sufficient enough so that they can pay their pro-rata share of the taxes owed.
2. **Sporadic, Onetime, or Special Dividends.** Companies with this type of dividend policy typically pay a dividend for specific reasons applicable at the time the dividend is paid. For example, the company may have volatile earnings depending upon the business cycle or an extremely profitable period or unusual, nonrecurring income that results in a special or onetime dividend.
3. **Targeted Dividend Payouts.** Companies paying targeted dividend payouts typically have either a target dividend payout ratio (e.g., 40% of after-tax earnings), a targeted dividend yield (2% of the concluded value of the business), or a constant-dollar dividend (i.e., $2 million dividend per year).

4. **Spinout or Spinoff of Subsidiaries or Assets.** Companies that spin out or spin off subsidiaries or assets take some subsidiary or division of the company and create a separate operating company. Interestingly, there have been a number of famous spinoffs of FinTech companies. One FinTech example is eBay and PayPal, but there have been others, including a number of payments companies that have been spun out of retail banks.

5. **Some Combination of Items 1–4.**

For banks, the question of whether to reinvest in the business or distribute cash is often uniquely different than for those FinTech companies. Often, banks are mature businesses that tend to have more limited growth prospects compared to FinTech companies, which leads them to often return cash flows and capital to shareholders in the form of dividends. For FinTech companies, the growth prospects are often higher than their traditional bank counterparts, and thus they often have more opportunities to create value through forgoing dividends and reinvesting earnings in capital projects that generate returns in excess of their cost of capital. However, mature banks do have the opportunity to take a portion of the cash flows generated and invest in these FinTech companies, or in their own technology groups to develop platforms that can capitalize on the potential growth within FinTech and ultimately create value for their institution.

Share Repurchases   Share repurchases may be a more favored use of capital than shareholder dividends when shareholders have diverse preferences in terms of what they desire for their shareholder return. For example, share repurchases allow those shareholders looking to sell their interest for whatever reason to be able to sell and then the remaining shareholders can benefit from capital appreciation following the repurchase. In order to facilitate repurchases, though, there must be a price that is deemed fair to both those selling shareholders and the remaining shareholders as well as cash flow available from the company to repurchase. Should the price paid for the repurchases be too high, then the selling shareholders benefit at the expense of those who remain after the repurchase. If the price paid is too low, then the remaining shareholders benefit at the expense of the sellers.

Selling In

Employee Stock Ownership Plans (ESOPs)   Another potential alternative to enhance liquidity is by selling a portion of the company to managers and employees through an Employee Stock Ownership Plan. ESOPs are often an important omission in the boardroom as a number of companies lack an understanding of the possible ways that an ESOP can solve a number of strategic and liquidity issues. ESOPs provide one option to maintain independence and enhance stock liquidity absent an outright sale or an IPO. ESOPs are a written, defined contribution retirement plan designed to qualify for some tax-favored treatments under IRC Section 401(a). While similar to a more typical profit-sharing plan, the fundamental difference is that the ESOP must be primarily invested in the stock of the sponsoring company (only S or C corporations).

ESOPs can acquire shares through employer contributions (in either cash or existing/newly issued shares) or by borrowing money to purchase stock (existing or newly issued) of the sponsoring company. When compared to other retirement plans, the ability to borrow money to purchase stock is an attribute that is fairly unique to ESOPs. Once holding shares, the ESOP obtains cash via sponsor contributions, borrowing money, or dividends/distributions on shares held by the ESOP. When an employee exits the plan, the sponsoring company must facilitate the repurchase of the shares, and the ESOP may use cash to purchase shares from the participant. Following repurchase, those shares are then reallocated among the remaining participants.

While ESOPs or some variant of them may be prevalent in other countries and their tax attributes will vary depending upon the country, ESOPs can potentially provide significant tax benefits here in the United States and we will discuss those briefly. Similar to other profit-sharing plans, contributions (subject to certain limitations) to the ESOP are tax-deductible to the sponsoring company. The ESOP is treated as a single tax-exempt shareholder. This can be of particular benefit to S corporations, as the earnings attributable to the ESOP's interest in the sponsoring company are untaxed. The tax liability related to ESOP plan holder's accounts is at the participant level and generally deferred similar to a 401(k) until employees take distributions from the plan. When leverage is involved (i.e., the ESOP borrows money to purchase shares), the potential tax benefits can be extremely large as the ESOP is able to effectively deduct (and get the associated tax benefit on) both principal and interest payment.

Both publicly traded and privately owned companies (C or S corporations) can sponsor ESOPs, but the benefits are often more profound for private institutions that are not as actively traded because the ESOP can promote a more active market and enhance liquidity more for the privately held shares.

An ESOP can help to solve a number of strategic issues, including the following:

- **Facilitating Stock Purchases and Providing Liquidity Absent an Outright Sale/IPO.** ESOPs can help create an "internal" stock market. By creating an "internal" stock market, the transaction activity between existing shareholders and the ESOP, which serves as a buyer, can promote confidence in stock pricing. For C corporations, the selling shareholder may even have the ability to sell their shares in a tax-free manner subject to certain limitations.[2]

- **Providing Employee Benefits.** ESOPs can provide a beneficial tool to reward and attract key employees. ESOPs offer the benefit of stock in the company absent any direct cost to the employees by providing them with common stock. The structure of ESOPs varies, but ESOPs typically tie rewards directly to the long-term performance of the company. A recent study by Ernst & Young found that the total return for S corporation ESOPs from 2002 to 2012 was a compound annual growth rate of 11.5 percent compared to the total return of the S&P 500 over the same period, which was 7.1 percent.[3] The measure of S corporation ESOP returns considers cumulative distributions as well as growth in value of net assets and the net of those distributions (i.e., growth in the underlying value per share).
- **Creating Long-Term Shareholder Value by Properly Aligning Incentives between Employees and Shareholders.**
- **Augmenting Capital.** While it typically occurs more slowly than through a private placement or a public offering, an ESOP strategy can provide certain tax advantages that can help to build capital and/or pay down existing debt.

Despite the potential benefits to an ESOP, there are some potential negatives to them. Here we have listed a few:

- Plans are regulated primarily by the Department of Labor and also the IRS (Internal Revenue Service) can review plan activities.
- The sponsoring company will need to have sufficient cash flow to be able to provide contributions to the ESOP so that the ESOP can manage its repurchase obligation as the ESOP participants receive cash (not stock) for their vested retirement plan payouts.
- There are some administrative costs with setting up and maintaining the plans.
- An ESOP can spread ownership/transparency to the employee base, which for some companies can be viewed as a negative.
- There can be some dilution to the existing shareholder if newly issued shares are purchased by the ESOP.

For those considering an ESOP, the first step is a feasibility study of what the ESOP would look like once implemented at your company. Parts of the study would include determining the value of the company's shares, the pro-forma implications from the potential transaction/installation, as well as what after-tax proceeds the seller might expect. This will help to determine whether the company should proceed, wait a few years to implement, or move to another strategic option. There are typically a number of parties involved in implementations, including, among others, the appraiser/valuation provider, trustee, attorney or plan designer, and administrative committee.

Selling Out

Initial Public Offerings (IPOs) Initial public offerings offer another way for shareholders of private companies to achieve liquidity. Typically, the private company transforms to a public one after completing the public offering as the shares are sold to institutional investors and then to the public after being listed on an exchange. The motivation for initiating an IPO is not always to achieve liquidity for shareholders. Other motivations can include raising capital or expanding access to capital for the company. One offset to these potential advantages for shareholders is that IPOs can be relatively costly to undertake the process and public companies are often required to disclose greater financial information to the public on an ongoing basis (which can also be costly to provide and comply with disclosure requirements).

The IPO of Netscape, a computer services company that was relatively well known for a web browser that it created, in the mid-1990s was a seminal moment in the technology industry. Netscape was founded in April 1994 and in approximately 18 months had an extremely successful IPO despite not yet being profitable. The IPO was initially priced at $14 per share before being offered initially at $28 per share and then closing at $58.25 per share, which implied a valuation for Netscape at roughly $3 billion, at the end of the first trading day.

Due to its rousing success, Netscape's story received widespread attention and generated significant proceeds for many of its early investors and employees, including a book written by Michael Lewis entitled *The New New Thing* (W.W. Norton & Company; January 6, 2014). Netscape's story provided a template for many technology entrepreneurs and investors to follow. Netscape's template basically became the playbook for a number of technology companies, and its strategy was relatively straightforward: develop a blueprint for a technology solution that can be applied to a large potential market, pitch the blueprint to the venture capitalists, raise money, gather the team, execute the business plan and develop the product, and then prepare for an exit in the form of either an IPO or strategic sale. Ironically, though, this template seems to be met with resistance by some entrepreneurs today. Even Marc Andreessen, one of Netscape's founders, has been on record downplaying the role of the IPO in today's market environment.

A number of technology companies and entrepreneurs have attempted to follow Netscape's track and develop their technology platforms and business models, including a successful IPO as their primary exit strategy. However, that has started to change somewhat in recent years as technology IPOs have faced increased levels of scrutiny and many private companies are staying private longer as ample funding has been available, limiting their need to undertake the time-consuming and costly process to access capital and liquidity in the public markets.

While FinTech is an emerging and growing industry, there are examples of FinTech IPOs. Table 12.2 provides the largest FinTech IPOs of all time. Payments companies (Visa, First Data, and MasterCard) represent the largest FinTech IPOs in terms of proceeds raised. Insurance/healthcare solutions are also relatively well represented. Interestingly, some of the areas that receive most of the media attention, like alternative lending, blockchain, and wealth management solutions, have yet to raise enough proceeds in a public offering to make the list of top FinTech IPOs.

IS YOUR BUY–SELL AGREEMENT SOLIDLY BUILT?

This question is important for FinTech entrepreneurs and bankers alike to ensure that their companies are built to last. We have seen over the years a number of situations where a company's strategic options were impacted by improperly constructed buy–sell agreements. At Mercer Capital, we have a unique perspective on buy–sell agreements, having written a number of articles and books on them and also been involved in disputes where the buy–sell agreement and valuation issues are the centerpiece. While we are not lawyers who draft these agreements, we are often asked to interpret these agreements as part of a process whereby we value the company or an interest in the company per the terms of the agreement.

Technology companies can often have disputes over buy-sell agreements for a number of reasons, including:

- There are a growing number of companies with new ones being founded daily.
- A number are backed by sophisticated investors such as traditional incumbents (banks, asset managers, insurance companies) and private equity or venture funds and have experienced a number of funding rounds. We have previously noted that a number of venture and private equity investors often have specific agreements related to their investments that offer unique preferences and/or liquidation rights.
- A number of companies are very valuable, which leads to greater dollars to distribute, which is ultimately of concern to shareholders and makes the stakes relatively high if disputes arise.

TABLE 12.2 Top FinTech IPOs

Ticker	Name	IPO Price	IPO Date	Gross Proceeds	% Return Since IPO	6/30/16 Price	6/30/16 Market Cap. ($M)	6/30/16 Ent. Value	FinTech Niche
V	Visa Inc.	44.00	3/18/08	19,650.40	68.6%	74.17	176,889	189,733	Payment Processors
FDC	First Data Corp.	16.00	10/14/15	2,817.23	−30.8%	11.07	10,046	31,922	Payment Processors
MA	MasterCard Inc.	39.00	5/24/06	2,579.27	125.8%	88.06	96,752	93,643	Payment Processors
VRSK	Verisk Analytics Inc.	22.00	10/6/09	2,155.91	268.5%	81.08	13,635	15,710	Financial Media & Content
IMS	IMS Health Holdings Inc.	20.00	4/3/14	1,495.00	Acq'd	na	na	na	Insurance/Healthcare Solutions
INFO	IHS Markit Ltd.	24.00	6/18/14	1,475.84	35.8%	32.60	5,840	6,529	Financial Media & Content
LC	Lending Club Corp.	15.00	12/10/14	1,000.50	−71.3%	4.30	1,641	1,068	Alternative Lender
PINC	Premier Inc.	27.00	9/25/13	874.12	21.1%	32.70	1,490	1,242	Insurance/Healthcare Solutions
TRU	Trans Union	22.50	6/24/15	764.49	48.6%	33.44	6,108	8,514	Financial Media & Content
WDAY	Workday Inc.	28.00	10/11/12	732.55	166.7%	74.67	14,710	13,144	Payroll & Admin. Solutions

Sources: SNL Financial and Capital IQ

Most owners and founders are so focused on running their businesses that they don't like to think about reviewing their buy–sell agreement, but spending some time on this can be very valuable and fixing issues on the front-end can often be fairly inexpensive and painless. Once the agreement becomes triggered, however, it becomes expensive and time-consuming to resolve potential issues. Buy–sell agreements are often unclear as they pertain to valuation. A poorly constructed buy–sell agreement can lead to expensive fees to resolve a dispute. We have helped clients structure buy–sell agreements, do annual (or sometimes more frequent) valuation analyses to set transaction pricing for buy–sell agreements, and offer dispute resolution services when things go awry.

As a founder/owner, take a moment and pull out your shareholder or buy–sell agreement and read it. Is it perfectly clear what will happen if a triggering event occurs (say another large owner/shareholder dies, gets divorced, or has a corporate split with the other owners/investors)? Can you tell how the interest will be valued? Do you know roughly what the value will be? Can you identify who the buyer of the interest will be and do you know how that buyer will fund the purchase?

When reviewing your buy–sell agreement (or developing one for those who do not yet have one), we have listed some important items to review in order to ensure that the buy–sell agreement sets reasonable expectations for the value of the company.

- **The Buy–Sell Agreement Should Clearly Define the Standard of Value.** The *standard of value* is an important element of the context of a given valuation, as it often defines the perspective in which a valuation is taking place. Similar to how a public stock analyst or investor might compare what they think a stock is worth to its trading price, valuation analysts are often looking at a company's value according to standards of value, such as *fair market value* or *fair value*. The most common standard of value is fair market value, which is typical for tax-related valuation issues. Fair market value has been defined by the IRS and in a number of court cases. It is defined in the *International Glossary of Business Valuation Terms* as:

  > *The price, expressed in terms of cash equivalents, at which property would change hands between a hypothetical willing/able buyer and a hypothetical willing/able seller, acting at arms' length in an open and unrestricted market, when neither is under compulsion to buy or sell and when both have reasonable knowledge of the relevant facts.*[4]

The standard of value is so important that it is worth naming, quoting, and citing which definition is applicable. Without naming the standard of value, significant questions can arise in a dispute that could materially impact valuation. For example, fair value—which is often considered to be similar to fair market value—can have a number of different interpretations, ranging from different definitions of statutory fair value depending upon legal jurisdiction to the standard of value cited under Generally Accepted Accounting Principles (GAAP). For most buy–sell agreements, we recommend one of the more common definitions of fair market value, as there is a long history of interpretation of this standard in the courts as well as professional writing on the subject.

The buy–sell agreement should also blatantly clarify the *level of value* (Figure 12.2). Public stock market investors do not often have to consider what the appropriate level of value is. However, interests in private FinTech companies and banks typically do not have active markets trading their stocks and a number of FinTech companies are venture-backed, which can often result in different share classes, rights, and preferences associated with investors in different funding rounds. Thus, a given interest might be worth less than the pro-rata portion of the overall enterprise or the headline valuation number reported in the press based on the last funding round.

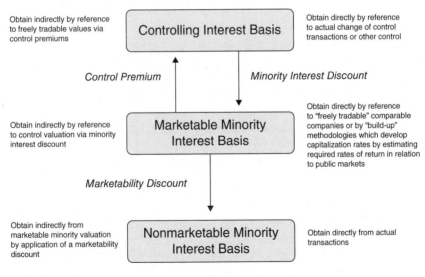

FIGURE 12.2 Levels of Value
Source: Mercer Capital

Appraisers and valuation specialists would likely attribute a portion of that difference in value to a lack of marketability.

Sellers typically want to be the bought-out pursuant to a buy–sell agreement at their pro-rata enterprise value (i.e., excluding consideration of the discount for marketability), but buyers may want to purchase at a discount. Unless the agreement is specific as to treatment of the level of value, the desire of the parties is typically secondary to what is actually laid out in the buy–sell agreement.

Fairness is also a consideration here. If a transaction occurs at a premium or discount to the pro-rata portion of the enterprise value, then there are typically winners or losers to the transaction. This may be appropriate in certain situations, but typically, the owners of banks and FinTech companies are joined together at arms' length and want to be paid based on their pro-rata ownership of the enterprise. The agreement, however, should be clear in terms of level of value. We often recommend including the level of value chart in Figure 12.2 and having an arrow pointing to the appropriate one in the buy–sell agreement.

- **The "As-of Date" for the Valuation Should Also Be Specified.** While this may seem obvious, the particular date of the valuation matters. Market conditions and company-specific events can change quickly over time and the date that the company is valued can have a significant impact on value. Furthermore, there is often disagreement as to whether the triggering event (and its potential impact on the company) should be considered in the valuation absent a specific instruction in regard to the valuation date. For example, if a "business divorce" is occurring or a significant founder passes away, should the valuation consider the potential impact on operations from that event (which may lower the valuation) or be valued on the day prior to the event occurring? While we will not go into all the details as to why selecting the valuation date is important, this provides just one example of how it can be important.

- **Appraiser Qualifications and the Selection Process Should Be Specified.** The appraisal community tends to include appraisers that fall into one of the following camps: "valuation experts" or "industry experts." Valuation experts typically have appropriate professional training, designations, and a scholarly understanding of valuation standards and concepts. Additionally, they tend to have experience advising and valuing private companies, which is different from working for public companies. This includes valuing minority interests appropriately, understanding buy–sell agreements and their implications, and explaining work in litigated matters. By contrast, FinTech industry experts are often known for their depth of particular industry knowledge and perspective on the market of typical buyers/investors and sellers.

Additionally, they tend to have transactions experience and regularly provide specialized advisory services to the FinTech industry. While there are pros and cons to each type of valuation professional, it is often best to specify that the valuation provider have a combination of both industry and valuation expertise. Ultimately, you need a reasonable appraisal work product that can withstand scrutiny from all parties and potentially judicial scrutiny.

Buy–Sell Agreement Example

Consider the following example. Assume a FinTech company is worth (has an enterprise value of) $30 million. There are three shareholders: the two founders—Tim and Richard—and a venture capital firm called NewTech Ventures. The two founders and NewTech each own one-third of the company. As such, the pro-rata interest of each shareholder is $10 million. If Tim and NewTech are able to force out Richard at a discounted value (let's say, $8 million, or a 20% discount to pro-rata enterprise value), and finance the action with debt, what remains is an enterprise worth $22 million (net of debt). Both Tim and NewTech now own 50 percent of the company and their interest is now worth $11 million ($22 million × 0.5). This $2 million decrement to value suffered by Richard is a benefit to Tim and NewTech Ventures.

This example illustrates why structuring a buy–sell agreement properly is important and also why these matters often get litigated as certain shareholders can attempt to enrich themselves at the expense of other investors.

So when you look at your buy–sell agreement or attempt to formulate one for your company, consider this question: "Does my buy–sell agreement create winners and losers?" If so, who are they? Is that appropriate and acknowledged by all parties? Should the pricing mechanism in the buy–sell agreement consider discounts and premiums or rely solely on the pro-rata proportion of the enterprise?

When crafting the buy–sell agreement, it is often unknown who will be exiting and who will be continuing. Thus, it is difficult to tell who will benefit or lose out in a transaction triggered under the agreement. It is still important, however, to think through the issue in advance and understand the implications so that the continuity of the business can be preserved and expensive ownership rifts can be avoided. There may be a compelling reason for the buy–sell agreement to have a pricing mechanism that discounts shares redeemed from departing shareholders as this may reduce the burden on the firm of remaining partners and promote firm continuity. As for buying out shareholders at a premium, the only argument for "paying too much" is to provide a windfall to former shareholders, which is hard to defend operationally.

Ownership tends to work best when it is structured in a way that supports the firm's operations and this certainly applies to the mechanics of a buy–sell agreement. It is often advised to attempt to avoid surprises to ensure the continuity of the company and avoid distractions. We often recommend to clients to keep the language in the buy–sell agreements up to date and also have a pricing mechanism that encourages annual valuations to be performed. If ownership sees consistently prepared appraisals over the years, then the ownership group will know what to expect should the agreement be triggered. They will know who will provide the valuation, what information will be analyzed, and how the valuation process as a whole will be constructed. While this will not eliminate the potential for disagreements over valuation, it can go a long way toward narrowing the difference of opinion and allow constructive feedback on the valuation methods and process over the years. Furthermore, this allows the board and management to measure valuation creation over time (by comparing the concluded values at different periods) and also serves to manage the expectations of owners as they will have a better idea of what price to expect in the event that they exit per the terms of the buy–sell agreement.

CONCLUSION

For those who are able to build a successful FinTech company or offering, this chapter provides insights into the process of determining the appropriate course of action once the company has matured and successful revenue generation has been achieved, which can often be as daunting as building the company itself. In prior chapters, we discussed acquisitions and partnerships with FinTech companies, but this chapter focused on strategic options for FinTech companies going a different route other than a third-party sale to a financial or strategic buyer. Additionally, the discussion of buy–sell agreements provides important tips that can be utilized by both FinTech companies and bankers to ensure that their companies are built to last. Poorly thought-out and improperly constructed buy–sell agreements can significantly limit a company's strategic and liquidity options.

NOTES

1. Certain material in this chapter was adapted with permission from "*Unlocking Private Company Wealth*," by Z. Christopher Mercer, FASA, CFA, ABAR (Peabody Publishing, LP, 2014).

2. For U.S. C corporations, the specific code is related to Section 1042 rollovers and the limitations include that the ESOP must own greater than 30% of each class of outstanding stock after the transaction date and the seller reinvesting the proceeds into qualified replacement property from 3 to 12 months after the sale.
3. "Contribution of S ESOPs to Participants' Retirement Security: Prepared for Employee-Owned S Corporations of America," *Ernst & Young*, March 2015, http://www.efesonline.org/LIBRARY/2015/EY_ESCA_S_ESOP_retirement_ security_analysis_2015.pdf.
4. American Institute of CPAs, *International Glossary of Business Valuation Terms*, http://www.aicpa.org/InterestAreas/ForensicAndValuation/Membership/ DownloadableDocuments/Intl%20Glossary%20of%20BV%20Terms.pdf.

CHAPTER 13

Is There a Bubble Forming in FinTech?

INTRODUCTION

Like many other sports, tennis is filled with prodigies who ultimately never consistently play at the professional level. As of the writing of this book, the top-ranked juniors from 2005 should be reaching their prime since the peak age for a tennis player is 27 (Table 13.1). However, none of the top-five junior players in the world at the end of 2005 were among the top-five professional players in the world at the end of 2015.

Novak Djokovic, the #1-ranked tennis player in the world (at year-end 2015) was ranked the #74 junior in the world in 2003. Yet, Djokovic went on to win many grand slams and hold the #1 ranking for a lengthy stretch of time. If gamblers were picking junior players, it is likely that Novak Djokovic would not have been the first, or even one of the first 50 players selected. While players like Djokovic were arguably under hyped as they rose through the professional ranks by virtue of their lower junior rankings, the other top juniors were conversely overhyped. Gael Monfils, the highest ranked player at year-end 2005, was ranked #24 in the world at year-end 2015. Of the other players who were ranked in the top five of juniors in the world at year-end 2005, none of them were ranked in the top 1,000 players at year-end 2015.

This example in tennis is instructive for bankers and FinTech entrepreneurs, because it provides perspective on the risks of early-stage investing and the importance of taking a balanced assessment of the FinTech industry. Only a fraction of the many promising FinTech companies may persist and the ones that do thrive and become mature, lasting companies may not be the ones receiving the most press and attention today. For bankers looking to develop FinTech offerings or invest/partner in a FinTech company, this chapter helps you develop a keen eye for the risks associated with FinTech companies and the FinTech industry generally.

TABLE 13.1 Tennis Junior and Professional Rankings

Ranking	Year-End Junior Rankings 2005	Year-End Pro Rankings 2005
1	Gael Monfils	Novak Djokovic
2	Eduardo Schwank	Andy Murray
3	Brendan Evans	Roger Federer
4	Woong-Sun Jun	Stan Wawrinka
5	Sun-Yong Kim	Rafael Nadal

Source: Junior Rankings—ITF Website; Pro Rankings—ATP Website

This chapter is also of special significance for FinTech entrepreneurs who, presumably like the lower-ranked players, can come to realize their weaknesses earlier in their careers and work hard to eliminate those weaknesses and then turn them into strengths. A quick tennis story on the rise of Novak Djokovic illustrates the power of honestly assessing weaknesses and turning them into strengths. I heard Andy Roddick discussing Novak Djokovic's game on a Periscope session during the 2016 U.S. Open. Roddick noted that he went back and reviewed his notes on how to play Djokovic when the two players first started playing each other on the tour. He said that the strategies that his notes indicated would be most successful when he played Djokovic early in his career were to make the match physical and wear him down mentally. It turns out that today those strategies are the exact opposite strategies employed by most players because those older strategies now play to his strengths. Djokovic improved his game from his early years on the professional tour. He now usually enjoys and wins the long physical matches and is arguably one of the toughest players mentally on tour. If Djokovic can grow and improve, so can FinTech entrepreneurs.

FACTORS LEADING TO A BUBBLE?

The majority of this book to this point has touted the promise of FinTech and the potential to achieve great success through leveraging the power of technology to deliver better, faster, and more efficient financial services to a large audience. However, there have long been skeptics of innovation and technology in the financial services industry. Former Federal Reserve Chairman Paul Volcker was quoted in 2009 as saying: "I wish somebody would give me some shred of evidence linking financial innovation with a benefit to the economy." Also, a renowned bank investor, J. Christopher Flowers, was quoted in the *Wall Street Journal* as saying:[1]

> *The tech idea [is that] you must get big fast and dominate a sector and must achieve a network effect … [however] in lending, this idea is not only wrong, it is very dangerous indeed. The lender that grows fast is the lender with future losses.*
>
> *Do not expect bitcoin to displace the U.S. dollar, and do not expect Visa to go broke.*
>
> *Banks in the U.S. are required at some level to settle all dollar transactions so there is no scenario where banks aren't part of the picture.*

Given the skepticism expressed toward FinTech in those quotes, let's take a look at challenges facing FinTech and then examine whether signs of a bubble are showing up.

- **The Majority of the Recently Hyped FinTech Lenders Have Not Experienced a Full Credit Cycle.** During any credit cycle there exists an expansion of credit that ultimately ends in contraction and pain for lenders that pushed the envelope too far. Because of this expansion, many skeptics view certain areas of FinTech as merely a new label for an age-old component of the expansionary portion of the credit cycle, whereby lenders loosen underwriting standards and credit expands. These cycles do ultimately come to an end, however; significant pain exists in the form of charge-offs and credit costs for those lenders that pushed the envelope too far. While we have yet to see the latest crop of alternative lenders over a full credit cycle, there is a debate brewing as to how they will hold up during a recession. Will the algorithms created hold up in a recession or will they prove to have their own flaws that will ultimately sink some of those lenders in the industry? While we do not yet know the answer to that question, it will be one to watch moving forward.
- **Banks Have Persisted a Long Time.** One other reason for skepticism of FinTech is that banks have been called "dinosaurs" and nonfinancial companies (including some notable tech companies) have been attempting to displace them for a long time. In the mid-1990s, Bill Gates famously called the banks "dinosaurs" and noted that banking services were a necessity but banks were not.[2] Microsoft has long tried, but largely been unable, to get into the money and banking space, even trying to buy Intuit in the mid-1990s before being blocked by the Justice Department. Microsoft Money, their personal finance software program, was discontinued in 2009 after trailing Intuit's Quicken for

an extended period of time and facing dwindling market share. Thus, the skeptics can point to the fact that banks have been fairly resilient over time and have historically focused on customer service and been heavy investors in technology, which has helped to stave off some competition.

- **Consumers May Still Prefer Traditional Financial Services.** One factor that has often been cited as a significant tailwind for the FinTech industry is that consumer preferences are shifting—consumers are increasingly showing interest in online and mobile financial services, which continues to drive the FinTech industry. However, there is some conflicting evidence in that regard.

  An FDIC survey released in March 2016 related to lending noted that community banks received higher customer satisfaction scores by a wide margin than online lenders. Consider the following insights from the 2015 Small Business Credit Survey from Federal Reserve.[3] Traditional banks were cited as still being the primary source for small-business loans and only 20 percent of employer firms applied at an online lender. The satisfaction rate for online lenders was low (15% satisfaction for the online lenders compared to 75% for small banks and 51% for large banks). The main reasons reported for dissatisfaction with online lenders was high interest rates and unfavorable repayment terms. As noted earlier in this book, traditional financial services companies (i.e., banks) have long invested in technology and often focus on customer service through their more people-heavy operation. Banks may be able to leverage both their people and the best FinTech innovations and still maintain the customer relationship and keep customers satisfied.

- **Banks Still Have Certain Advantages Over FinTech Companies.** Banks still have documented funding advantages that could serve them well competitively in a higher interest rate environment and, at this point, still serve as the primary financial services contact for customers, ultimately controlling the relationship. Globally, these trends may be a little more balanced, as less belief and trust exists in certain areas for traditional financial systems/institutions.

- **Regulatory Scrutiny of FinTech Could Increase.** It is often noted that the nonfinancial companies (like a number of FinTech companies) have significant regulatory advantages over more-regulated financial companies like banks and insurers since they do not face the same compliance burdens. This advantage, however, may change over time. While it is difficult to forecast how the regulatory dominoes will ultimately fall, consider some of the recent regulatory movements related to FinTech in the alternative online lending industry. The CFPB announced plans to regulate online lending in 2017. RICO and other lawsuits have popped up and are mounting against some online lenders. Many FinTech companies that do not have a bank charter have to consider different state requirements in the United States, like usury laws. A significant case related to online lending is going to the Supreme Court (*Madden v. Midland Funding*). The case will essentially test, and could set a legal precedent for, the viability of the relationships that many online lenders have with banks. Banks have historically had the ability to export the interest rate in their home state to other states and also sell the debt to nonbanks. Thus, a partnership with a bank has typically been underlying a number of alternative FinTech lenders (for example, Lending Club has a relationship with Web Bank).

- **Softer Public IPO Markets Will Likely Trickle into the Private Markets.** Square, a prominent FinTech company in the United States, effectively had a down-round IPO in late 2015 and the IPO market has been relatively soft since with no FinTech IPOs reported through the first half of 2016. The slowdown in the IPO market will make exits difficult for those highly valued private companies. We previously noted that M&A activity where deal values exceed $1 billion have been rare, even in frothy markets. This overhang of highly valued FinTech companies, and their inability or unwillingness to go public in a softer IPO market, will likely impact both valuations and funding for other private FinTech companies. Investors will achieve liquidity more slowly than expected as expectations are reset for the sector.

SIGNS THAT A BUBBLE MAY BE FORMING IN FINTECH

As previously discussed, optimism and investor interest in FinTech is growing and has been for some time. Against this backdrop, we examined valuation multiples within the FinTech industry over time to see whether public markets reflect this optimism. While key valuation drivers such as profitability, growth prospects, and risks vary among each FinTech niche, Figures 13.1 and 13.2 illustrate that perhaps a FinTech bubble is emerging as margins are down across various FinTech niches while valuation multiples have expanded.

CASE STUDY OF A FINTECH FAILURE

In prior chapters, we discussed successful FinTech companies. However, there have been high-profile failures in the FinTech space as well. We examine one in particular, Powa Technologies, a FinTech prodigy that

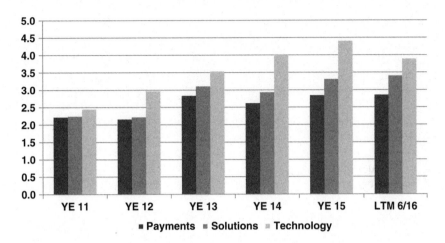

FIGURE 13.1   FinTech Public Company Pricing Multiples: Median Enterprise Value/EBITDA Multiples
Source: Capital IQ, Mercer Capital Research

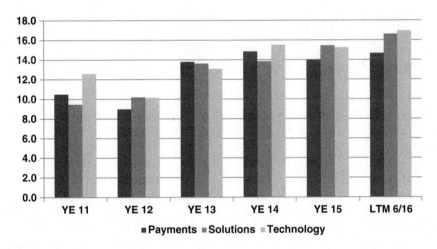

FIGURE 13.2   FinTech Public Company Pricing Multiples: Median EBITDA Margins
Source: Capital IQ, Mercer Capital Research

ultimately failed, to see what lessons can be learned from this failure.[4] We hope this discussion can assist FinTech entrepreneurs, investors, and partners strengthen their respective FinTech companies while addressing weaknesses early (so that they do not follow the example of Powa or the tennis prodigies discussed earlier).

Powa Technologies Case Study

In February 2016, British FinTech startup Powa Technologies went into receivership at the hands of Deloitte, signaling the collapse and failure of a once-promising startup. While tech (and even FinTech) startups fail on a regular basis, Powa was unique in that it represented a FinTech unicorn. It had risen to prominence and successfully acquired other FinTech companies while raising approximately $175 million in funds. For additional perspective on the hype surrounding Powa prior to its failure, British PM David Cameron had lauded Powa as a potential lightning rod for the UK's recovering post-recession economy.

Powa's founder and CEO at the time of its failure, called the collapse of his startup "the business equivalent of walking across the street and being hit by a car. It's one of those things that's completely random." While we would agree with the car-wreck comparison, we would not agree with his assessment that Powa's collapse was "completely random." We readily admit that the reasons for Powa Technologies' failure are myriad and varied. However, there were some specific issues and decisions that led to both the rise and ultimate fall of Powa.

Powa's story serves as a cautionary tale to FinTech startups and includes many valuable warnings of exactly what not to do when trying to raise capital, develop products, and grow your FinTech startup. We attempt to shed light on the collapse and also provide key takeaways to help prevent a repeat in other FinTech companies. Several of the more glaring issues that led to Powa's failure appear to be a complicated and tension-filled management structure, too much funding, too high of a burn rate, and a bad product. However, before we delve into these specific problems, let's begin with a brief historical overview of the rise and fall of Powa.

Brief History of Powa   Powa was focused on the payments niche and operated as an international commerce company. It focused on providing point-of-sale mobile and tablet payment solutions. In 2007, PowaWeb, the first of Powa's three key product offerings, launched. PowaWeb built online shops for retailers to market and sell their products over the Web. After PowaWeb's launch, PowaTag emerged. PowaTag was a mobile application that would allow people to purchase items anywhere by scanning QR (Quick Response) codes, picking up audio waves, or taking a picture of advertisements. In 2012, after failing to acquire Paddle, a mobile payments provider, to write the code for PowaTag, Powa began licensing technologies from other companies and bolting it all together to build a prototype of PowaTag. Around this time, Powa Technologies, the umbrella company that would raise money for and manage the different suite of products, was starting to get put together.

In July 2013, Powa secured $76 million (USD) in equity funding in a Series A round. Powa also developed PowaPOS, an app to give iPads Square-like functionality linked to PowaTag through the same type of device-attached card reader utilized by Square. Things became such a mess in this division that on New Year's Eve 2013, almost the entire PowaPOS team, many of whom were working on the holiday, were laid off, just months after the significant Series A round of funding. Despite this massive firing, investors invested $20 million more in equity and $60 million in debt into the company in the first quarter of 2014.

The year 2014 would prove to be a pivotal one for the company, as PowaTag officially launched in March 2014, and the MPayMe deal would be executed in July of that year. The MPayMe acquisition was structured as an all-stock transaction that reportedly placed a $2.7 billion valuation on Powa in June 2014, elevating Powa into the rarefied air of being a FinTech unicorn. The capital continued to flow in from investors with an additional $41 million coming in 2015. However, the end of 2015 also meant the repayment of the $60 million in debt that investors had provided Powa previously. Powa could not repay this debt, as it had just $250,000 in the bank at the end of 2015. Through the new year into 2016, the debt was never repaid, much of the staff was laid off, and those who were not laid off were never paid. In February 2016, Deloitte was sent in to be administrators and Powa was effectively dismantled, leading to the end of Powa.

Some Takeaways from Powa's Story

Again, several of the more glaring issues and lessons to be learned from Powa's failure appear to be too much funding, too high of a burn rate, poor executive leadership, a complicated and tension-filled management structure, and a bad product.

Beware of a High Burn Rate   Powa maintained an outward appearance of functionality and long-term viability, highlighted by various debt and equity fundings from investors. However, the combination of all the funding and a desire to maintain a strong outward appearance, along with certain management decisions, ultimately contributed to Powa's downfall. After the $76 million funding in July 2013, Powa moved offices to two floors of the Heron Tower in London, a move that cost the company around £2 million in rent per year. Looking back at the company's collapse, one of Powa's chief competitors commented on the move: "The Heron Tower is not a place to put an entrepreneurial venture, a startup. Especially one that's pre-revenue." The blunder essentially summed up the style of Powa's management in that Powa was trying to portray the appearance of a powerful and stable company when in reality the still-nascent startup would never in its life be able to afford tenancy in the Heron Tower. This over-compensatory style was again apparent in the extravagant Christmas parties, complete with all-you-could-drink Veuve Clicquot champagne (which costs upwards of $50 a bottle). In the words of one former employee, "You don't serve champagne all night for a startup. You just don't." Again, Powa's spending habits greatly outsized the revenues of this infant company.

Powa also acquired a similar Chinese company known as MPayMe. However, both the fundings from investors and acquisition of MPayMe would become problematic for Powa. Specifically, Powa's management structure became extremely muddled as a result of both the investor fundings and the MPayMe acquisition. According to a former Powa employee, the MPayMe acquisition was also troubled in that the product acquired from MPayMe turned out to be "a bit of a dud."

Beware of Poor Executive Leadership and Management Structure Many of Powa's troubles can be attributed to their management. Their management did not have as much background in the technological processes behind their product like many tech-startup CEOs.

Not only did the company suffer due to the incompetence of its leadership, but the management structure of Powa also created a muddled and confusing work environment, often leaving employees unsure of their responsibilities or to whom they reported. This complicated structure came as a result of the funding rounds from investors and the acquisition of MPayMe, as both events brought extra baggage outside of the material gains from which the company would supposedly benefit.

Many senior positions were filled with supporters of Powa's CEO in upper-level positions, which allowed the CEO to enjoy almost complete autonomy until investors began to fill positions with people who they thought could steer the company toward profitability. The CEO's team and the investor's people never meshed, leaving the upper-level management of Powa in disarray.

Also contributing to the managerial confusion within the upper ranks was the acquisition of MPayMe in July 2014, which brought a whole Asia-Pacific department into the management structure. Further, Powa acquired offices across the globe in Italy, France, Mexico, and New York and appointed friends and family to governing roles in each. Despite this worldwide presence, the company was still not generating revenue, and the widespread belief among former employees is that this global expansion was more of Powa's attempt to paint themselves as a worldwide power on scale with Apple and Google in efforts to gain retail clients, consumer adoption, and new investors. According to Deloitte's insolvency report, this also juiced the payroll to almost £25 million by 2015—a level of overhead that was difficult to sustain. To sum, one former product developer put it this way: "You'd go to the Christmas party and be talking to someone who's vice president of PowaTag in Spain or Greece or whatever. All these people with these titles. It's insane. All these people were on the payroll." The attempts of Powa management to build this façade of strength and viability through a global presence coupled with an inability to work with the top investor's chosen people contributed to a confusing and ineffective management structure that would play a key role in Powa's downfall.

Beware of a Bad Product Much of Powa's collapse can be attributed to this: the products were subpar and there was simply no market for them. As previously mentioned, Powa licensed technology from other companies and bolted it all together to create PowaTag. The technology behind PowaTag was reportedly rudimentary and consistently failed. One former employee noted: "It was hosted on someone's box at home. It had to be restarted every day." Bear in mind that this was an app that stored customers' credit card information across the world. Powa's management difficulties trickled all the way down to the technology driving his products.

The MPayMe acquisition added a product that was widely considered in the mobile payments and FinTech realms to be a flop. One former MPayMe employee who stayed on through the acquisition gave a perfect summation of the technological flaws in the deal: "Powa made a Frankenstein out of the technology. There was the technology there but Powa wanted to merge it in a very different way and do very different things and keep adding things." Powa took incompatible technologies, tried to make something out of nothing, and was left with a shoddy product that didn't have much functionality. It was debatable whether the market or consumers even needed the products that Powa had developed. It was innovation for the sake of innovation. Powa tried desperately to create a market for the product and encourage consumer adoption, but Powa struggled with attracting and retaining customers.

CONCLUSION

In prior chapters, we discussed a number of factors contributing to the excitement and interest in FinTech but this last chapter examined the potential over-exuberance in the sector and challenges for the sector as it continues to evolve and mature. Powa's story provides valuable lessons. By taking an honest assessment of the challenges facing FinTech and learning from a FinTech failure, we hope to help bankers and FinTech entrepreneurs realistically assess the opportunity and market potential for whatever FinTech niche they focus on. We hope that banks, investors, and FinTech entrepreneurs utilize this information to better identify weaknesses of FinTech companies early and work to turn those weaknesses into strengths to establish a mature, profitable, and lasting company.

NOTES

1. J. Christopher Flowers, "'FinTech' Will Mostly End in Tears," *Wall Street Journal*, February 25, 2016, http://www.wsj.com/articles/fintech-will-mostly-end-in-tears-christopher-flowers-says-1456411711#:LZ6fDmSYRFBjKA.
2. Amy Cortese, Kelly Holland, "Bill Gates Is Rattling the Teller's Window," *Bloomberg*, October 30, 1994, http://www.bloomberg.com/news/articles/1994-10-30/bill-gates-is-rattling-the-tellers-window.
3. U.S. Federal Reserve System, "2015 Small Business Credit Survey: Report on Employer Firms," Washington, DC, 2016, https://www.newyorkfed.org/medialibrary/media/smallbusiness/2015/Report-SBCS-2015.pdf.
4. Sources for Powa Technologies case study include:
   Business Insider: http://www.businessinsider.com
   Money: http://money.cnn.com
   Crunchbase: http://crunchbase.com

Index

Page references followed by f indicate an illustrated figure and t indicate table